Differentiating Instruction for Students With Learning Disabilities

3rd Edition

Differentiating Instruction for Students With Learning Disabilities

New Best Practices for General and Special Educators

William N. Bender

CORWIN

A SAGE Company

CORWIN
A SAGE Company

FOR INFORMATION:

Corwin
A SAGE Company
2455 Teller Road
Thousand Oaks, California 91320
(800) 233-9936
www.corwin.com

SAGE Publications Ltd.
1 Oliver's Yard
55 City Road
London, EC1Y 1SP
United Kingdom

SAGE Publications India Pvt. Ltd.
B 1/I 1 Mohan Cooperative Industrial Area
Mathura Road, New Delhi 110 044
India

SAGE Publications Asia-Pacific Pte. Ltd.
3 Church Street
#10-04 Samsung Hub
Singapore 049483

Acquisitions Editor: Jessica Allan
Editorial Assistant: Lisa Whitney
Permissions Editors: Jason Kelley and Karen Ehrmann
Project Editors: Amy Schroller and Veronica Stapleton
Copy Editor: Dan Gordon
Typesetter: Hurix Systems Pvt. Ltd.
Proofreader: Dennis W. Webb
Indexer: Karen Wiley
Cover Designer: Candice Harman

Copyright © 2012 by Corwin

Library of Congress Cataloging-in-Publication Data

Bender, William N.
Differentiating instruction for students with learning disabilities : new best practices for general and special educators / William N. Bender. – 3rd ed.

p. cm.
Includes bibliographical references and index.

ISBN 978-1-4129-9859-8 (pbk.)

1. Learning disabled children—Education. 2. Individualized instruction. I. Title.

LC4704.5.B46 2012

371.9'043—dc23

2012023287

12 13 14 15 16 10 9 8 7 6 5 4 3 2 1

Contents

Preface

Differentiated instruction has become one of the—if not *the*—most widely adopted instructional approach since the concept was articulated by Dr. Carol Tomlinson in her seminal work, *The Differentiated Classroom* (Tomlinson, 1999). Not only has this instructional approach captured the hearts and minds of educators across the nation, it has been applied to one degree or another in virtually every state and in many nations around the world (Bender, 2009a; Bender & Waller, 2011a; 2011b; Berkeley, Bender, Peaster, & Saunders, 2009).

In fact, differentiated instruction has now been enshrined in various response to intervention (RTI) initiatives in nearly every state since many state RTI plans have differentiated instruction embedded within them as the basis for Tier 1 instruction in the general education classroom (Berkeley et al., 2009).

> Differentiated instruction has become the most widely adopted instructional approach in recent years.

This relatively simple idea that teachers should present varied instructional options and activities based not only on the academic content to be covered but also on the learning styles, preferences, strengths, and weaknesses of the learners in the class has clearly taken root (Bender, 2012a, 2008; Tomlinson, Brimijoin, & Narvaez, 2008), and today it is difficult to find a teacher that is not re-creating his or her instructional approach with an eye toward increasing the variation of instructional activities and assessment practices in his or her classroom.

> This idea that teachers should present varied instructional options based not only on the academic content to be covered, but also on the learning styles and preferences of the learners has clearly taken root.

Moreover, it is difficult to find anywhere in the history of educational reforms in this nation any comparable fundamental change in instructional paradigm that was not based in either legislation or a court-mandated educational transition. Differentiated instruction is, indeed, a major transition of instruction that has been and continues to be based on a grassroots movement among educators seeking a more effective way to teach the highly diverse students found in most classrooms today (Bender, 2012b; Bender & Waller, 2011b). Thus, Dr. Tomlinson has done a great service to all educators and, more importantly, to all students in this nation and around the world with the development of this instructional approach.

As this book is published in 2012, it is safe to assert that the concept of differentiated instruction has not only been widely adopted but has indeed grown up (Sousa & Tomlinson, 2011; Tomlinson, 2010)! In fact, the meaning of the term *differentiation* has changed or migrated to some degree over time from the initial construct as proposed in 1999, and understanding this change over time is critical to understanding the differentiated instructional construct. In fact, there are several notable changes in the theoretical basis for differentiated instruction, as well as multiple other educational initiatives and transformations in instructional practice, that are impacting teachers' collective efforts to differentiate the instruction in their classrooms (Bender & Waller, 2012b). Thus, the concept of a new *differentiated instruction*, as introduced herein, seems very apropos.

> Differentiated instruction today emphasizes many different conceptualizations of learning styles, student learning preferences, and ability differences.

For example, unlike the initial work on differentiated instruction, today's differentiation is not tied exclusively to one learning style approach any longer (Bender & Waller, 2011a; Sousa & Tomlinson, 2010, 2011). Rather, differentiated instructing emphasizes many different conceptualizations of learning styles, student learning preferences, and ability differences. Also, both increased application of instructional technologies and the more recent response to intervention initiative (RTI) have impacted the differentiated instructional approach to such a degree that discussion of any one of these factors in isolation—differentiated instruction, technology in the classroom, and RTI—is virtually meaningless (Bender & Waller, 2011a). In today's classroom, each of these factors impacts the other, and thus, they must be considered together in order to make meaningful instructional recommendations for teachers.

This book represents an initial attempt to explore how differentiated instruction has been transformed by the cross-fertilization of these recent educational initiatives. The various chapters emphasize instructional suggestions for educators working with students with learning disabilities and other disabilities in the general education-inclusive class as well as with nondisabled students who may be struggling in the curriculum. Thus, any educator with a focus on the primary and elementary grades may find this book useful, including

General education teachers
School psychologists
Professional learning communities

Special education teachers
School administrators
Other educational administrators

DESCRIPTION OF THIS BOOK

This book is intended as a professional development book for practicing teachers and, possibly, a supplemental book in college instructional methods courses. With a strong focus on 21st century teaching practices, the book provides numerous instructional strategies for teaching within the context of the Common Core State Standards (www.corestandards.org/the-standards), standards which have been adopted by many states as one foundation of the school curriculum. Each chapter in the book will present specific instructional strategies related to these standards and intended for the general education class.

Many of these strategies will emphasize technology applications as well as the most modern and relevant differentiated instructional practices. Various interest boxes will be presented for supplementary information as needed, and numerous teaching tips, holding specific instructional guidelines for specific teaching tactics will be included in each chapter.

Chapter Descriptions

Chapter 1: *Differentiated Instruction: Then and Now.* This chapter will briefly describe the history of differentiated instruction as a concept, beginning in 1999 and moving through 2012. The chapter will open with an extended discussion of several things that have impacted the differentiated instruction concept, including increased emphasis on brain-compatible instruction and less on the multiple intelligences paradigm. Then, a variety of brain-friendly instructional examples are provided. Next, technology will be described as one factor that can increase and enhance differentiated instruction, along with implementation of Common Core State Standards and the response to intervention (RTI) instructional approaches. Further, the case will be made that these three instructional innovations—differentiation, RTI, and increased use of technology, are mutually supporting in today's classrooms. Then the application of differentiated instruction specifically for students with learning disabilities and other learning challenges is discussed.

Chapter 2: *Universal Design and Differentiated Instructional Models.* This chapter presents the concept of universal design as the basis for effective classroom organization, showing how universal design will assure access to the general education curriculum for students with learning disabilities and other learning problems. Initially, the chapter describes methods for organizing the class for effective differentiation. Finally, four models of differentiated instruction are described, including modification of a traditional lesson plan using learning centers for differentiation, project-based learning as a differentiated instructional model, and the newest model of differentiated instruction, the "flipped" classroom.

Chapter 3: *Technology and the New Differentiated Instruction.* This chapter will describe a variety of innovative technology-based instructional tactics appropriate for differentiating classroom activities. Initially, a description of the changing model of knowledge for the 21st century will be presented, which will lead to a focus on technology-based instructional ideas, including webquests for differentiating instruction, class blogs, and using wikis in the classroom. Next, several specific instructional tools will be described in detail, including use of social networking for instruction, simulation and gaming formats, the flipped classroom, and Khan Academy—an anytime, anywhere teaching and learning tool. Finally, these tech-based teaching tools will be discussed in terms of the new differentiated instruction and how these tools are transforming the teaching and learning process.

Chapter 4: *Response to Intervention and Differentiated Assessment Strategies.* RTI will be described as a recent innovation that is working for students with learning disabilities and other learning challenges across the nation. RTI is described in terms of the three-tier pyramid with an emphasis on differentiated instructional assessments in Tier 1 coupled with multiyear universal screening measures. Next, progress monitoring practices in differentiated instruction is discussed, and progress monitoring in Tiers 2 and 3 is described in detail. Next, a case study RTI procedure is presented, with an emphasis on the assessment practices within RTI. Finally, a brief discussion on grading in differentiated instruction is presented, and specific options for grading differentiated instructional activities are provided.

Chapter 5: *Instructional Support Strategies in Differentiated Classes.* Provision of a variety of instructional supports for students with learning disabilities and other learning challenges is critical in differentiated classes for all students with academic deficits because such supportive strategies allow teachers to differentiate the lessons based on students' needs. This chapter presents a variety of supportive instructional techniques, including scaffolded instruction, content enhancements, story maps, graphic organizers, study guides, classwide peer tutoring and reciprocal teaching.

Chapter 6: *Cognitive Strategy Instruction for Differentiated Classes.* In addition to the instructional support strategies above, the research on metacognition has presented an array of additional strategies for the differentiated class. This chapter presents several metacognitive instructional strategies that have been proven to work for students with learning disabilities and other academic deficits. These may be used in the general education class, in special education settings, and in Tiers 1, 2, or 3 in an RTI framework. Strategies include implementation of a cognitive strategies model and self-monitoring. A case study RTI procedure will be described in which an eighth-grade student with reading comprehension problems received a Tier 2 cognitive strategies intervention to increase reading comprehension.

Next, as schools move into 21st century teaching, personal responsibility for learning has been increasingly emphasized, and self-regulation strategies for planning and monitoring of one's own cognitive understanding and behavior have become increasingly important. Self-monitoring and self-regulation of learning for differentiated classes are presented in detail, along with guidelines for implementation.

Appendix: *Intervention Curricula Used for Differentiated Instruction and RTI.*

The Goal

Schools will continue to move into several new and uncharted areas over the next decade, including implementation of the Common Core State Standards, the growing emphasis on the flipped classroom, Internet-based learning, the use of Facebook, Twitter, or other social media, or continuing RTI implementation, including implementation in the upper-grade levels. It is clear that all educators need an understanding of how these innovations fit within their efforts to provide differentiated instruction for all students. Many of the changes are already under way in education, and most will provide excellent opportunities for teachers to structure highly differentiated instruction in their classes.

However, it is one thing to understand and implement any of these single innovations; it is another thing altogether to understand how they fit within the "whole" of differentiated instruction in the classroom, and the latter understanding is critical.

The goal of this book, therefore, is to provide specific instructional strategies for a variety of primary and elementary instructional situations that integrate these innovations in such a way as to result in provision of highly differentiated instruction for students with learning disabilities and others who may struggle in the general education classrooms. I sincerely hope and honestly believe that this book will be of use in that regard.

About the Author

 **William N. Bender** is an international leader who focuses on practical instructional tactics with an emphasis on response to intervention (RTI) and differentiated instruction in general education classes across the grade levels. In particular, Dr. Bender has written more books on RTI than any other author in the world, two of which are best sellers. He has now completed seven books on various aspects of response to intervention, as well as a professional development videotape on that topic. He completes between 40 and 50 workshops yearly in the United States, Canada, and the Caribbean. In the fall of 2010, he was selected to work with the Ministry of Education in Bermuda to establish its nationwide RTI framework. One of his recent books, *Beyond the RTI Pyramid*, was a 2010 finalist for the Distinguished Achievement Award for Excellence in Educational Publishing.

Dr. Bender uses practical strategies and easy humor to make his workshops an enjoyable experience for all, and he is frequently asked to return to the same school or district for additional workshops. He consistently receives positive reviews of his professional-development workshops for educators across the grade levels. Dr. Bender believes his job is to inform educators of innovative, up-to-date tactics for the classroom, rooted in current research, in an enjoyable workshop experience. He is able to convey this information in a humorous, motivating fashion.

Dr. Bender began his education career teaching in a junior high school resource classroom, working with adolescents with behavioral disorders and learning disabilities. He earned his doctorate in special education from the University of North Carolina and has taught in leading universities around the nation, including Rutgers University and the University of Georgia. He is now consulting and writing full time and has published over 60 research articles and 23 books in education.

Differentiated Instruction 1

Then and Now

DIFFERENTIATED INSTRUCTION: THE FIRST DECADE

Both general education teachers and special education teachers are generally familiar with the concept of differentiated instruction because of the highly diverse learning characteristics displayed by the students in general education classrooms today (Bender, 2008; Bender & Waller, 2011b). Since Tomlinson wrote the initial book on differentiated instruction in 1999, teachers across the nation have begun to implement a wider variety of activities in their classes, based on the differentiated instructional paradigm (O'Meara, 2010; Sousa & Tomlinson, 2011; Tomlinson, 2010). While any group of students is likely to demonstrate considerable variation in their learning characteristics, the learning characteristics that are displayed by many kids with learning disabilities and/or other learning disorders within the general education classroom are likely to further necessitate a variety of learning activities in most general education classes.

As every veteran teacher realizes, students with learning disabilities and other learning disorders may be less engaged in the learning task, unable to cope with multiple instructions, and poorly organized in their thinking and work habits when compared with students without disabilities. Approximately 75 percent of students with learning disabilities are males, and because males are more physically active than females at many age levels (Bender, 2008; King & Gurian, 2006), the mere volume of physical activity shown by males with learning disabilities in the typical classroom can enhance the difficulties these students have. When these deficits are coupled with severe academic deficits, the result can be very challenging for general education and special education teachers alike. Thus, these teachers are hungry for tactics and ideas that work for these challenging students. The differentiated instructional approach, while appropriate for virtually all general education classes, is particularly helpful to students with this array of learning challenges (Bender, 2008).

Origins of Differentiated Instruction

> Differentiated instruction is best conceptualized as a teacher's response to the diverse learning needs of students.

The concept of differentiated instruction was originally based on the need for teachers to differentiate instruction to meet the needs of diverse learners in the general education class (Chapman & King, 2005; 2003; O'Meara, 2010; Tomlinson, 1999; 2003). This includes students with learning disabilities as well as a number of other mild and moderate disabilities, since students with mild and moderate disabilities are quite likely to be included in general education classes. Differentiated instruction was and is best conceptualized as a teacher's response to the diverse learning needs of students in the general education classes (Tomlinson, 2010; 1999; Tomlinson & McTighe, 2006).

Teachers must know the learners in the class, understanding not only such things about each learner as her learning abilities, her academic levels, and her individual learning styles and learning preferences but must also show a concern for each student by tailoring instruction to meet her unique needs. In creating the concept of differentiation, Tomlinson (1999) incorporated a wide range of recent research on how diverse students learn. The concept was primarily founded on Dr. Howard Gardner's concept of multiple intelligences, coupled with the more recent instructional suggestions emerging from the brain-compatible research literature (Gardner, 2006; Goleman. 2006; Moran, Kornhaber, & Gardner, 2006: Sousa & Tomlinson, 2011; Tomlinson, 1999). With this emphasis on diverse learning styles as a backdrop, Tomlinson encouraged teachers to personalize the instructional activities in order to challenge students with a highly interactive, challenging, and interesting curriculum. Teachers were encouraged to consider students' unique learning styles and then differentiate the educational activities presented in the class to provide for those divergent learning styles.

In particular, Tomlinson encouraged differentiation in three areas:

1. *Content* (what is learned)

2. *Process* (how the content is mastered by the student)

3. *Product* (how the learning is observed and evaluated)

The learning content involves what students are to master and what we want the students to accomplish after instruction (Tomlinson, 1999; Tomlinson, 2010). The academic content that students are expected to master is today delineated in state-approved curricula or (for many states) within the Common Core State Standards (www.commoncorestandards/thestandards). Thus, the content, in many ways, is a "given" in education today and typically cannot be varied a great deal by the teacher. However, the presentation of that content can be varied, and teachers might choose to present content in a variety of forms including modeling the content, rehearsal, choral chanting, movement associated with the content, educational games, or student-developed projects associated with the content. Of course, these variations should be established with specific learners and their needs in mind, and all have been discussed in the literature on differentiation (Bender, 2008; Chapman & King, 2003; 2005; Gregory, 2008).

Differentiated instruction also emphasized the learning process that students must complete in learning the content (Tomlinson, 1999). Of course, different students learn in different ways—some through movement associated with the content, and others through visual aids or graphic organizers, while others learn via outlining (Bender, 2008; 2009a; Sousa & Tomlinson, 2011). In short, the learning process might vary from student to student, so teachers are encouraged to offer a variety of learning options and fit those options to the learning process that best meets the needs of individual students in the class.

Finally, the learning product is of paramount importance because varied demonstrations of learning allow the teacher to determine the students who have mastered the material and those who may need more time and continued instruction (Tomlinson, 1999). Again, the learning styles of the students in the class should help determine what types of products the teacher may wish to accept as demonstrations of learning. In the differentiated learning classroom, it would not be uncommon for a given unit of instruction to have four or five different types of culminating projects that students may choose in order to demonstrate their knowledge of the topic. Art projects, role-play minidramas for groups of students, library or web-based research, digital media portfolios, multimedia projects, as well as paper-and-pencil projects, written reports, or oral reports, all represent excellent projects that students may complete to demonstrate their knowledge (Bender & Waller, 2011b). The various assessment options associated with differentiated instruction are discussed throughout the text.

Using this early view of differentiated instruction, teachers have been expected to modify the instruction in these three areas—content, process, and product—in order to address the individual learning needs of all of the students in the class (Bender, 2008; Tomlinson, 1999; 2010). Furthermore, the teacher's relationship with, and knowledge of, the students in the class was considered the basis for the differentiation, and so the relationship between the teacher and the pupil was and is viewed as critical for effective instruction. Only a solid positive relationship and fairly complete knowledge of the student's abilities, learning styles, and preferences can provide an effective basis for differentiated instruction.

> Teachers have been expected to modify the instruction in these three areas—content, process, and product—in order to address the individual learning needs of all of the students in the class.

Multiple Intelligences Theory And Differentiated Instruction

As noted above, Tomlinson based many of her ideas on the theory of multiple intelligences of Dr. Howard Gardner (2006, 1983; Tomlinson, 1999). In short, Tomlinson described the diverse learning needs of students in terms of the various abilities (which Dr. Gardner referred to as intelligences), so in many ways, the early discussions of differentiation were in the early years, clearly tied to the multiple intelligence theory (e.g., Bender, 2008; Chapman & King, 2005). For that reason, some discussion of the multiple intelligences theory is necessary, in order to understand the early perspectives on differentiated instruction.

Dr. Howard Gardner's work on intelligence in children (Gardner, 2006; Moran et al., 2006) has served a crucial function in education, since his work, and other work on learning styles and learning preferences, has refocused how educators understand student learning. Essentially, Gardner postulated eight different intelligences, which he refers to as relatively independent but interacting cognitive capacities (Gardner, 2006; Moran et al., 2006). The eight intelligences that Dr. Gardner considers confirmed are presented in Box 1.1 below. Dr. Gardner has likewise tentatively identified a ninth intelligence (moral intelligence), but does not, as yet, consider the existence of that intelligence confirmed (Gardner, 2006; Sousa & Tomlinson, 2011).

BOX 1.1: GARDNER'S MULTIPLE INTELLIGENCES

Verbal-linguistic: An ability to understand and use spoken and written communications, abstract reasoning, symbolic thinking, and conceptual patterning. Individuals with this strength make excellent poets and attorneys. This intelligence is highly emphasized in schools.

Logical-mathematical: Ability to understand and use logic and numeric symbols and operations, recognize patterns, and see connections between separate pieces of information. These individuals tend to excel in math and related fields such as computer programming.

Musical: Ability to understand and use such concepts as rhythm, pitch, melody, and harmony. These individuals often are highly sensitive to sounds, and will excel in music composition, but note that this intelligences does not necessarily mean the individual has performing talent in each of these areas.

Spatial: Ability to orient and manipulate three-dimensional space. Judgments based on spatial intelligence allow some individuals to shoot a basketball through a hoop 30 feet away with relative ease. These individuals can excel in architecture, mapmaking, and games requiring visualization of objects from differing perspectives.

Bodily-kinesthetic: Ability to coordinate physical movement, or use the body to express emotion. Students with this strength often excel in athletics.

Naturalistic: The ability to distinguish and categorize objects or phenomena in nature, master taxonomy, or demonstrate extreme sensitivity to nature. The ideal occupation for a person with this strength is zoologist.

Interpersonal: An ability to understand, interpret, and interact well with others. Students who seem to "come alive" when working in small-group work represent this type of learner, and the ideal occupation for this person include politics and/or sales.

Intrapersonal: The ability to interpret, explain, and use their own thoughts, feelings, preferences, perceptions, and interests. This ability can assist persons in any job, since self-regulation is one component of success in almost every task. These persons succeed in reflective professions (e.g., authors) and entrepreneurship.

Moral intelligence (the potential ninth intelligence): An ability to contemplate phenomena or questions from a superordinate, moral perspective, beyond sensory data, such as contemplations of the infinite. This is the more recent of these intelligences described, and there are still questions about the reality of this as a separate intelligence.

As described above, these abilities or intelligences seem to exist in almost everyone to some degree, and almost everyone demonstrates strengths in several different intelligences (Gardner, 1983; Moran et al., 2006). Focusing on these intelligences and planning instructional activities with these in mind will, it is believed, result in a wider array of educational activities in the classroom, and various researchers proposed that teachers should consider these intelligences in planning every lesson (Bender, 2008; Chapman & King, 2005; Moran et al., 2006).

We should point out that Gardner's work represents one theory of intelligence and that even the existence of these eight (or nine) separate intelligences has not been independently validated (Sousa, 2006, 2010), and various researchers have questioned these intelligences, and/or the relevance of this theory for education (see the discussion by Sousa, 2010). It is fair to assert that these intelligences are based on Dr. Gardner's expertise and observations, rather than on solid, empirical research. Thus, subsequent research may show that, in reality, only five or six of these nine exist, or that these intelligences are merely behavioral response differences and not actual distinctions in thought processes within the brain. For that reason, some caution is in order here.

> Gardner's work represents one theory of intelligence, and even the existence of these eight (or nine) separate intelligences has not been independently validated

However, even with those cautions in mind, Gardner's work has highlighted several points on which almost all educators agree. First, students do seem to learn in highly diverse ways, and knowledge of these different ways of learning can offer the opportunity for teachers to build instructional activities that involve a number of varied cognitive capabilities. It was in this realm that Tomlinson (1999; 2010) utilized multiple intelligences theory as the basis for advocating increased differentiation in curricular activities.

Secondly, expanding the range of educational activities in the traditional classroom will, in all likelihood, result in enhanced learning, as students with varied learning styles become more cognitively engaged with the content (King & Gurian, 2006; Marzano, 2010; O'Meara, 2010; Silver & Perini, 2010a; 2010b). For these reasons, many practitioners, including this author, have advocated use of this multiple intelligence construct for educational planning purposes over the years (Bender. 2008, 2009a; Sousa & Tomlinson, 2011).

In fact, even Gardner and his colleagues have cautioned against "reductionistic" thinking and educational planning based on this theory (Moran et al., 2006). When presented with this theory, some educators immediately began to plan nine different versions of each instructional activity, and this was clearly not Dr. Gardner's intent (Moran et al., 2006). Rather, these capacities must be viewed in terms of relative strengths and weaknesses that interrelate with each other. Some students demonstrate a particularly strong intelligence in one area, whereas others seem to demonstrate strengths in a "cluster" of intelligences, and effective educational planning should generally offer a variety of opportunities to engage with the learning content using a variety of the learning styles.

Rather than planning nine versions of the same lesson, teachers who wish to address these multiple intelligences are well advised to consider planning in terms of longer units of instruction (Bender, 2008; 2009a). Within a five- or 10-day instructional unit, teachers can provide activities that address the learning styles represented by various intelligences in order to devise an interesting array of highly diverse educational activities. Those various activities would then be targeted to the strengths of the different learners in the class. Wiliam (2011) suggested that students be taught about their own learning styles in order to encourage them to challenge themselves in task selection by choosing tasks that may not be particularly congruent with their own learning style. Teaching Tip 1.1 presents a sample of the types of activities that might be used in a middle-elementary class in a mathematics unit that would tap strengths in each of these intelligences. In a two-week unit on fractions, teachers should be able to implement each of these instructional ideas as either individual or small-group work.

The New Differentiated Instruction

With that brief summary of differentiated instruction and multiple intelligences theory in mind, teachers today must realize that there have been a number of shifts in emphasis that impact differentiated instruction teaching practices today (Bender, 2008; O'Meara, 2010; Sousa & Tomlinson, 2011). Further, several factors that are independent of the differentiated instructional concept

Teaching Tip 1.1

Multiple Intelligence Teaching Suggestions for Mathematics

Verbal-linguistic: Write a description of several fractions, and/or draw a picture to illustrate each.

Logical-mathematical: Describe and evaluate a recipe, then multiply it by two to serve twice as many people.

Musical: Use a chant to learn the steps in reducing fractions, or to memorize multiplication or division math facts. Have students write a "rap" about how to reduce improper fractions.

Spatial: Visualize large objects, and mentally divide them into fractional parts. Draw those objects and fractional parts of them.

Bodily-kinesthetic: Mount a large circle on the wall, from the floor to approximately head high. Have a student stand in front of the circle and use his or her body to divide the circle into fractions. Standing with hands by one's side, the body divides the circle into halves-head to foot. Holding one's arms out straight to each side divides the circle into fourths and so on.

Naturalistic: Explore the core of an apple, cutting it into fractional parts.

Interpersonal: Playing musical chairs, discuss the improper fractions in the game (i.e., five persons circling four chairs is the improper fraction of 5/4). Another idea is to have pairs of kids create fractional parts together by cutting up circles/squares.

Intrapersonal: Have these introspective children keep a daily journal of each experience in their home lives where they experience fractions (e.g., "I wanted more cake last night, so I ate 1/2 of the part that was left over").

Moral intelligence: Have this child reflect on the relationship between one person and the groups to which he or she belongs ("I am 1/22 of this class, and 1/532 of this school, while our class is 22/532 of this school"). Write down these reflections and share them with the class.

have likewise impacted this instructional approach to such a degree that educators today should become aware of these factors, what this author refers to as the new differentiated instruction. This section presents a variety of factors that have impacted the differentiated instructional concept since 1999.

Learning Styles, Learning Preferences, or Intelligences?

As indicated above, the original differentiated instructional concept was developed, to a considerable degree, with the multiple intelligences theory of Dr. Howard Gardner as the basis (Gardner, 1983; Tomlinson, 1999), and while the multiple intelligences construct has served a critically important function in development of this instructional approach, educators today look to a wider variety of learning styles and learning preferences than are typically presented within multiple intelligences theory (Sousa & Tomlinson, 2011; Tomlinson, 2010; Tomlinson, Brimijoin, & Narvaez, 2008; Wiliam, 2011). Thus, to some extent, the very basis of differentiated instruction, as well as for planning differentiated educational tasks within the classroom, has changed somewhat since 1999 (Bender & Waller, 2011b; Sousa & Tomlinson, 2011; Tomlinson, 2010; Tomlinson et al., 2008).

For example, in some of the recent books and chapters on differentiated instruction the multiple intelligences theory is not mentioned at all (O'Meara, 2010; Tomlinson, 2010; Tomlinson et al., 2008), while other books include multiple intelligences along with one or more alternative learning style theories or perspectives on intellectual processing (Sousa & Tomlinson, 2011). This seems to indicate a shift toward more diverse perspectives on learning style, and a wider attention to other student variations within the classroom as the basis for forming differentiated instructional groups (Bender & Waller, 2011b; Sousa & Tomlinson, 2011).

Even the definitions of the terms used in this discussion seem to be somewhat clouded in the literature. In this book, the terms learning style, learning preference, and multiple intelligences are used as if they are roughly synonymous, since most educators, at least in the experience of this author, consider multiple intelligences as one perspective in the broader learning style literature. However, other proponents might advocate against such usage, considering learning styles to be fundamentally different from abilities or intelligences. Learning styles or preferences in some of the literature may, for some, represent choices students tend to make regarding their preferred learning environment (lighter versus darker rooms, or completing only one task at a time versus doing many tasks simultaneously; see Sousa & Tomlinson, 2011). In contrast, the term "intelligences" may be limited to mental processing styles that are relatively independent of the environment, such as the multiple intelligences in Dr. Gardner's original multiple intelligences theory (2006; 1983).

Further, at least two alternative learning or intelligences approaches are considered as appropriate bases for planning the differentiated lesson. First, Robert Sternberg's (1985) triarchic theory of intelligence suggests that students process information and ideas in one of three ways, analytic, practical, or creative, as described in Box 1.2. This description of three "intelligences" has been specifically highlighted recently as one basis for differentiated instructional planning (Sousa & Tomlinson, 2011).

BOX 1.2: STERNBERG'S TRIARCHIC THEORY OF INTELLIGENCE

Analytic intelligence—emphasizes "part to whole" thinking and is typically strongly emphasized in many school tasks. A strength in this area aids in delving into the components or specific aspects of a task or concept.

Practical intelligence—is sometimes described as contextual understanding and emphasizes how concepts apply in real-world settings. A strength in this intelligence would allow a student to problem solve and apply his understandings in different situations.

Creative intelligences—this can best be summarized as "out of the box" thinking. Rather than problem solving with an eye to real-world needs, the creative thinker tends to refocus or reenvision the environment such that novel solutions present themselves.

BOX 1.3: SILVER, STRONG, AND PERINI'S LEARNING STYLES

Mastery style. Students with this learning style proceed in a step-by-step fashion, focusing on practical implications of the content. These students are highly motivated by success, take pride in developing new understandings, and respond well to competitive and challenging learning tasks.

Understanding style. Students with this style question the content, analyzing the implications of it and fitting the pieces of a construct together. These students want to make sense of the academic content and respond well to puzzles, games, or discussions of controversy.

Self-expressive style. Students with this learning style demonstrate innovative thinking and imagination when undertaking a learning task. They long to be unique in their thinking and original in their approach to any task, seeking understanding that only they have reached. These students respond well to choices in their work and creative assignments.

Interpersonal style. Students with this learning style learn best in the social context, exploring their own feelings or the feelings and understandings of others. These students thrive in cooperative learning situations and are highly emotive in sharing their feelings.

Another conceptualization of students' mental processing styles has been proposed by Silver, Strong, & Perini (2000). These researchers advocated consideration of four learning styles that impact the motivation shown by learners in the classroom, and within that context these authors recommend specific types of instructional tasks for various learners (Silver & Perini, 2010a, 2010b). Box 1.3 presents the four learning styles identified by Silver et al. (2000), and suggestions for the types of learning tasks that might work for various learners.

While other views of abilities, intelligences, and/or learning styles and preferences that impact learning could well be presented in this context, these several perspectives seem to be capturing most of the attention in various discussions on differentiated instruction. Several things are clear in this literature. First, most educators today believe students learn in a variety of ways, and that attention to these learning styles and preferences will positively impact student engagement with the academic content and ultimately student achievement (Bender, 2008; O'Meara, 2010; Silver & Perini, 2010b; Sternberg, 2006; Sousa, 2010; Tomlinson et al., 2008). Next, educators around the world are today encouraged to implement differentiated instruction in order to provide learning activities that address some of these varied learning styles and preferences. For example, as reported by Berkeley, Bender, Peaster, and Saunders (2009), virtually every RTI plan implemented in the various states stressed differentiated instruction as the cornerstone of general education instruction.

Thus, discussions of differentiated instruction today focus more broadly on differences in general learning styles and individualized or small-group learning center instruction for either heterogeneous or homogeneous groups based on these learning styles. One might well say that, in contrast to 1999, the differentiated instructional paradigm is now free from dependency on only one theory of intelligence (Sousa & Tomlinson, 2011).

> Most educators today believe students learn in a variety of ways, and attention to these learning styles and preferences will positively impact student engagement with the academic content and ultimately student achievement.

Brain Physiology, Learning, and the New Differentiated Instruction

In addition to the broadening theoretical basis for differentiated instruction, there are other changes in emphasis within the broader differentiated instructional paradigm. In particular, the work on the physiology of learning process has come to influence the differentiated instructional approach much more since 1999 (Sousa & Tomlinson, 2011). Of course, much of the work on the physiology and neurochemistry of learning has been undertaken since the original differentiated instructional concept was described by Tomlinson (1999), and this research, both theoretical and practical in nature, has clear implications for differentiating instruction in both reading and mathematics (Bender, 2009a; 2008; Caine & Caine, 2006; Coch, 2010; Devlin, 2010; Shah, 2012; Sousa, 2010; Sousa & Tomlinson, 2011).

> Much of the work on the physiology and neurochemistry of learning has been undertaken since the original differentiated instructional concept was described by Tomlinson.

Often referred to as brain-compatible learning, this research is now providing a more solid basis for differentiated instruction than did the multiple intelligences theory in isolation. Thus, a more research-based theory for differentiated instruction is developing, and has been discussed as a more solid scientific basis for differentiated instruction (Sousa & Tomlinson, 2011; Bender & Waller, 2011a). More information on this brain-compatible research, and the differentiated instructional suggestions stemming from that research, is presented later in this chapter.

Next, differentiated instruction today is more broadly focused than the original differentiation concept (Tomlinson, 2010; Sousa & Tomlinson, 2011). Initially,

> Brain-compatible learning is now providing a more solid basis for differentiated instruction than did the multiple intelligences theory in isolation.

differentiated instruction focused on the three areas presented above, differentiated content, process, and product (Tomlinson, 1999), and differentiated instruction groups were based on the various multiple intelligences in order to strengthen student learning. However, today while differentiated instruction still stresses these three ideas, other areas are likewise considered essential for differentiated instruction, including respect for the learner, a powerful, engaging curriculum, flexible groupings for academic tasks based on student interest, student readiness, as well as learning preferences, ongoing assessment and a positive learning environment, attuned to student needs (Sousa & Tomlinson, 2011). As these areas continue to increase, the concept of differentiated instruction continues to broaden over time.

Recent Initiatives Impact Differentiated Instruction

With these modifications of the original differentiated instructional concept in mind, there are at least two other factors that have impacted differentiated instruction. First, the differentiated instruction concept has been and will be transformed, based on the increasing use of technology in the classroom (Bender & Waller, 2011b). While differentiated instruction has always emphasized consideration of students' learning styles, strengths, and the formation of instruction groups based on those, the increased availability of technology, social networking, and computerized curricula in the classroom today allows for a totally differentiated instructional program.

In fact, placing students individually in appropriate, engaging, well-designed computer-based curricula might be envisioned as the epitome of differentiated instruction, since such well-designed curricula do deliver individualized instruction that is highly targeted to students' individual needs and based on their individual academic levels. In many modern computer programs, educators can vary the amount of stimulation that the program delivers to the student during the lesson, thus addressing some of the factors associated with varied learning styles. These might include variations in the way problems are presented (e.g., the amount of color, or noise, or animation used), or the level of instructional assistance provided. Even the timing may be varied in modern computer-based curricula (i.e. the rate of presentation of the questions, etc.).

All of these possible variations allow educators to tailor the computer-based instructional presentation to students with various learning styles, and thus, this can be considered highly differentiated instruction (Bender & Waller, 2011b). While some computer-based instructional programs have offered many of these variations for at least 25 years, today most programs do, and teachers are becoming adept at using these options to provide differentiated instructional assignments for their students. Thus, computer- and Internet-based instruction today hold much more potential for allowing teachers to differentiate instruction than was the case in 1999.

However, technology is impacting instruction in many ways today that go far beyond merely effective computer-based instructional programs. Various social networking options (e.g., Facebook, Twitter, or Ning), use of wikis or class blogs for instructional collaborations, and creation of content offer instructional options that have not, as yet, been conceptualized as methods for differentiating instruction. Indeed, most of the recent books focused on modern instructional technology in the classroom have not mentioned differentiated instruction at all (Ferriter & Garry, 2010; Richardson & Mancabelli, 2011). Clearly this oversight needs to be addressed, as not only can individual computerized curricula aid in our efforts to differentiate instruction, but more recently developed (and developing) networking technologies can aid the differentiated effort as well, as students choose their role in various learning projects in their effort to create their own learning content (Bender & Waller, 2011a). Students are demonstrating, via their nonschool behaviors, that they love social networking, and as educators grow in our understanding of how these social networking tools may be used in education, many opportunities for increased differentiation of instruction are likely to result. The impact of technologies for teaching on differentiation is presented in more detail in Chapter 3.

> Most of the recent books focused on modern instructional technology in the classroom have not mentioned differentiated instruction at all.

Another instructional innovation that has transformed and continues to transform education today is the response to intervention initiative (RTI). RTI represents a mandate to deliver multi-tiered levels of supplemental instruction for students in the classroom, in order to assure that students' instructional needs are met with the exact level of instructional intensity necessary to assure their success (Bender, 2009b; Bender & Crane, 2010; Bender & Shores, 2007). Of course, the provision of supplemental, intensive instruction is much less necessary if a wider variety of instruction needs are met within the general education classroom. That is why, in many states, the differentiated instructional paradigm was "written into" or required by the various state plans as the basis for all Tier 1 instruction within the RTI initiative (Berkeley et al., 2009). More detail on the impact of RTI on differentiated instruction for students with learning disabilities is presented in the assessment chapter, Chapter 4.

Finally, the implementation of Common Core State Standards in education by the 46 states that have chosen to participate in the Common Core is likely to impact how teachers differentiate instruction in their classes. For this reason, a brief introduction to the Common Core State Standards and the issues surrounding them is presented below.

Conclusion: The New Differentiated Instruction

These factors, taken together, have resulted in a new understanding of differentiated instruction. The increased emphasis on the physiology of learning using modern instructional technologies for teaching implementation of Common Core State Standards and differentiation within the RTI paradigm—a paradigm that is driving education today—have all merged to create a new differentiated instructional paradigm, and in this instance, the whole is greater than the sum of the parts (Bender & Waller, 2011a). That is, each of these instructional innovations has become transformed by interaction with these other factors, and the resulting educational procedures currently evolving do not greatly resemble traditional educational practices.

COMMON CORE STATE STANDARDS AND DIFFERENTIATION

> The Common Core State Standards promise to significantly impact how instruction is undertaken over the next decade.

By 2012, 45 states had decided to adopt the Common Core State Standards (Toppo, 2012). Only Texas, Alaska, Nebraska, Minnesota, and Virginia have not adopted these standards, meaning that most teachers will be working within the context of the common core standards. Clearly the Common Core State Standards promise to significantly impact differentiated instruction over the next decade, so some understanding of those standards is essential for determining how teachers might differentiate their instruction.

The Common Core State Standards were developed by the National Governors Association Center for Best Practices and the Council of Chief State School Officers in collaboration with teachers, school administrators, and curriculum experts in order to provide a clear and consistent framework to prepare our children for higher education and/or the workforce (see http://www.corestandards.org/the-standards).

Initially, standards were developed by expert teams, and input was solicited from many sources including various teacher organizations, higher education educators, civil rights groups, and advocates for students with disabilities. Following the initial round of feedback, the draft standards were opened for public comment, and nearly 10,000 responses were considered in preparing the final standards. The standards in reading and mathematics were finalized and initially released in 2010. These standards represent, in participating states, the instructional content that students are expected to learn. Further, the standards are intended to provide appropriate benchmarks for all students, regardless of where they live. They are described by the developing agency as clear and consistent, rigorous with an emphasis on higher-order skills, and evidence based.

Because these standards are intended to represent a common core for instruction across states, in some cases there is little difference between the current state standards in reading and/or mathematics and the Common Core standards. For example, the Common Core standards still call for fluency in addition and subtraction by the end of Grade 3, and that is quite common in many existing state standards (Wurman & Wilson, 2012). In that sense, implementation of these standards may be more involved in some states than in others.

Still, implementation activities involving the Common Core are ongoing, and as of Spring 2012, various organizations have partnered together for curriculum development and professional development activities. For example, in May 2012, Universities and school districts from 30 states have partnered together to foster implementation of the Common Core State Standards for Mathematics, though the scope of this partnership has yet to be determined (Sawchuk, 2012).

In addition to the Common Core State Standards, and the Standards for Mathematical Practice, two different teams at the national level are developing common assessments for the Common Core State Standards for Mathematics and for English Language Arts (Shaughnessy, 2011). Once these different assessment frameworks are developed, it is anticipated that all participating states will choose which framework to implement in addition to their Common Core instruction. While that work is ongoing as of 2012, the implementation of these Common Core assessments in reading and mathematics is currently scheduled for 2014. Information on these assessments in mathematics is presented at the website of the National Council of Teachers of Mathematics (http://www.nctm.org/uploadedFiles/Research_News_and_Advocacy/Summing_Up/Articles/2011/AchieveCOMAPPARCC(1).pdf#search=%22Common Core Assessment Plans%22). As this discussion indicates, much work is ongoing as of 2012 in reading and mathematics instruction, and this will impact how teachers deliver differentiated instruction in their classes for the next decade.

As this indicates, a major national effort is under way to implement the Common Core State Standards. While most educators are supportive of the Common Core State Standards, there are many who have raised concerns about the Common Core standards, even prior to the implementation date of 2014 (Loveless, 2012; Tucker, 2012; Ujifusa, 2012; Wurman & Wilson, 2012). In early 2012, Tom Loveless published a report, "How Well Are American Students Learning?" as one of the Brown Center's Reports on American Education, published by the Brookings Institution (http://www.brokings.edu/reports/2012/0216_brown_education_loveless.aspx).

That Brown Center report that was largely critical of the idea that setting rigorous academic standards enhances academic achievement, though that conclusion was based on academic achievement data related to previous state standards in various states rather than the Common Core standards themselves, as the Common Core State Standards have yet to be implemented, as of 2012. Still, that conclusion ignited a firestorm among educational leaders (Hess, 2012; Loveless, 2012; Tucker, 2012). Specifically, Loveless (2012) argued that adoption of earlier state standards was not related to achievement scores on the National Assessment of Educational Progress from 2003 through 2009. Further, he concluded that there was little evidence that setting standards can close achievement gaps between groups (Loveless, 2012).

Independent of the debate on the impact of the Common Core on student achievement, other concerns with these standards have arisen, and several advocacy groups in education have gone on record as opposing these standards (Ujifusa, 2012). The Common Core State Standards were intended to be more simple and streamlined than the standards adopted by the individual states previously while demanding increased performance, but some have suggested that standards in mathematics for many states (e.g., California and Minnesota), were more rigorous than the Common Core State Standards (Wurman & Wilson, 2012). Clearly, this critique, if true, would defeat the purpose of the entire Common Core standards effort, and needless to say, this major national effort is likely to cost millions of dollars across the nation.

In conclusion, it is not yet known how effective the implementation of the Common Core State Standards will be over the next decade. However, all teachers in participating states can anticipate extensive involvement with these standards, and thus, this will impact teacher's efforts to differentiate instruction. Thus, any description of differentiated instruction must be framed in the context of the Common Core State Standards in reading and mathematics.

BRAIN-COMPATIBLE INSTRUCTION IN THE DIFFERENTIATED CLASSROOM

As indicated previously, the emerging research on brain functioning has provided a solid foundation for differentiated instruction since the concept was introduced in 1999 (Bender, 2009a; Bender & Waller, 2011b; Shah, 2012; Sousa & Tomlinson, 2011). While related in a general way to the concept of multiple intelligences, the literature on brain-compatible instruction is much more solidly grounded in the neurosciences (Caine & Caine, 2006; Shah, 2012; Simos et al., 2007; Sousa. 2006, 2010). However, like multiple intelligences, the instructional ideas stemming from the neurosciences provided Tomlinson (1999) with another foundation for differentiated instruction (Sousa & Tomlinson, 2011).

Brain-compatible instruction has emerged since 1990, primarily based on improvements in the medical sciences (Caine & Caine, 2006; Shah, 2012; Simos et al., 2007; Sousa, 2010). In fact, much of our increasing understanding of the human brain has come from the development of the functional magnetic resonance imaging techniques (a technique that is sometimes represented in the literature as the fMRI). This is a non-radiological technique—and thus a relatively safe brain-scanning technique—that has allowed scientists to study the performance of human brains while the subjects concentrated on different types of learning tasks. The fMRI measures the brain's use of oxygen and sugar during the thinking process, and, from that information, physicians can determine which brain areas are most active during various types of educational tasks (Sousa, 1999). For example, specialists have now identified brain regions that are specifically associated with various learning activities such as language, reading, math, motor learning, music appreciation, or verbal response to questions in a classroom discussion (Sousa, 2006, 2010).

Caine and Caine (2006), two leaders in the field of brain-compatible instruction, refer to learning in terms of *cognits*, which are defined as organized configurations of brain cells that activate together and result in a unified thought. These may range from simple cognits, which represent a single fact, to much more involved cognits that might be activated to handle more complex information. From this perspective, the teacher's role is to provide instructional experiences that are rich in learning potential and thus develop more and/or increasingly complex cognits.

For example, having a student complete a written problem involving the addition of negative 2 plus positive 3 activates a number of different cognits within the brain, and thus can result in learning. However, having that same student "walk through" the same addition problems using a number line of positive and negative integers on the floor activates many more cognits within the brain, and thus results in higher impact learning—both increased understanding and enhanced memory. Further, Caine and Caine (2006) have specified the types of high impact activities students should engage in when presented with new material in the class. Students should

- undergo sensory and emotional experiences tied to the content, because sensory and emotional tags associated with content learning enhances memory;
- make associations with previous knowledge and their own experiences;
- articulate questions and develop a focus that leads to planning their activities on the content;
- perform some movement or action related to understanding the content or produce some product associated with it; and
- be challenged with high quality curricula that are minutely more challenging than tasks the student is known to perform independently.

GENERAL CONCLUSIONS FOR BRAIN-COMPATIBLE TEACHING

Thus, the neurosciences are now providing some general information that will inform instructional practices in the differentiated class (Bender, 2009a; Doidge, 2007; Merzenich, 2001; Shah, 2012). First, studies are now under way using the fMRI technology to attempt to predict which kindergarten students might experience reading difficulties in later school years (Shah, 2012). This diagnostic application of neurosciences may provide information that allows educators to intervene earlier in the education process for those students. Also, several actual curricula have been developed using the emerging insights from the neurosciences (Doidge, 2007; Shah, 2012). Thus, both the diagnostic process and educational interventions for the differentiated classroom are now based, in part, on this emerging area of science.

Some authors have even presented syntheses on what this brain-compatible research may mean in the classroom, and while there is little consensus, several tentative conclusions have emerged. First, engaging our students' brains in active, deep thought on the content is critical for higher level conceptual learning (Bender, 2008; Doidge, 2007; Merzenich, Tallal, Peterson, Miller, & Jenkins, 1999; Merzenich, 2001; Shah, 2012). While many different proponents have provided instructional guidelines, the key is to engage students' brains with critical content in a fashion that stimulates maximum brain involvement. Teaching strategies and activities that engage brains in that fashion seem to enhance student achievement overall (Doidge, 2007; Merzenich et al., 1999; Merzenich, 2001; Shah, 2012; Silver & Perini, 2010a; Sternberg, 2006; Tate, 2005), since they are more likely to lead to long-term retention, than more traditional instructional techniques.

> The key to teaching is to engage students' brains with critical content in a fashion that stimulates maximum brain involvement, and teaching strategies and activities that engage brains more enhance student achievement overall.

Next, extensive cognitive engagement with the critical content in an instructional unit may be more critical in learning than "content coverage" for overall mastery of the content (Bender & Waller, 2011b; Shah, 2012).

Therefore the idea of "teaching less content, but teaching it more thoroughly" is a sound teaching principle across the public school grades (Fogarty & Pate, 2010).

Next, effective teaching involves creating exciting, innovative differentiated learning activities that will actively engage today's students with the learning content in a rich, meaningful, highly involved manner (Bender, 2008; 2009a; Doidge, 2007; Shah, 2012; Tomlinson & McTighe, 2006). Today's students expect and respond to nothing less than the stimulation they have grown used to in today's digital, media rich, highly interactive and technological world, and teachers must structure their instruction to approximate that modern world, in order to reach students today. Thus, using brain-compatible teaching ideas, coupled with modern technologies to engage our students is now critical. Teachers must create differentiated learning activities that emulate the high tech world of our students, and on that basis instruction is much more likely to be more effective (Bender & Waller, 2011a, 2011b; Gregory, 2008).

Next, to the degree possible, teachers should create "authentic" learning environments in which students actually "experience" the content and/or produce the content, rather than merely read about it, discuss it, or study it (Larmer, Ross, & Mergendoller, 2009). Interactive activities such as creation of podcasts, Internet searches, and group projects based on web-based collaborative development tools are likely to enhance learning much more than traditional "read, discuss, and test" instruction. Such "experiential learning" will result in deeper understanding and longer-term learning of the content in question (Sternberg, 2006).

Recent Discoveries on Learning

While this single text cannot present the exciting array of recent findings from the neurosciences, several additional discoveries bear directly on discussions of the ways students experience learning in the classroom. First, within the last several years, a set of neurons commonly called "mirror neurons" have been identified within the human brain (Goleman, 2006; Sousa. 2006). These neurons allow human beings to create internal, mental simulations of what is going on in the minds or emotions of other people in their environment. Thus, when two people interact, their minds are actually influencing each other (Goleman, 2006), and they are likely to increasingly reflect each other's moods and emotions. In fact, they are quite likely to begin to "match" each other on such things as voice volume, voice tone, emotional intensity, or even facial expression and body language, depending on the degree and level of intensity of the interaction. Thus, when teachers or students are unhappy in the context of an educational activity, the other students in the class are somewhat predisposed to reflect that in their own moods, emotions, and possibly even their actions (Sousa, 2006, 2010).

Next, brains perform at their best when they are highly motivated and involved and experiencing "manageable" stress (Goleman, 2006). Should a student experience too much stress (e.g., when presented with a math problem he or she cannot do and is expected to perform that problem on the dry-erase board in front of the whole class), energy is shunted into the emotional centers of the brain, and the cerebrum or "cognitive area" of the brain actually demonstrates reduced brain activity. Thus, higher order thinking—which takes place in the cerebrum—decreases when students are overstressed in the classroom.

With these neuroscience concepts in mind, it is easy to understand why some instructional environments don't work for many students, including many students with learning disabilities. Students with learning disabilities and other learning problems are more likely to be stressed in the classroom environment and may therefore engage less with the academic content. Taken together, what these findings suggest is that if students do not experience their learning as a warm, positive environment that challenges them at an appropriate level—a level of task which, while challenging, is at least within the realm of the possible for them—those students will actually become less capable of learning as the brain activity in the cerebrum decreases. Thus, every teacher is obligated to ask, "How do all of my students—particularly students with learning disabilities or other learning challenges—experience learning in the context of my classroom?"

Specific Instructional Guidelines for Struggling Students

In addition to these issues raised by the neurosciences, other researchers have suggested that the research on brain-compatible instruction has developed to a point where specific teaching suggestions can be made. On the basis of this research, teachers across the nation have begun to restructure their classroom practices based on these guidelines (Moran et al., 2006; Sousa. 2001, 2010). Although various authors make different recommendations, the 10 tactics for a brain-compatible instruction classroom, presented in Teaching Tip 1.2, represent the accumulated thought in this area (Bender, 2008; Moran et al., 2006: Shah, 2012; Sousa, 2010; Sousa & Tomlinson, 2011; Sternberg, 2006).

Teaching Tip 1.2

10 Tactics for Brain-Compatible Teaching

1. Create a Safe and Comfortable Environment
2. Use Comfortable Furniture, Lighting, Ambiance
3. Offer Water and Fruits Where Possible
4. Encourage Frequent Student Responses
5. Teach Using Bodily Movements to Represent Content
6. Teach With Strong Visual Stimuli
7. Use Chants, Rhythms, and Music
8. Offer Appropriate Wait Time
9. Offer Student Choices
10. Foster Social Networking Around Learning Content

From *Differentiating Instruction for Students With Learning Disabilities: Best Teaching Practices for General and Special Educators*, Second Edition, by William N. Bender. Thousand Oaks, CA: Corwin, 2008. Used with permission.

Create a Safe, Comfortable Environment. Research on learning has demonstrated that the brain serves as a filter on several levels. First, the brain selectively focuses on sounds, sights, and other stimuli that threaten our safety, often to the exclusion of other stimuli. A second priority is information resulting in emotional responses, and only as a last priority does the brain process information for new nonthreatening learning tasks (Sousa. 2001). Thus, based on this filtering or prioritizing brain function, several implications for the classroom come to mind. Clearly, students must not be distracted by a sense of danger in their learning environment: They must feel safe and comfortable in order to be prepared to focus on new material (i.e., the school curriculum) that, by its very nature, is usually not threatening. For students who come from violent homes or communities, who may be picked on at school, or who may frequently feel punished by the school environment, learning new material will be almost impossible. However, physical safety is not enough; for students to feel comfortable, students must feel emotionally secure. Thus, a positive personal relationship with the teacher is paramount. Only in the context of such a comfortable, caring relationship will students with learning disabilities turn their attention to mastering new tasks.

Of course, this holds serious implications for students with learning disabilities because some students may suffer from a sense of frustration in certain classrooms. Students with disabilities may even experience some school classes as "hostile terrain" in which they are frequently punished by either their continuing failure in learning tasks or by the teacher. Clearly, this classroom environment will not support strong academic success for those students.

Use Comfortable Furniture and Lighting. As a part of structuring a comfortable learning environment, many teachers bring "house furniture" into the classroom and set up reading areas with a sofa and perhaps several comfortable chairs. Lamps are also used in brain-compatible classrooms for more "home-like" lighting, and some research has suggested that lighting closer to the red end of the light spectrum functions like a "wake-up" call for the brain.

A moment's reflection on the hardness of the wooden desks in most of our nation's classrooms—desks where students must sit for up to five hours each day—makes this a critical concern for many teachers. How would any adult like to sit at those wooden desks for five or six hours each day for an entire year? A different type of furniture can make our classrooms more user-friendly and facilitate learning.

Offer Water and Fruits If Possible. Research has shown that the brain requires certain fuels—oxygen, glucose, and water—to perform at peak efficiency (Sousa, 2001, p. 20). Up to one fourth of the blood pumped in our bodies with each heartbeat is headed for the brain and central nervous system, and water is critical for even blood flow. Furthermore, water is essential for the movement of neuron signals through the brain (Sousa, 2006). Finally, we now know that fruits are an excellent source of glucose for the brain, and research has shown that eating a moderate amount of fruit can boost performance and accuracy of word memory (Sousa, 2001, 2006). Thus, in brain-compatible classrooms, individual water bottles are usually present on the desks for students to take a sip whenever they need to: water is not a once-an-hour privilege in the brain-compatible class. Also, many teachers offer light fruits as snacks.

Encourage Frequent Student Responses. Students will learn much more when work output is regularly expected from them because students are generally much more engaged in the process of learning when they must produce a product of some type. In fact, students with learning challenges need more practice with newly learned concepts than do other students (Shah, 2012), and this usually means that students should produce more. Note once again the differentiated instructional emphasis on the products of learning. Students must be required to do assignments, either in the form of projects, class work, or homework on any new material that is presented. The frequency of work expected from the students will be a major determinant of how much information students retain. However, the required work output doesn't have to be an entire page of problems—more frequent output of only a few problems each time will be much more useful in the learning process for students with learning disabilities (Sousa, 2001, 2006). More frequent, shorter assignments also give the teacher additional opportunities to check the students' understanding of the concepts covered.

Teach With Bodily Movements to Represent Content. Have you ever wondered why motor skills such as swimming seem to be retained for life, even without routine practice, whereas use of a foreign language quickly atrophies if it is not practiced? Recent brain research has shown that motor skills represent a deeper form of learning than merely cerebral learning, which is why movement is now recommended as a highly effective teaching tool (Sousa, 2010). Motor skills, once learned, are remembered much longer than cognitive skills that do not involve a motor response, and this suggests that, whenever possible, teachers should pair factual memory tasks with physical movements.

> Recent brain research has shown that motor skills represent a deeper form of learning than merely cerebral learning, which is why movement is now recommended as a highly effective teaching tool.

The emerging research on the human brain has addressed this question concerning motor learning versus higher order cognitive learning, and two findings have emerged (see Bender, 2008). First, learning of motor skills takes place in a different area within the brain—the cerebellum, which involves a more basic level of thought than thought in the cerebrum, such as the learning of languages. Secondly, the brain considers motor skills more essential to survival. Because our ancient ancestors often had to run away from predators or, alternatively, had to hunt for their own food in order to survive, motor learning, which generally takes place in the cerebellum, has been prioritized by the brain as a survival skill. Thus, cognitive facts that are frequently paired with motor movements are learned in a deeper way and typically retained longer. In contrast, language or reading skills such as interpreting the shape of the letters in a word takes place in the cerebrum, and is generally interpreted by our brains as a lower priority than movement and other survival skills. Even in the upper grades, various memory tasks can be represented by physical movement, and this will greatly enhance retention for students with learning disabilities as well as most other students (Sousa, 2010).

An example of a movement technique for learning the location of the continents is presented in Teaching Tip 1.3. Note how this movement associates specific bodily orientation with locations of the continents on a world map. This use of movement to teach content is appropriate across the grade levels, and involves a change in the process of learning for students who seem to do better with physical movement as a learning support. The contents of other maps can easily be represented with body parts, as can various other learning tasks (e.g., parts of a business letter or personal letter, or any content in which concepts are graphically related to each other—e.g., parts of a cell).

Teaching Tip 1.3

Teaching With Movement: Locations of the Continents

Chapman (2000) shared an instructional strategy for middle and upper grades using movement to teach locations of the continents. While facing a map of the world on the wall, the students should be told to imagine their bodies superimposed over that map. In that position, the following movement and chanted lines will facilitate learning the locations of the continents. Note that the body parts focused on by the movements below represent the actual locations of the continents on the map.

1.	Extend the left arm with hand open, pointing away from the body	Say "This is North America, where we live."
2.	Move right fist to touch forehead.	Say "This is Europe."
3.	Stick right hand out, palm up, and touch that with the left fist.	Say "This is Asia."
4.	Put both hands on hips.	Say "This is the equator."
5.	Put hands together over one's belt, making a diamond (i.e., thumbs up and touching each other, and index fingers pointing down touching each other).	Say "This is Africa."
6.	Move the thumbs together (while holding the position above).	Say "Part of Africa is above the equator."
7.	Move index fingers (while holding the position above).	Say "Part of Africa is below the equator."
8.	Stick out left leg.	Say "This is South America."
9.	Stick out right leg.	Say "This is Australia."
10.	Bend over and point to the floor.	Say "This is Antarctica. It's cold down there!

Adapted from Chapman, C. (2000). "Brain Compatible Instruction." A paper presented on a nationwide tele-satellite workshop. *Tactics for Brain Compatible Instruction,* the Teacher's Workshop. Bishop, GA.

Teach With Strong Visual Stimuli. Although teachers have known that visual stimuli often enhance learning, this commonsense insight has been confirmed by the brain-compatible instructional literature (Sousa, 2006). There is evidence that boys, in particular, respond more positively to strong, color-enhanced visual stimuli and that boys' brains and visual receptors may be more attuned to moving stimuli than young girls' (King & Gurian, 2006). Therefore, teachers should use color enhancements, size, and shape enhancements in developing lesson materials posted in the classroom because the human brain and central nervous system are specifically attuned to seek out novelty and differences in stimuli (Sousa, 2001, 2006). Thus, highlighting the topic sentence of the paragraph in a different color for students with learning disabilities can be of benefit for them in describing the topic of the paragraph. Likewise, using different colors for different parts of speech (red for nouns, blue for verb, green for adjectives, etc.) can facilitate learning. Also, if possible, teachers should use moving stimuli such as video examples to illustrate academic content.

However, to make color an effective learning tool, the teacher and the student (or the class) should specifically discuss why certain aspects of the material are colored differently and the importance of those colored items. Many computer-driven instructional programs are making use of this technique today and include color highlights or size variations to teach syllabication and other reading skills. Again, this represents a modification of the learning processes for students with various learning challenges.

Use Chanting, Rhymes, and Music. Because music and rhythms are processed in a different area of the brain from language, pairing facts to be learned to a musical melody, or a rhythmic chant, can enhance learning (Tate, 2005). Most adults, on reflection, can remember the song that was frequently used to memorize the ABCs—the tune to *Twinkle, Twinkle Little Star*—and many students used that same song for other memory tasks in the higher grades—the periodic table or division math facts. Again, teachers have used this insight for a number of decades, but the emerging research on the human brain has documented the basis for enhanced learning when music and rhythms are used to enhance memory for the academic content (see Tate, 2005).

Assure Appropriate Wait Time. Students have learned that teachers will often call on the first one or two students who raise their hand after the teacher has asked a question in class. Thus, all that students with learning disabilities have to do is remain "invisible" for a few seconds (i.e., not raise their hand and not look toward the teacher), and the teacher will usually call on someone else. On average, teachers will wait only one or two seconds before calling on someone for an answer, and this period of time between the question and when an answer is called for is defined as "wait time" (Sousa. 2001).

However, students process information at different rates, and the brain research has demonstrated the importance of waiting for a few seconds (perhaps seven to 10 seconds) after asking a question prior to calling on someone for the answer. This increased wait time gives students who process information more slowly and deliberately a period of time to consider their answer and, it is hoped, raise their hand to volunteer a response to the teacher's question. For this reason, adequate wait time can be a critical component of learning for students with learning disabilities, many of whom do process information more slowly than others in the class.

Offer Student Choices: Various educators today emphasize the importance of student choice in the activities they undertake (Larmer, Ross, & Mergendoller, 2009). In short, if teachers want their students to make reasonable and informed choices when they are not in the context of the school, teachers must offer choices within the classroom, and coach students in making informed choices. Such choices may involve the options for demonstrating competence or understanding a set of facts or other choices among assignments on a particular topic, and in a highly differentiated classroom, students will be offered many choices and are likely to use their own understanding of their learning styles and preferences to make such choices.

Use Social Networking for Learning. It has often been noted by veteran teachers that having students explain new information to other students can enhance learning, and the emerging research on the human brain has once again supported this instructional procedure. Further, the frequency with which most students today participate in social networking indicates a general preference for social learning opportunities within the classroom (Rushkoff & Dretzin, 2010). Teachers should get in the habit of presenting some information in shorter time frames and then let students discuss that information together, thus enhancing the opportunity for social networking on the academic content. In fact, the brain research suggests presenting new information at the beginning of the period for between 10 and 20 minutes (Sousa, 2001), and then pausing to ask students to reflect together on the new information.

Further, students are demonstrating by their own actions that they enjoy learning in the context of a social environment. Most students today engage in social networking using Facebook and other such platforms for many hours each week, and, on average, teenagers in 2012 text approximately 3,000 times per month, or over 100 times daily (Bender & Waller, 2011a; List & Bryant, 2010; Rushkoff & Dretzin, 2010). As more student choice is offered in the classroom, students are quite likely to choose social networking as one basis for learning, and this represents an option for providing differentiated activities that could not have been foreseen previously. The use of social networking for instruction using modern communications technologies is discussed in more detail in Chapter 3.

Efficacy of Differentiated Instruction

With all of the emphasis now placed on brain-compatible, highly differentiated instruction, it may come as a surprise that the research supportive of differentiated instruction is still somewhat limited. To date, there has been no systematic empirical research on differentiated instruction and its potential impact on student achievement. In an educational world of "show me the data," this lack of empirical research for differentiated instruction is somewhat surprising. In particular, more than a decade of time has now passed since differentiated instruction was introduced in 1999 (Tomlinson, 1999), and one may well ask, where is the supportive research?

In response, there is a growing body of evidence, much of which is anecdotal, that is suggestive of the positive impact of differentiated instruction

(King & Gurian, 2006; Tomlinson et al., 2008). This limited research does suggest the positive impact of differentiated instruction coupled with increased brain-compatible instructional activities on student achievement (Caine & Caine, 2006; Doidge, 2007; King & Gurian, 2006; Lee, Wehmeyer, Soukup, & Palmer, 2010; Merzenich, 2001; Merzenich et al., 1999; Tate, 2005; Tomlinson, 2010; Tomlinson et al., 2008; Silver & Perini, 2010b; Sousa, 2005, 2009, 2010; Sternberg, 2006).

> There is a growing body of anecdotal evidence that is suggestive of the positive impact of differentiated instruction.

As one example, Tomlinson and her coauthors (2008) presented evidence of academic improvement in two schools as a result of implementation of differentiated instructional practices. Conway Elementary School and Colchester High School were described as two ordinary schools in different districts of the United States, though student performance at Colchester High was somewhat weaker than achievement at Conway Elementary, prior to the initiation of differentiated instruction (Tomlinson et al., 2008). Results are presented in terms of percentages of students demonstrating advanced or proficient scores on normative assessments for several years prior to the implementation of differentiated instruction and for several years after implementation.

Data at Conway Elementary School indicated that decidedly more students are achieving proficiency and/or testing at the advanced level after a three-year implementation of differentiated instructional practices. In fact, the data after the first year of implementation, showed a decided increase in student achievement (Tomlinson et al., 2008). All of these data clearly show no substantive change in other schools' achievement during these years, but when Conway Elementary implemented differentiated instruction, student achievement scores jumped as much as 30% in some academic areas.

Data for Colchester High School include the number of students passing the statewide assessment in reading, writing, and mathematics. Again, these data represent the percentage of students meeting educational goals both before and after differentiated instruction was implemented. These assessment results from Colchester High compare scores in the specific core subjects of reading, writing, and mathematics, and, in every area, students' achievement increased after the school implemented differentiated instruction.

Other results document the efficacy of brain-compatible teaching tactics within a differentiated instructional paradigm. For example, in a schoolwide implementation study, King and Gurian (2006) described a school in Colorado in which teachers noted a sharp achievement gap—a gap of 21% points on the state reading test—between young males and young females. Males were falling behind females consistently in the reading curriculum, and the faculty became concerned and began to study the matter. They looked into research on brain-based gender differences and concluded that their instructional practices favored the brain-based learning styles of young girls more than the learning styles of young boys. Further, they concluded that the actual reading curriculum in use likewise favored the learning styles and preferences of young girls.

In particular, when students were presented with an array of reading materials, males and females chose different topics (King & Gurian, 2006). Males chose to read topics with more conflict between characters and very clear role distinctions between heroes and villains. They often chose reading topics with a hint of danger, aggression, and stories that involve clear winners and losers, including reading material on topics such as NASCAR, football, atomic bombs, battles, or animals fighting (King & Gurian, 2006). In contrast, females tend to avoid reading material that represents high levels of overt conflict, preferring topics such as relationships, deep friendships, or fantasy material (e.g., mermaids and unicorns). Further, the teachers then investigated the stories in the basal reading curriculum and found that the stories that appealed to young girls' interests clearly outnumbered the stories that would appeal to boys.

With this information in hand, the faculty collectively determined to supplement their reading curriculum with additional stories that were of more interest to males (King & Gurian, 2006). Also, having studied the differentiated instruction and brain-compatible instructional literature, teachers began to teach with more attention to novel stimuli, conflict, and movement-based instruction, as recommended within that literature. As a result of these differentiated instructional modifications, the school was able to effectively close the reading achievement gap between young males and young females in only one year. While this is clearly an anecdotal example, this result nevertheless does indicate the potential for highly differentiated brain-compatible instruction to enhance academic achievement (King & Gurian, 2006).

> As a result of these differentiated instructional modifications, the school was able to effectively close the reading achievement gap between young males and young females in only one year.

THE NEW DIFFERENTIATED INSTRUCTION

As this summary indicates, the construct of differentiated instruction has changed somewhat since its inception in Tomlinson's critically important book (1999). Today, many views of learning styles and preferences are used as the basis for differentiation, and factors such as academic variation are used, in addition to learning style preferences, when forming instructional groups for differentiated activities in the classroom. Further, both technology and the RTI initiative have impacted teachers' differentiated instructional efforts, since each can greatly enhance the delivery of highly targeted instructional support for all students in the class. Thus, this author has chosen to use the term *The New Differentiated Instruction* to emphasize these modifications to the differentiated instructional paradigm, and to represent what differentiated instruction may mean in the years to come.

WHAT'S NEXT?

In the next chapter, I present the concept of universal design as a basis for classroom organization for differentiated instruction. The instructional practices noted above, such as using movement for instruction, and effective use of modern instructional technologies will also be highlighted. Finally, four different models for differentiating instruction in the context of a universally designed classroom are described to illustrate the newly emerging options for differentiating instruction.

Universal Design and Differentiated Instructional Models 2

UNIVERSAL DESIGN

While various models of differentiated instruction abound, one principle that is driving how teachers structure the class and conduct their instruction is the principle of universal design. An interface of universal design principles, as delineated below, and the differentiated instruction construct provides one of the most effective backdrops for discussing various differentiated instructional models.

Accessing the General Education Curriculum

Facilitating access to the general education curriculum and Common Core standards for students with learning difficulties involves much more than merely placing students in general education classes. In most cases, various barriers to learning, physical, emotional, and/or academic may need to be alleviated in order to help students with learning disabilities and other disorders to benefit from general education classes. This often involves various modifications to lessons and/or other accommodations in the class.

The concept of universal design has been promoted as the most effective way for teachers to address these barriers and organize their classes and curricula for differentiated instruction in order to assure that all learners, including struggling learners, have equal access to the general education curriculum (Abell, Bauder, & Simmons, 2005; Acrey, Johnstone, & Milligan, 2005; Pisha & Stahl, 2005). The concept of universal design originally dealt with universal construction design intended to alleviate physical barriers for individuals with disabilities, but the concept quickly expanded to include universal design for curriculum and assessment practices in schools (Acrey, Johnstone, & Milligan. 2005; Rose & Meyer, 2006), as well as design of activities within the school curricula, both hard-copy materials and computer-based learning environments for education. In particular, universal design of the classroom learning environment, including

> Facilitating access to the general education curriculum and common core standards for students with learning difficulties involves more than merely placing students in general education classes.

technology-based learning environments, as well as the instructional activities provided within each, provides an effective basis for differentiating the learning tasks for students with learning disabilities and other students of various academic challenges (Abell, Bauder, & Simmons, 2005; Acrey, Johnstone, & Milligan, 2005).

As inclusive class placements for students with learning disabilities have become increasingly popular since 2000, more and more students with learning disabilities are included for longer periods of time in the general education class. Unfortunately, little change has been noted in some classes relative to how general education teachers delivered instruction (Abell, Bauder, & Simmons, 2005), and developing an understanding of universal design concepts will assist all teachers in structuring their classes for increased differentiation.

Universal Curriculum Design

Perhaps an example of universal design would help illustrate this important concept. Imagine a student with a learning disability—specifically a reading disability—as well as a vision problem. In short, reading is quite likely to be a significant challenge for that student in any reading-dependent subject area. The principle of universal design would suggest that curriculum materials for that student should be designed such that his or her understanding of the content in the textbooks is not limited by virtue of that disability. In that sense, universal design assists schools in assuring that students with learning difficulties have access to the general education curriculum.

In this example, the school should order textbooks that are available both in print and online, and, presumably in the online version of the texts, the text size could be modified to make the print larger, which in turn would alleviate some of the negative effects of the vision problem. Moreover, such texts might be equipped with various features to facilitate and enhance cognitive understanding of the reading content. In some software, features that allow students to access definitions of text terms instantaneously or verbal pronunciations of unknown words would assist struggling students.

In such a text, if a student doesn't understand a word, he or she can merely click on it, and a definition would appear on the screen. In some curricular programs, the student might also hear the correct pronunciation of the term. Thus, this type of universally designed text, delivered via computer technology, could alleviate both the visual problems and the cognitive disabilities in understanding new vocabulary terms.

Universal design principles have been presented in a variety of ways (Abell, Bauder, & Simmons, 2005; Acrey, Johnstone, & Milligan, 2005; Rose & Meyer, 2006), and these typically include several factors:

- *Equitable Use:* The same means of use should be provided for all users, identical use where possible.

- *Flexibility in Use:* Options should include clear choices for users and adaptability of use.
- *Simple and Intuitive Presentation:* Use should be intuitively obvious, eliminate complexity, accommodate a wide range of literacy and language skills, and provide prompting and feedback on use.
- *Perceptible Presentation:* Information should be presented in several redundant modes such as visual, verbal, pictorial, and tactile.
- *Tolerance for Error:* Elements should be arranged to minimize the possibility of errors.
- *Appropriate Size and Space:* Use should provide clear line of sight for important information and adequate space for the use of adaptive devices.

When these universal design principles are applied to school curricula, a number of instructional strategies have been recommended (Abell, Bauder, & Simmons, 2005; Acrey, Johnstone, & Milligan, 2005; Pisha & Stahl, 2005). These include

- frequent summarization of big ideas and concepts;
- implementation of scaffolded supports for instruction;
- implementation of explicit instructional strategies based on clear goals and methods of instruction;
- streaming of lecture notes and assignments for students online where possible
- use of digital books and text materials;
- utilization of built-in academic supports (e.g., Web 2.0 tools, spell-checker, grammar checker, calculator);
- use of electronic communications (teacher to/from student, and teacher to/from parents); and
- provision of various assessment accommodations.

More recent technology innovations allow us to add to this list. For example, web-based curricula allow students to access the same curricula at home or in any online environment. In contrast, instructional software a decade ago was, in large measure, housed only on computers at schools. Further, the recent advent of "cloud computing" allows multiple students access to academic work anytime and anywhere, and students now have the option of working collaboratively. Clearly these venues that make school tasks more accessible represent great leaps forward in universal design, as these instructional tools tend to maximize accessibility to the general education curriculum for students with learning disabilities.

With the universal design concept as a background organizer, this chapter continues with a focus on organizing the classroom for differentiation and then suggests four relatively new organizational approaches for differentiation: modification of the traditional, whole-group lesson plan, learning centers for differentiation, project-based learning as a new example of differentiating instruction, and the "flipped" classroom. Because of the increasing emphasis on universal design, teachers should expect to see that overriding concept as the governing factor for classroom organization and instruction over the next few decades. Thus, each of these four approaches to differentiated instruction will be discussed with the concept of universal design in mind. First, however, the chapter presents suggestions for room arrangement that facilitate universal access to the curriculum.

ROOM ARRANGEMENT FOR DIFFERENTIATED INSTRUCTION

> Room organization must be guided by concerns about the need to differentiate instruction, the types of activities planned, the number of students in the class, and the behavioral or academic problems demonstrated by those students.

Considerations of room organization for both inclusive general education and special education classes must be guided by concerns about the need to differentiate instruction, the types of activities planned, the number of students in the class, and the behavioral or academic problems demonstrated by those students. Both inclusive general education classes and special education classes can be arranged based on a few straightforward considerations, even though these might involve different numbers of desks.

In an ideal classroom, space would be allocated for instructional tasks and organized to allow for multiple learning activities at the same time. Although not every classroom has optimum space, Figure 2.1 presents a suggested room arrangement for a general education class, including desks, learning centers, study carrels, computers, and so on, which should help facilitate differentiated instruction.

Whole-Group Instruction

This suggested room arrangement includes areas for whole-group and small-group instruction, as well as individual seatwork, technology-based instruction, and multimedia work spaces, floor space for movement-based learning, and individual work in study carrels. Perhaps the most notable feature is the semicircular desk arrangement in the whole-group instructional area. While whole-group instruction tends to decrease somewhat as teachers move more into differentiated instruction, many teachers do whole-group "mini-lessons" on difficult conceptual material, and such mini-lessons tend to be whole-group lessons that may last from 15 to 20 minutes.

In this room arrangement, the whole-group lesson area is where one typically finds a whiteboard or interactive whiteboard and desks for all students. In

> While whole-group instruction tends to decrease somewhat as teachers move more into differentiated instruction, many teachers do whole-group "mini-lessons" on difficult conceptual material.

this arrangement, students with challenging behaviors should be seated near the teacher but not together, because they would model inappropriate behaviors for each other. Furthermore, using this arrangement, the teacher can more easily monitor students' behavior visually. Specifically, the teacher can visually monitor most students' work while assisting a particular child; he or she should merely remain outside or behind the semicircle.

Figure 2.1   Recommended Room Arrangement for Differentiated Instruction

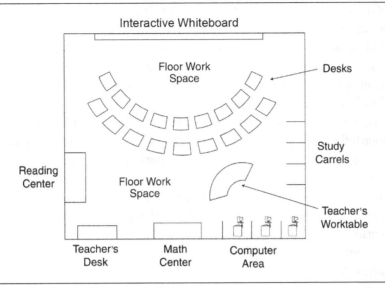

From *Differentiating Instruction for Students With Learning Disabilities: Best Teaching Practices for General and Special Educators*, Second Edition, by William N. Bender. Thousand Oaks, CA: Corwin, 2008. Used with permission.

This arrangement allows the teacher to face almost all members of the class almost all of the time (even when leaning over a student's shoulder to assist on a particular assignment). This ease of visual monitoring will tend to improve behavior and assist students with learning disabilities in the class. With three students assigned to sit at the reading center table and three in the study carrels for whole-group work, the work space in this class can accommodate a general education class size of 24 students. A similar semicircular arrangement is also appropriate for special education classes, which generally include smaller numbers of students.

Learning Centers

Many classrooms currently include learning centers, and in most classrooms these learning centers provide adjunct educational activities to supplement ongoing instructional units in the classroom. That is to say, in most classrooms today, learning centers are not the primary method of instructional delivery. In those classes, learning centers would be used by some students at the same time as the teacher leads other students in other instructional activities in a given instructional unit, and the activities within the learning center are typically considered supplemental activities within that instructional unit. In contrast, there are classrooms in which virtually all instruction is delivered in learning centers, and while learning centers work in both contexts, in the second type of class, the learning centers would be considered as the primary model for differentiating instruction. That differentiated instruction model is presented in some detail later in this chapter, whereas this section describes learning centers as an adjunct to unit-based instruction.

When learning centers are used as an adjunct to the unit-based instruction in the class, the learning centers should be developed to allow for modifications and adaptability within the curriculum. In that context, the activities and information in the learning center can provide one way to address the diverse needs of a wide variety of learners, including students with learning disabilities (Bender, 2008; Gregory, 2008; Gregory & Kuzmich, 2005). For the elementary education classroom, learning centers in both reading/language arts and math would be a minimum requirement. Other teachers, depending on their class grade level and teaching responsibilities, may also include a center for science, history and social science, and/or other subject areas.

As these examples suggest, in content areas (e.g., in this case, history) in departmentalized schools, the learning centers should be based on general concepts or issues within the topic that are not particular to a given unit of study. Thus, in the history centers mentioned above, the teacher would place materials in these centers that were appropriate for the various historical periods and/ or different units of study. Although those materials may change when studies of one period conclude and another historical period begins, the learning center names and orientations should remain constant across educational units throughout the year.

The materials that should be included in each learning center should be obtained on a continuous basis and subsequently labeled and organized in a way to facilitate the student's retrieval of appropriate materials. As noted previously, the universal design principles emphasize flexibility of use for curriculum materials. Thus, students with learning disabilities should be taught *how* to obtain their own work materials from the learning center because this will assist them in the development of organization skills as well as instill an ability to focus on the specific task at hand. In that sense, the learning centers must be a model of efficient organization of materials.

Activities in the learning centers vary widely. In most cases, educational games may be identified for the centers, or manipulatives might be available. Most learning centers include materials to develop art projects in various subject areas, and posters might be in the centers for various subjects (e.g., a timeline in the history center, a periodic table or model of a solar system in science, or a times table chart in the mathematics center). Most teachers also develop sets of worksheets that may be used, either individually or by small groups of students, and place these worksheets in the learning centers as well. Also, teachers should seek out the media specialist and inquire whether materials are available for long- or short-term loan to a particular class. In many cases, with special permission, the teacher may be able to check out materials for use for a week, a multi-week instructional unit, or a month. Teachers will also want some materials for lower level readers to use. This will enable almost all students to obtain assignments from the learning center.

In each learning center, teachers should provide some instructions for the students working there. Many teachers post "activity cards" on the wall in each learning center that instruct the students on the activities that must be accomplished to receive credit for completing the work in that center. Other learning centers include small dry-erase boards on which assignments may be written. To make these learning centers accessible for students with learning disabilities, teachers should keep the instructions for these activities simple and clear. Also, classes may have various levels of assignments present on these activity cards and instruct some students to complete the "Level 1" activities while others complete "Level 2" or "Level 3" activities. Again, such differentiated instruction must be provided to meet the needs of students with learning disabilities or other diverse learning needs.

Teacher's Worktable and Desk

As shown in Figure 2.1, the teacher should have a worktable located such that the teacher can scan the entire room while working with one student or a small group of students at a time. This will greatly facilitate the teacher's use of small-group, teacher-directed instruction, as well as RTI interventions at the Tier 2 or Tier 3 level. Although this requires that the worktable be located somewhere where teachers can see virtually the entire class, it does not have to be the focal point within the front area of the class.

Generally, teachers should not use the teacher's desk as their worktable. The desk is typically used for writing assignments and grading papers at the end of the day, along with grading and other tasks (e.g., attendance sheets). Consequently, teachers' desks tend to be cluttered with a lot of noninstructional material—some of which may be confidential. If students are working with a teacher on that desk, the opportunities for misbehavior are multiplied. In contrast, the worktable can be kept clear of everything except the instructional materials currently in use.

Small-Group Instruction Areas

Many social activities, such as sharing time, group games, or class projects, require or may best be facilitated by a small-group instruction area. This may involve table workspaces or open floor spaces for movement activities. In some classes, those floor spaces may be carpeted since students across the primary and elementary age range seem to enjoy working on the floor. These small-group instruction areas generally include some nearby shelves for storage of ongoing project work.

Internet Accessibility and Computer Area

Internet accessibility is critical for education today, and in 2012, schools across the nation are ramping up their Wi-Fi networks to assure that students in their area are not left on the wrong side of the digital divide. Therefore, the use of computers, educational tablets (e.g., iPads), and/or other multimedia instructional tools (e.g., digital cameras) has increased rather dramatically in recent years, and this trend fosters many opportunities for differentiated instruction. Further this trend is likely to increase over the next decade. In fact, while Wi-Fi was still quite limited in many schools in 2011, one would be hard-pressed to find a modern classroom without some computers or multimedia equipment, and these ever-evolving technology options provide teachers today with critically important tools for offering differentiated instruction to students with learning difficulties.

> The use of computers, educational tablets, iPads, and/or other multimedia instructional tools (e.g., digital cameras) has increased rather dramatically in recent years, and this trend fosters many opportunities for differentiated instruction.

In most classrooms, computers will typically be located along the wall since the electrical outlets may determine where they are placed. In consideration of disciplinary issues for students with learning disabilities, the teacher should make certain that there is ample room between these computer workspaces, such that hyperactive, distractible, and/or aggressive students cannot find too many opportunities for misbehavior. In many cases, computers are located in study carrels, and these can prevent mischief for many students.

Study Carrels

Study carrels are essential in classes that include students with learning disabilities and related attentional disorders because these students tend to be easily distracted by any movement in the class. Generally, several study carrels can be lined up along one wall and used for individual seatwork for certain children. Students may feel better about using these areas if they are labeled a "student office." If the class includes a student who is reluctant to work in a study carrel but would benefit from it, the teacher might create a "private office" environment for him or her, merely by labeling a study carrel with that student's name. One important fact to remember is that if a student with a learning disability needs a place to work that is free of visual distraction, one must be provided to assist the student in his or her classwork.

In addition to limiting the visual distractions that may be present in the work area, teachers should note that many students with learning disabilities are quite disturbed by auditory distraction. Consequently, soft music played continuously in class becomes a type of background noise and may facilitate higher work output from those students. However, one person's relaxation is another person's distraction. In some instances, teachers may wish to provide soft music through earphones to only one or two students. Regardless, teachers should carefully consider the impact of such music on all of the students in the class and make decisions accordingly.

Conclusion

As this description suggests, teachers should give careful consideration to how they physically organize the class for differentiated instruction. However with such considerations and some degree of intentional planning, highly differentiated instruction is much easier to provide. In the room arrangement described above, for example, one group of students who prefer movement-based learning might be working on a project in the open floor space while another group with strengths in linguistic skills works at the interactive whiteboard. Three or four students might be working individually on computer-based curricula while the teacher works with five students at the teachers' worktable. In that example, it is clear that highly differentiated instruction is provided based on the organization of the workspace within the classroom, and, clearly, having these organized workspaces will help in the delivery of such instruction.

With this workspace in mind, educators must now decide how to deliver differentiated instruction in order to assure access to the general educational curriculum. At least four different models for differentiated instruction are available, including modification of traditional whole-group lessons, learning centers, project-based instruction, and the flipped classroom.

DIFFERENTIATED INSTRUCTION MODEL I

Modification of the Traditional Lesson Plan

Modification of the traditional lesson plan has been discussed throughout the literature on differentiated instruction and, thus, may be considered the earliest approach to differentiation (Bender, 2008; Bender & Waller, 2011b; Sousa & Tomlinson, 2011; Tomlinson, 2001, 2003, 1999). While other differentiation models have been discussed over the last decade, certain other models (e.g., project-based learning) have been described only recently as differentiated instruction models (Schlemmer & Schlemmer, 2008). For that reason, it is quite appropriate to discuss modification of the traditional lesson plan as the first model for differentiated instruction.

The traditional whole-group lesson plan, presented in Box 2.1, is quite familiar to every teacher, because this format for a whole-group lesson has been in use since the late 1960s. This lesson plan includes a series of sequenced instructional phases in a traditional lesson, and this has been the primary model for instructional delivery since the 1970s, in most classes. In fact, as recently as 2012, most instructors' manuals in virtually every subject area in the schools included some version of this whole-group lesson plan format; thus, it is not a stretch to assert that this whole-group instructional model has become "the" instructional model for the general education classroom.

However, this traditional whole-group lesson plan was developed at a time when general education classes were much less academically diverse than today. Specifically, researchers of the late 1960s and 1970s who developed the traditional instructional plan based their work on the types of classrooms and the types of students who were then prevalent in those classrooms, and in that context of relatively homogeneous students, the traditional lesson plan worked very well.

> The traditional whole-group lesson plan was developed at a time when general education classes were much less academically diverse than today.

For example, if a teacher taught in Grade 5 in the early 1970s, he or she could realistically assume that most of the students in that class were working on reading and math somewhere between Grade Level 3 and Grade Level 7—a very limited range of academic diversity indeed, by today's standards. While there would have certainly been some differences in the children's math or reading skills, there was a fairly narrow level of academic diversity within most classes at that time, since many students with special needs were excluded from the general education classes during the 1960s and 1970s. Specifically, students with learning disabilities were often educated for some portion of the school day in resource rooms, and students with other disabilities were not in the general education class at all during those years.

BOX 2.1: PHASES IN THE TRADITIONAL WHOLE-GROUP LESSON PLAN

Orientation or introduction. Teacher uses three to five minutes to introduce a new topic, often with one or more high-interest activities, a video segment, or brief interest-heightening activity.

Initial instruction. This phase typically involves a 15- to 20-minute presentation of new information. To begin initial instruction, the teacher moves from introductory activity to a second example or instance. This phase often involves teacher modeling of a problem, or "think aloud" strategies where teachers verbally discuss steps in completing the work or critically important aspects of the topic.

Teacher guided practice. In this phase, the teacher typically assigns some work for the students to complete involving the content taught in the previous phase, and that 10 to 15 minutes practice is guided by the teacher, who moves around the room helping students individually.

Independent practice. In this phase, more practice problems or additional readings/research on the topic are assigned. This phase may be done as a part of classwork later during the period or as homework in the traditional whole-group lesson.

Check and reteach. At some point, either last in the instructional period, or the next day after students complete independent practice at home, the teacher would check that work to assure student understanding and then reteach that work as necessary for the students that didn't understand it.

From *Differentiating Instruction for Students With Learning Disabilities: Best Teaching Practices for General and Special Educators,* Second Edition, by William N. Bender. Thousand Oaks, CA: Corwin, 2008. Used with permission.

In contrast, in today's fifth-grade class it is quite likely that students' achievement levels in reading and math range from Grade Level 1 up through Grade Level 8, 9, or even 10. Thus, teachers today face highly diverse general education classes, and it is clearly time to reconceptualize how instruction is delivered. Thankfully, Tomlinson's work (1999, 2010) allows us to plan lesson activities in classes that are not based on the whole-group lesson plan concept of "one set of lesson activities for all students." In fact, that "one size fits all" instructional approach is no longer the norm. Rather, the differentiated classrooms of today present a much wider array of activities, targeted at individual learners, in order to address the issues of more varied learning styles, learning preferences, and the wider academic diversity in today's schools.

> Tomlinson's work allow us to contemplate classes in which whole-group work based on one set of lesson activities for all students is no longer the norm.

Once teachers grasp that the traditional lesson plan in their instructional manuals is outdated by 50 years and doesn't fit well with today's highly diverse classes, it becomes a priority to learn how to differentiate instruction in order to meet the needs of a more diverse group of learners. In point of fact, teachers will never see less diverse groups of kids in their classes than they see today. Further, academic diversity seems to be increasing yearly as more students from non-English speaking homes enter the schools. Thus, teachers need to provide a wider array of different instructional activities in order to accommodate such diversity in the general education classes.

Planning a Differentiated Lesson

Because most school curricula present some version of the traditional, whole-group lesson plan, many teachers, particularly in upper elementary, middle and high school grades, are more comfortable beginning with that traditional lesson plan model and then moving toward increased differentiated activities. As noted above, as late as 2012, many teacher's manuals included some version of the traditional whole-group lesson plan, involving different "phases" for each daily lesson. While the terms may change from one curriculum to another (e.g., some texts use essential questions or "activate their understanding" rather than the terms "introduction to the lesson" or "orientation to the lesson"), the fact is, teachers have been planning whole-group lessons for decades based on this traditional lesson plan.

Further, that traditional lesson plan involves several specific assumptions:

1. All learners need the same instruction, because they are academically on the same general academic level.

2. All students will work together in a series of whole-class activities.

3. Students will all move through these phases of instruction at the same rough pace.

In today's highly diverse classes, these are no longer valid assumptions, and this clearly indicates a need for a more diverse array of educational activities in the classroom.

A Differentiated Lesson Plan Example

In order to provide a comparison model of a differentiated lesson, imagine the following instructional lesson in Ms. Nyland's third-grade math class. The class includes 22 students, five of whom are special education students. Two of those students have learning disabilities, with an overlay of hyperactive behavior, and the three others have other disabilities. Further, four of the other students in that class are highly advanced academically, and two of those are identified as gifted students. In schools today, this would seem to be a typical class.

In this scenario, Nyland is teaching a math lesson concerning the aggregation of data, the creation of a tally table, and the eventual formulation of a frequency table summarizing those data. Box 2.2 shows a traditional whole-group lesson on the left and a series of differentiated lesson activities on the right for the same lesson. To begin this lesson with an attention-grabbing orientation activity, Ms. Nyland might ask students to identify their favorite dinosaur, since dinosaurs frequently capture students' attention. She might hold up a picture of one of the five most recognizable dinosaurs and have a student at the dry-erase board begin to tally how many students like the T. rex. That student might draw a T. rex on the board and beside that picture put tally marks indicating the number of students that liked that type of dinosaur best. Next, Ms. Nyland would hold up another picture (perhaps an allosaurus, a raptor, or a stegosaurus), and the student would draw a picture of that animal under the T. rex and put tally marks beside it to represent the number of students who indicate it as their favorite.

Once Ms. Nyland has three to five pictures, and associated tally marks on the dry-erase board, she may then say something like, "How can we summarize these data so they make sense?" Ms. Nyland would then ask for suggestions from the class, and she will eventually develop a frequency table with dinosaurs in one column, tally marks in the second column, and digits representing the actual count of the tally marks for that dinosaur in a third column. She would make certain she used the vocabulary associated with the lesson (e.g., tally

BOX 2.2: TRADITIONAL WHOLE-GROUP LESSON AND DIFFERENTIATED LESSON ACTIVITIES

Typical Phases of a Traditional Lesson	Differentiated Lesson Activities
A. Introduction	
Cover tally tables and frequency tables	After the intro, break out one group (Omega group) to create a tally table on the floor, then rejoin main group
B. Teacher-Guided Instruction	
Teach tally tables vs. frequency tables	Tear out a second group (Beta group) Complete Step 2 Activity to stand in the tally table on floor sorted by favorite colors
C. Teacher-Guided Practice	
Have main group complete practice worksheet	Have two groups work together to evaluate each other's work
D. Independent Practice	
Have students complete the independent practice	Omega and Beta groups rejoin mainline instruction or move into another enrichment activity
E. Check	
Have all students complete a quick check quiz to document understanding	Have Omega and Beta groups describe their activities to the whole class and complete a quick quiz
F. Reteach Content as Necessary	

From *Differentiating Instruction for Students With Learning Disabilities: Best Teaching Practices for General and Special Educators*, Second Edition, by William N. Bender. Thousand Oaks, CA: Corwin, 2008. Used with permission.

table, frequency table), and she would then point out the advantages of being able to collect and aggregate data. She might then conclude the orientation phase of instruction by saying something like, "Let's look at another example where we aggregate data in our class."

After this brief orientation activity, the traditional direct instruction lesson would suggest that Ms. Nyland begin the second phase of the lesson, the initial instruction on tally tables. She would begin that with another example of data aggregation, and again use the terminology and model the aggregation process. She would ultimately discuss both tally tables and frequency tables, using several more examples. However, while interesting orientation activities may hold students' interest for a brief time, including students with learning disabilities or attention disorders, many of those students are likely to lose interest in the lesson as Ms. Nyland begins the second instructional phase. Thus, they have effectively withdrawn from class mentally.

Also, other students may pay less attention as the whole-group lesson progresses. For example, after the orientation to the lesson and prior to initial instruction, some of the more advanced students may have already understood the concept. Those students may remember similar prerequisite concepts and couple those insights with a quick look ahead in the text. Thus, both advanced students and students with learning problems may become less engaged with the lesson content during the whole-group lesson format.

If five students with disabilities and four advanced or gifted students cease to pay attention in Ms. Nyland's class, she has effectively lost nearly one half of her classroom! Nine of the 22 students have stopped participating in the lesson, simply because Ms. Nyland taught the traditional, whole-group lesson plan, just as instructed in the teacher's manual.

The differentiated lesson plan offers an alternative approach that is much more likely to keep all of these learners engaged with the lesson content. Rather than begin the second phase of the traditional whole-group lesson, Ms. Nyland should present a different lesson activity for some of the learners in the class, as she continues the traditional whole-group lesson with the other students. In fact, Ms. Nyland can probably identify some students who have already understood the concept as well as others who have not, and, if those students possess similar learning styles and generally work well together, those students should be provided a differentiated activity that will keep them focused on the lesson content. For example, if three gifted or advanced students in the class and two students with learning disabilities had similar learning preferences (e.g., all enjoyed learning through movement and small-group interaction), Ms. Nyland could easily form a heterogeneous differentiated group for those students and assign them a differentiated lesson activity.

In order to quickly form that differentiated group, a group referred to as the Omega Group in Box 2.2, Ms. Nyland might check to see what students might have the general concept using a question like, "Do you think you could structure a tally table to collect data and then transfer those data to a frequency table?" For the students who indicate they could, she would place those students in different activities dealing with the concept, and she might also place a few children who do not understand the concept in the same differentiated group. If that group works well together and concentrates on an assigned learning task, the students who know the content will be "teaching" the students who do not understand the concepts, while Ms. Nyland continues the traditional lesson format with others in the classroom.

The Omega Group

The names for the differentiated groups in the class should be nonsequential and should not indicate a quantitative or qualitative judgment on the skills or the intellect of the group. Rather the class should understand that different groups are frequently formed to complete alternative learning activities that are on the general topic of study. In this example, Ms. Nyland would have previously developed an assignment sheet for the Omega group involving the structure of a frequency table. The Omega group students would be instructed to move to a separate section of the room to begin their group project to develop a grid on the floor that represents the structure of another frequency table, creating the grid with masking tape. In that way, rather than losing the attention of these students, members of that differentiated group would be discussing and focusing on the column and row structure of a frequency table. Teachers rarely have to create these alternative differentiated activities. Most modern curricula include project alternatives, which are usually described in the teacher's manuals as "enrichment" activities or "reteaching" activities. Ms. Nyland need only select an appropriate activity and provide any necessary materials to the Omega group.

In this example, students are assigned to review the frequency table on the dry-erase board (the table developed in the orientation activity the class just completed, involving the dinosaurs) and construct a grid for a similar table on the floor using masking tape. The enrichment assignment description in the students' text provides instructions for the Omega group.

> *This activity requires some floor space (15' by 15') and a roll of masking tape. Students will place masking tape on the floor to develop an outline for a frequency table. The rows will represent choices of students' favorite color for tennis shoes (teachers should select five specific colors as options). One column will be used for preferred color (red shoes, white, black, green, or blue shoes). The second column will be used for students to stand beside their preferred color of shoe, and the third for the numbers representing the count of persons preferring the various colors. Use the masking tape to develop an appropriate five-by-three grid for this activity.*

Based on a set of instructions such as this, the students in the Omega group should be provided with a roll of masking tape and then should begin this activity in one corner of the room. Given that the next instructional phase—the teacher-directed phase—typically takes approximately 15 minutes, the group activity for Omega group should be planned with that time frame in mind. The Omega group students would have to jointly plan what the frequency *table* would look like using the model on the dry-erase board, and plan for how big the boxes are going to be in order to hold various groups of students, and how the categories in the tally table should be organized. Thus in the finished frequency table grid developed by the Omega group, the box on the left is the "category" box, and that box need be only large enough to accommodate the pictures of items of various colors. In contrast, the box in the middle must be large enough for a number of students to stand in, as they stand by their preferences. The box on the right end will hold only a digit or two that summarizes the data in the middle box, so it can be somewhat smaller. The point is that the Omega group has to figure all of this out—including the number of categories and the relative size of the boxes—while working as a group. Thus, rather than mentally withdrawing from the lesson, these students are likely to be highly engaged with the lesson content. That high level of engagement is the focal point of differentiated lessons; differentiation is designed to hold students' interest in the lesson activity by using students' learning preferences and styles along with exciting and engaging lesson content.

Of course, it is possible for the Omega group to make a mistake in their work. They may develop a five-by-three grid but forget to consider the relative size of the boxes. In fact, the challenge for the Omega group in making this grid is a more complicated activity than merely copying the frequency table structure on the dry-erase board, and the students will need to carefully consider how to build a frequency table. Generally, teachers can correct such errors with a quick visual scan of the work and a one sentence reminder, such as "Remember that the box in the middle must be large enough for several students to stand in!"

The Mainline Instructional Group

Thus, after only a five-minute orientation to the lesson and prior to having actually "taught" the lesson for everyone in the class, Ms. Nyland has already differentiated the lesson. She has formed two groups for instruction; the Omega group and the mainline group, comprised of the rest of the class. As the Omega group does its work. Ms. Nyland will engage in teacher-led initial instruction as she normally would for the mainline group, using modeling and additional problem examples to teach about tally tables and frequency tables. She may use a variety of activities from the instructor's manual, but she should make certain that a variety of activities are offered that are at least as engaging and as interesting as the work the Omega group is doing.

Further, in order to hold the students' attention, Ms. Nyland might consider reorienting the class furniture a bit. If she placed the Omega group in the front left corner of the classroom (perhaps because that is where she had some space for small-group work), she should then move to the back right corner and tell the mainline group to, "Turn your desks around so you can see the floor activity we'll be doing." By doing that, she accomplishes two critical things:

1. She has oriented the mainline instructional group to have their backs to the Omega group—and thus both groups are more likely to pay attention to their assigned task.

2. She has placed herself in a position to lead instruction for the mainline group and still visually monitor the Omega group.

Finally, we should note that the efficacy of Ms. Nyland's instruction in the mainline group is likely to increase as she does more differentiated activities in the class. In a math class of 22 students, if she selected five students for the Omega group, only 17 students would remain in the mainline group during the initial instruction, and they are likely to be more homogeneously grouped. Consequently, Ms. Nyland's instruction is likely to be more highly targeted to those students that she is teaching in the mainline group, since targeted instruction is facilitated by small instructional groups. Also, Ms. Nyland will be less distracted by gifted or advanced students who might become bored in the whole-group lesson activities.

> Differentiated instruction is strategically targeted instruction aimed at the learning needs of individual students in the class, and encourages the teacher to offer more highly targeted instruction.

This is, of course, the main strength of differentiated instruction—it is strategically targeted instruction aimed at the learning needs of individual students in the class, and encourages the teacher to offer more highly targeted instruction. In this sense, differentiated instruction is "higher impact" instruction than merely following the traditional lesson plan from the teacher's manual.

The Beta Group

However, merely offering one group of students a different task does not constitute differentiation, and we should consider what happens after Ms. Nyland completes the initial instruction for the mainline instructional group. By 20 minutes into the lesson, Ms. Nyland will have completed both the lesson orientation and the initial instructional phase for the mainline students. Also, the Omega group will probably have completed its work in designing the new grid for the frequency table on the floor. Thus, at this point in the traditional lesson it is probably time to form another group for another differentiated activity.

Again, with a few judicious questions, Ms. Nyland can identify a second group of perhaps five or six other students from the mainline group who, by that point in the lesson, understand the data aggregation concept and do not need the next phase of the traditional lesson—teacher-guided practice. She might call this group the Beta group. Again, Ms. Nyland would select this group from the mainline group and provide a differentiated assignment for them. As shown in Box 2.2, this assignment might be to "test out" the grid on the floor that was created by the Omega group with one or two new examples of a frequency table.

Of course at this point in the lesson, the Omega group will also need another assignment. It would be perfectly appropriate to use them to work with the Beta group to develop these activities for later classroom use. However, Ms. Nyland may wish to give them a separate assignment that involves writing several data aggregation problems for subsequent classroom use, or she may merely invite them to rejoin the mainline group of students for the next 15 minutes or so.

As this example indicates, Ms. Nyland is offering highly differentiated instruction, targeted at individual students based on their learning styles and individual needs. Also, note that in this example Ms. Nyland presented a differentiated activity shortly after the class began rather than much later after teacher-led practice phase of the lesson, which has been the traditional time for small-group work. Specifically, after Ms. Nyland oriented the students to the lesson, she created the Omega group for a differentiated activity, and after the initial instruction phase she tore out the Beta group for another differentiated activity. Thus, after 15 to 20 minutes, five students in the Omega group will be doing a second differentiated assignment and the Beta group will be doing its first as Ms. Nyland continues instruction for the mainline instructional group. At that point, the mainline group will include only 11 students, and they will be receiving highly focused, direct instruction from Ms. Nyland. Thus, these 11 students will get the additional attention they need from the teacher.

As indicated in this example, good differentiated instruction takes place well before the class begins. Differentiation is planned when teachers develop their lesson plans, when they include a wide array of differentiated instructional activities for each phase of the lesson, based on the specific instructional needs, academic variations, and learning-style preferences of the students in the class. Of course, Ms. Nyland should continue to differentiate the lesson throughout the lesson period, and she may form a third differentiated group at some point. However, most classes typically have no more than three different groups doing different tasks at any one point in time.

Guidelines for Differentiated Instruction

Teachers are, at times, concerned with the time it takes to plan multiple activities for the class, and certainly relying on the traditional lesson plan is easier than planning a dynamic, differentiated lesson. However, teachers must understand that the essence of differentiated instruction is presentation of lesson activities that engage the learners, and planning such lessons may take a bit more time, initially. However, not every daily lesson needs to be highly differentiated. In fact, many whole-group activities can and do actively engage almost all learners. Activities such as gaming activities, video/computer-based presentations, debates, interactive simulations, role play, and many other whole-class activities are excellent instructional activities for the entire class, and when a teacher is using these activities, little differentiation will be necessary to keep all students focused on the learning content. In middle and upper grades, as a general guideline, teachers should use some of the engaging activities above for one or two periods weekly and consider planning and implementing a highly differentiated lesson on other days.

As these examples show, in a differentiated class, the instructional groups are quite fluid, frequently formed for specific short-term tasks, and then merged again into the mainline instruction. Teachers should never be reluctant to form a differentiated group for brief, specific activities or to re-include those same students in the mainline instruction when the differentiated task is completed. This fluid aspect of the lesson, with different students frequently moving into different activities, is the very essence of a differentiated lesson.

With these ideas in mind, we can now identify the general guidelines for modifying a traditional whole-group lesson in order to transform it into a differentiated lesson. Note that these are merely guidelines and that every teacher should, based on his or her understanding of the individuals in the class as well as the demands of the subject content, adapt these to the specific needs of the students. These guidelines are presented in Teaching Tip 2.1.

Guidelines for Differentiating the Whole-Group Lesson Plan

- *Subdivide Early and Often.* Provide as many differentiated activities as possible, because these activities engage the students much more. Teachers employing differentiated instruction will typically subdivide their class much earlier in the lesson than is usual in the direct instruction model, and will do so much more frequently. Teachers should form either a homogeneous group or a heterogeneous group of students for an alternative instructional activity after each phase in the traditional lesson plan. For heterogeneous groups, teachers should select some students who have grasped the concept and some who haven't by exercising judgment concerning who can work effectively in a group and who can or will work together.

- *Never Plan Just One Activity When You Need Two or Three!* The academic diversity in today's elementary classes often necessitates the presentation of the same content in multiple ways, so each time a teacher plans one activity, he or she should consider planning at least one more variation and subdivide the class based on learning styles, preferences, and academic levels, with some students doing one and some doing the other.

- *Use the Various Differentiated Activities More Than Once in the Unit.* In the example above, the Omega group was the first to develop a frequency table on the floor. On subsequent days within that unit of instruction, other students in other groups may also be assigned the same type of activity. Further, it is perfectly acceptable for a particular student to be included in several groups doing the same activity.

- *Modify Alternative Activities to Address Different Learning Styles.* The teacher in the example above, while using the grid activity in her class, provided an activity that emphasized several learning styles, including spatial, logical/mathematical, and interpersonal. *Use what you have in the local community!* Using examples in the students' community can involve students more and motivate them to complete the math.

- For example, in farming communities, tying math problems to local crop sales can be quite effective. For students in urban areas, describing math problems in terms of the types of clothes or tennis shoes that are in vogue can motivate students more than simply using whatever math problems are on the page. If students live near a major historical park, teachers should consider history examples that could be tied to that local resource, with an emphasis on something like, "What national history took place in our town?"

- Teachers in every field should use examples from the community whenever possible. One interesting type of assignment for some differentiated groups is to rewrite each of the math word problems in a particular unit using some local example. The others in the class can then use those problems for their practice work. This results in more "authentic" learning than some of the math problems presented in the standard math texts.

- *Tie Students in Emotionally.* We now know that prior to learning the student must sense emotional safety in the learning environment. Further, if teachers can tie the content of a lesson to an emotional hook, students will become more focused on that content.

- *Use Differentiated Instruction for Inclusive Classes.* Students with significant disabilities are included in virtually all general education classes today, and differentiated instruction provides the best basis for instruction in those classes. Thus, differentiated instruction is often described as the best practice for Tier 1 instruction in all subject areas at all grade levels (Bender, 2012a). Moreover, in inclusive classes with both a general educator and a special educator in the class, the monitoring of the differentiated groups is much more easily managed!

- *Continue Some Traditional Lessons.* Teachers in higher grades should not attempt differentiated lessons each and every day. While lectures seem ineffective with many students today, other types of activities, as noted in the text above, do result in high levels of engagement for virtually all learners in the class. These whole-group activities should certainly be continued.

- *Teachers Should "Test the Waters" of Differentiated Instruction Tentatively.* Once a teacher decides to attempt differentiated instruction, he or she should try this approach in a successful class—a classroom that seems to be working well. The teacher should also initially do this in an area of the curriculum that students know well. This will effectively increase the teacher's comfort zone and will be more likely to result in a pleasant teaching experience than trying this new teaching paradigm in a challenging class. Also, testing this idea in a class that is not presenting challenges is more likely to result in initial success. After that, teachers can expand into other, more challenging classes. Moreover, teachers who have moved into this slowly—and have seen it work as both they and the students grow to understand this instructional system—have stated that teaching is simply much more fun this way!

From *Differentiating Instruction for Students With Learning Disabilities: Best Teaching Practices for General and Special Educators*, Second Edition, by William N. Bender. Thousand Oaks, CA: Corwin, 2008. Used with permission.

Results of Differentiated Instruction

Teachers who have chosen to move into differentiation for instruction have generally found that many of the anxieties they had about such instruction did not materialize. For example, many teachers are initially concerned about the issue of management of varied groups within the classroom. Of course, every class includes some students who, at least initially, should not be selected for these less-supervised differentiated activities, since their behavior patterns necessitate closer teacher supervision. However, teachers typically find that after the class as a whole gets accustomed to the differentiated lesson format, even students with behavioral challenges can participate meaningfully in differentiated activities.

In fact, one teacher provided me with the following idea of how to get a child with verbal aggressive tendencies to participate in a differentiated group. After she moved to differentiated instruction for three days a week, she continued to exclude him, knowing that he would eventually ask, "Why can't I ever work over there?" That not too subtle request put the teacher in a perfect negotiating position to work with that child. Thus, the teacher

- waited until the child requested to be placed in a differentiated group; and
- negotiated with the child about his or her problem behavior.

Next, because the training of most teachers in schools today was based on the traditional whole-group lesson plan, some teachers have difficulty moving into differentiated instruction because they suspect that less learning will take place in differentiated groups. Some teachers even view these less-supervised differentiated groups as disasters waiting to happen. However, experience with this type of instruction will show the inaccuracy of these fears. Even highly skeptical teachers, upon trying this approach, have subsequently stated that, once they moved to a differentiated instruction format, they found that students do learn from each other in the differentiated group activities and that this instructional format results in increased student learning overall.

Finally, the ultimate reason to undertake differentiation stems from the fact that this is highly effective teaching. All teachers are under pressure today to address either the Common Core standards or state standards, and high quality differentiated instruction is the best way to do that, as this learning format will result in improved instruction and higher achievement compared to whole-class, traditional instruction (Tomlinson et al., 2008). Box 2.3 lists other typical results reported by teachers once they begin the transition to a truly differentiated classroom.

BOX 2.3: RESULTS OF DIFFERENTIATING THE WHOLE-GROUP LESSON PLANS

- *Provision of varied instruction.* This approach offers the most effective instructional option for presenting appropriate instruction for all students in today's classes.
- *Increased involvement of advanced students.* The advanced kids in this procedure will be more challenged and thus less likely to get bored and engage in problem behaviors.
- *Varied behavior management concerns.* Management of an increased number of instructional groups will be a concern, and the teacher should move into differentiated instruction slowly for this reason. However, students who would otherwise be bored with traditional lessons will be more engaged in this instructional model, and it is possible that these behavior management results will effectively even things out for the teacher in the differentiated lesson.
- *Improved instruction for those who need it.* As the mainline group gets smaller, the instruction for that group is likely to improve since the teacher is concentrating on a smaller group. Thus, the teacher is providing increased support for the students who really need the help on a particular lesson. This will tend to increase learning—thus increasing test scores—on average for the entire class (see the data provided by Tomlinson, Brimijoin, & Narvaez, 2008).
- *Provision of the best instruction for everyone.* Differentiated instruction encourages teachers to offer the most effective enrichment/instruction to kids across the ability spectrum. Teachers must make the mainline group activities as varied, as novel, and as exciting as any of the alternative assignments for the tear-out groups.

(Continued)

(Continued)

- *Effective use as a model for inclusive instruction.* Teachers can readily see the comfortable fit between the use of multiple differentiated groups and the demands of the inclusive classroom. Differentiated instruction provides one of the most effective models for inclusion of students with learning disabilities that is currently available.
- *Teachers become used to teaching this way.* Once teachers try this instructional model, particularly if they test this model in an academic area within their comfort zone, they typically find that they enjoy this type of teaching. While all teachers differentiate to some degree, teachers who devote themselves to this approach often state that they would not like to return to teaching in a traditional fashion.

DIFFERENTIATED INSTRUCTION MODEL II

Learning Centers

While modification of the traditional, whole-group lesson was the first differentiated instruction model, it is not the only one. In fact, the new differentiated instruction can take many forms in the classroom, and various instructional delivery methods have been presented for differentiated instruction over the years (Bender, 2008; Gregory, 2008; Tomlinson, 1999, 2010). For example, learning centers have been used not only as a supplement to unit instruction but also as a primary delivery method for highly differentiated instruction (Bender & Waller, 2011b). Rather than using learning centers to support unit-based instruction or on an occasional basis as "project activity areas," many teachers use learning centers as their primary method for delivering all instruction in a given subject area, and this can result in a highly differentiated lesson. In these classes, as in the example described below, very little whole-group instruction ever takes place. Rather, differentiated instruction via learning centers involves instruction that is differentiated based on learning styles and the formation of relatively homogeneous academic groups for reading and language arts instruction in the elementary class.

The Organization of Learning Centers for Differentiated Instruction

In this model of differentiated instruction, teachers should use students' individual learning styles, along with their academic achievement levels in either reading or mathematics, to divide the class into four relatively homogeneous groups (Bender & Waller, 2011b). Each group will work in a learning center for 15- to 20-minute time slots and then save their work in that center and move to another center. At the end of each 15-minute segment, teachers would instruct all students to save their work and then tell each homogeneous group of students which center to move to. Once in that center, students would begin the work in that location as per assignments previously developed by the teacher for that specific group. In this fashion, the teacher can move from center to center helping students individually and facilitating instruction rather than deliver a traditional whole-group lesson for all members of the class. Further, the center work would be directed at the learning style and achievement levels for each small group of students, thus providing a higher level of differentiated instruction, targeted to the needs of the students in that particular small group.

Here is an example of this learning center model for differentiated instruction in reading. In establishing a technology-rich environment for differentiated instruction, a minimum of four reading/language arts learning centers should be established, including the reading center, the computer center, the writing and spelling center, and the special projects center. If the elementary teacher likewise wishes to use learning centers to differentiate mathematics instruction, various math learning centers may also be necessary, including centers for operations, story problems, measurement, and perhaps other areas depending on the grade level. For this example, a set of learning centers for language arts and reading instruction is described.

The Reading Center. Various reading materials should be included in the reading center, and these might include sequenced reading stories as well as graphic novels (which seem to immediately engage students' attention today), picture books, or "speak-and-read" books, which are read to the student. Various manipulatives might also be included that allow students to create words from letters or groups of letters or word-phrase cards with which students can create whole sentences.

The Computer Center. In the computer center, students will work relatively independently and on individual work targeted at their individual academic reading level. Six or seven computers should be located in individual study carrels along one wall, and each should be equipped with research-based, reading instructional software programs to teach both reading and language arts. Because most reading instructional software curricula include screening assessments that place a student at his or her instructional level, teachers need only place students within that curricula and make certain that they open their program and begin work on the appropriate reading story or language arts exercise each day. The individualized reading assignments in the computer center serve to provide high quality guided reading instruction to each student at exactly his or her individual level. Further, students' progress can be checked by the teacher after class since modern instructional software stores students' performance data.

The Writing and Spelling Center. In the writing and spelling center, various activities may be included dealing with writing skills or language arts skills, including phonics, spelling patterns, challenging spelling words, root words and prefixes/suffixes, or other word attack skills. Also, activities dealing with sentence, paragraph, or theme formation may be included to enhance writing skills, depending on the grade level of the class.

These activities should include some worksheet activities as well as some activities intended for small groups and/or manipulative activities such as "construct a word" from letters and/or syllables. When students leave this center, they are instructed to place their work in their personal folder and take the folder with them to the next center. This allows the teacher to review that "hardcopy" work after class.

In the writing center, students are challenged to write something every time they go to the center. Because this primary teacher teaches the class around thematic units, the writing assignment often involves writing several sentences or, for more advanced students, a paragraph about the theme of the unit. When students leave that center, they place their writing, either finished or unfinished, in their personal folder.

The Special Projects Center. In the special projects center, the teacher might include a wide variety of projects, including poems, cartoons, art projects, stories, or other projects that relates to the thematic unit of the class. Students might be required to read a poem in pairs and discuss it together. Then, they might individually write some type of reflection about that poem or story in their writing journal. In many cases, the assignments from the special projects center and the writing center are highly related to each other.

Content in Each Learning Center

Setting up the learning centers as the basis for differentiated instruction is relatively easy. Each center should include, at a minimum, a table by the wall to hold learning center materials and a large poster label on the wall naming the center. The computer center, obviously, likewise holds the computers or tablets (e.g. iPads) and appropriate software. Each center should also include a small dry-erase board on which the teacher can write individual assignments for various students or one assignment for each of the small groups.

Each center usually includes a storage box of some type, with 10 to 15 file folders in the box. Each file folder should be labeled with the name of the center, a sequenced number, and the title of a specific activity (e.g., Writing Center; Folder 12; journal reflection on the poem, "The Tree"). Each folder might include a worksheet or manipulative activity or directions for an activity. Further, each activity in each center should be developed to require approximately 15 to 20 minutes.

Moving Students Through the Learning Centers

At the beginning of the reading and language arts instructional period, three of the four differentiated groups should be instructed to begin their work in a learning center. A paraprofessional in the class may be used to monitor students' academic work and behavior in the various learning centers, or teachers can monitor that work while leading small-group work for the other group at the teacher's worktable. Of course, one of those three differentiated groups should always be assigned to the computer center, and modern software tends to keep virtually all students highly engaged in the learning activities, including students with learning disabilities. Thus, less teacher monitoring will be needed for students in the computer center than for students in the other learning centers.

Of course, in this differentiated instruction model, students will move from one learning center to another every 15 to 20 minutes. Thus, students should be encouraged to complete their assignments and check their work in each center during that time frame. For worksheets and other hard-copy assignments in various centers, students can place their checked work in their individual folders for the teacher to check at a later time. In the computer center, students will store their work within the software itself for teachers to check later.

One teacher devised a "two-minute warning" that signaled students to prepare to change learning centers (Bender & Waller, 2011b). Two minutes prior to the end of the 20-minute period allocated for an activity, the teacher would say "two minute warning" to the class. That meant that the class was to draw their work to a close and save it either in their personal folder or on the computer software. After their work was saved and their books and materials were closed and stored in the center, students were taught to face the teacher. When the teacher saw each child facing in her direction, she assigned the groups to the next learning center.

Using this system, the teacher typically worked with one group or another during each 15- to 20-minute time slot on intensive small-group instruction at the teacher's worktable. When center work began, the teacher called one of the four homogeneous groups to the worktable to work in teacher-led, intensive instruction for the next 20-minute period. Thus, the teacher was working with four to six students in a relatively homogeneous group at any given time.

As teachers implement response to intervention programs around the nation, this learning center model for differentiation has proven highly important. In every class, some of the homogeneous groups of students will include more challenged readers than other groups, and those groups may need a Tier 2 reading intervention, which, of course, will probably require more of the teacher's instructional time. By having all students work in learning centers, teachers can more easily address that need.

In the example above, the teacher addressed the need for intensive Tier 2 interventions by merely working with the Tier 2 instructional group for an extra 20-minute period each day at the teacher's worktable. This time requirement was offset because many of the more advanced students did not require as much of the teacher's small-group instructional time, and those more advanced groups were called to the teacher's worktable only two or three times each week.

When each group came to the small-group work at the teachers' worktable, a supplemental reading curriculum designed for teacher-led small-group work was used. Thus, this teacher targeted each student's areas of strength and weakness while meeting the requirements of providing Tier 2 RTI instruction for some readers in the class.

Advantages of Learning Centers for Differentiated Instruction

In using this learning center approach to differentiate instruction, teachers never need to lead the whole group in reading instruction! Thus, in this type of differentiated instruction, the teacher becomes a planner and facilitator for everyone's reading instruction, and works with every student in some small-group format at least several times each week. In fact, students taught in this differentiated fashion are likely to receive higher quality instruction overall than they would in a whole-group reading lesson since so much instruction is directly targeted to their specific needs.

Further, in this technology-rich classroom, software-based guided reading lessons tend to be exactly focused at the individual reading levels of particular students, and the same can be said of the intensive work with the teacher at the teacher's worktable. This would suggest that this approach meets the needs of today's diverse students in most general education classrooms better than traditional whole-group instruction.

There are a number of other advantages to using learning centers as the basis for differentiation. First, implementing differentiation through learning centers is an "RTI friendly" reading instructional system. As mentioned above, every student was assessed almost continuously both in the computerized program and by the teacher during the intensive reading small-group work. Thus, for students in a Tier 2 or Tier 3 intensive intervention, progress monitoring added no extra assessment burden to the teacher.

Secondly, learning centers placed more of the responsibility for learning on the students (Gregory, 2008). As long as the teaching/learning process is based on a view of students as passive learners (i.e., the targets of group lessons, lectures, or discussions led for the whole class by the teacher), only limited learning is likely to take place, particularly among struggling students. However, a learning center approach makes students responsible for their own learning activities. Further, with most students, having some choice among assignments in the learning centers is even more likely to foster active student participation, and this factor is likely to enhance learning overall.

Next, a learning center approach is adaptable to many subject areas (Gregory, 2008), even in the higher elementary, middle, and secondary grades. For example, in the class described above with four learning centers for reading centers, two of those learning centers can likewise include mathematics activities (e.g., the computer center and the writing center). Those centers might also include activities in science or history/social studies work. This teacher could also add a learning center for mathematics calculations and a learning center for problem solving. The computer center, if equipped with appropriate software, can easily serve as a learning center in any subject area. Further, by using the writing center assignments to stress subjects such as science, history, and health activities, virtually every Common Core curriculum area can be covered. Thus, learning centers may serve as the basis for differentiated instruction in all primary and elementary subject areas.

DIFFERENTIATED INSTRUCTION MODEL III

Project-Based Learning

Project-based learning (PBL) was not discussed as a model for differentiated instruction until recently (Schlemmer & Schlemmer, 2008). However, this approach has been around for several decades, and today PBL does provide a 21st century instructional approach that greatly facilitates differentiated instruction while at the same time fostering high levels of student engagement (Barell, 2010; Bender, 2012a; 2012b; Larmer & Mergendoller, 2010; Schlemmer & Schlemmer, 2008). PBL is an exciting, innovative instructional format in which students select a driving question that frames their project, and the teacher refines the curricular standards to fit within that project. Within the project time frame, students also select many tasks that must be accomplished, as well as aspects of various assignments, and that selection process typically results in students choosing learning activities that are particularly compatible with their learning styles and preferences. For that reason, some researchers consider project-based learning to be one method for differentiating instruction (Bender, 2012b; Schlemmer & Schlemmer, 2008).

PBL may be defined as using authentic, real-world projects, based on a highly motivating and engaging question, task, or problem. Each project is likely to take considerable time and should be developed in order to teach students academic content in the context of students working cooperatively to solve the problem and complete the project (Barell, 2010). Student inquiry is heavily integrated into project-based learning, and because students typically have some choice in selecting their group's project and the methods they would use to solve their projects, they tend to be more highly motivated to work diligently toward a solution to these problems (Belland, French, & Ertmer, 2009; Boss & Krauss, 2007; Larmer, Ross, & Mergendoller, 2009; Mergendoller, Maxwell, & Bellisimo, 2007). This typically results in high levels of engagement with the academic content involved in solving the problem or completing the project, as well as higher levels of academic achievement (Barell, 2010; Larmer & Mergendoller, 2010; Mergendoller et al., 2007).

> Project-based learning (PBL) may be defined as using real-world projects, based on a highly motivating and engaging guiding question, task, or problem to teach students academic content in the context of students working cooperatively in order to solve the problem.

PBL has been used in virtually every subject area and grade level, up through adult learning situations (Bender, 2012b; Boss & Krauss, 2007; Larmer, Ross, & Mergendoller, 2009), though PBL has been implemented more frequently in science and mathematics. Because PBL increases motivation to learn, teamwork, and collaborative skills, it is now recommended as a 21st century differentiated instructional teaching approach (Cole & Wasburn-Moses, 2010; Partnership for 21st Century Skills, 2009; Schlemmer & Schlemmer, 2008). Further, with the advent of modern social networking and communications technologies, project-based learning has received increasing attention (Boss & Krauss, 2007). Several brief introductory videos on PBL are available at the website (Edutopia.org/project-based-learning), and these are strongly recommended as a quick introduction for PBL.

Teachers should note that other terms have been used through the years for this instructional approach (e.g., problem-based learning, inquiry learning, authentic learning), and some educators prefer one term rather than another (Bender, 2012b). Proponents of PBL also disagree on the essential components of PBL, though the general list presented in Box 2.4 presents the general components of most projects. In spite of these disagreements, the instructional approach remains the same: students identifying and solving real-world problems that they consider important, and developing various projects to address those problems (Bender, 2012; Boss & Krauss, 2007; Larmer, Ross, & Mergendoller, 2009).

BOX 2.4 COMPONENTS OF PROJECT-BASED LEARNING

- *A project anchor.* An "anchor" is used to frame the project. Anchors may be a one or two paragraph narrative that describes a project, or a video segment that presents a problem to be solved via PBL. Some teachers use excerpts from newscast or media reports that describe a problem or project.
- *A driving question.* A driving question should be identified or developed to work with the project anchor as the major focus of the project. Teachers may develop these, or students may develop these as a first step in the project. Virtually any topic imaginable can be researched and investigated at various levels of depth, and the anchor and driving question together should help define the depth necessary for project completion. In fact, framing the project is critical for the success of PBL instruction.

   In an example described by Larmer and Mergendoller (2010), a teacher introduced a study of infectious disease in a biology class by using a video of a beautiful beach with a sign saying: "Beach Closed: Contaminated Water." Next, a discussion was held about why beaches are occasionally closed and the types of diseases and/or pollution that might result in closed beaches. In this example, both the anchor and the driving question were selected by the teacher, but student choice was exercised later in planning the research activities to address the issue of getting the beach cleaned up. Other teachers provide merely an anchor that presents a general problem and begin the instruction by having students articulate the driving question. Still other teachers might provide an anchor and then articulate two or three driving questions that become the basis of work for different groups of students.

- *Student choice and student voice.* Student dedication to the project is critical for both motivation and project success, making student choice a critically important component of a PBL instruction (Larmer & Mergendoller, 2010). Student choice fosters student participation in and ownership of the project. In terms of differentiated instruction, student choice is likewise critical. When students are presented with many small tasks required in a long-term class project, they, like all human beings, will choose tasks that fit their learning styles and preferences.

   Of course, when and how to provide students choices are instructional decisions that must be made by the teacher, and thus, the teacher can likewise exercise some control over how tasks are split up among groups of students. Again, this is likely to foster activities for differentiated groups where the groups are based, in part, on learning styles and preference.

- *Specific processes for investigation and research.* Teachers use a wide variety of instructional procedures in the investigation phase or step of the PBL process, including all the usual instruction techniques (modeling problem solution, discussions). However, more recently, technologically based instructional strategies (e.g., webquests, wikis, online discussion groups) are playing an increasing role in PBL (Boss & Krauss, 2007).

- *Student inquiry and reflective thinking.* Reflective thinking is encouraged in most PBL projects. Teachers frequently use an individual journal, or perhaps a wiki, to foster development of ideas and deeper understanding of the content. Reflective thinking, both individually and in teams, is considered critical in PBL.

(Continued)

(Continued)

- *Collaboration and teamwork.* Proponents of PBL insist that authentic (i.e., real world) tasks be selected as the basis of study and that teamwork to address those tasks and issues mirrors the working world of the 21st century. Thus, collaboration and teamwork are critical components of most PBL projects.
- *Feedback and revision.* Feedback is a critical component of PBL instruction, and the teacher serves as facilitator and coach in PBL projects and not as an information delivery system (i.e., lecturer). Feedback is critical, and much of this comes informally from the teacher. However, feedback should also come from the other students on the PBL project.
- *Publication of project results.* In PBL, as in life, one works to produce something, perhaps a model low-sunlight garden on the school campus (an actual project done by a fifth grade in a charter school in Atlanta) or a report to the school board about the feasibility of developing a second student parking lot next to the school (including the environmental impact study and appropriate engineering recommendations). When students attack an actual problem in the real world and produce a project to address that problem, then the product or project should be published. This is one reason students are so highly motivated to participate in PBL studies; they perceive that PBL projects make a real difference.

From *Differentiating Instruction for Students With Learning Disabilities: Best Teaching Practices for General and Special Educators*, Second Edition, by William N. Bender. Thousand Oaks, CA: Corwin, 2008. Used with permission.

A PBL Example

The following PBL example is fictional, but does illustrate how teachers generally endeavor to tie learning to current events. Note that in this PBL example learning activities are directly tied to a tornado in Birmingham, Alabama, and thus, students are likely to be motivated to help learn about tornadoes in order to assist in rebuilding their school. Finally, most PBL projects today, as illustrated in this example, are heavily tied to 21st century technology tools for learning. In this example, both webquests and wikis were planned for the students during the PBL experience, and these teaching strategies are explained further in the next chapter. These modern teaching tools help every student access the curricular content, much more so than merely delivering this content via a textbook and lecture presentation.

An Emphasis on Real-World Problems

Part of the allure of PBL is that students are more likely to engage in study of real-world problem-solving examples than in traditional instruction (Bender, 2012b; Boss & Krauss, 2007; Larmer, Ross, & Mergendoller, 2009). For example, Boss (2011) provided a real-world example of a PBL project that seemed to spontaneously "arise" in an earth science class in Indiana. When studying the impact of misuse of environments (specifically deforestation related to erosion

BOX 2.5: A SAMPLE PBL PROJECT

After the Tornado: Helping Rebuild Our School!

Project Anchor. At approximately 6:00 p.m. on April 27, 2011, an EF5 tornado, a storm that was slightly over a mile wide, tore the heart out of our city of Birmingham, Alabama. Winds were officially measured at 190 miles per hour. Many persons were left homeless, and many businesses were destroyed. Ultimately, 26 people died in Birmingham, and 128 persons in total were killed as a result of this terrible series of tornadoes and storms in Alabama. Our school, Andrew Jackson Elementary School, was completely destroyed.

We shall rise again from the ashes! For ourselves and the thousands of students who attended Andrew Jackson Elementary School before us, we will help in rebuilding this school. While we will be going to school elsewhere for some time, but we shall dedicate ourselves to helping in this relief effort for our school while learning the science behind tornadoes and weather patterns. The purpose of this project is to help our school rebuild from the destruction of this storm. Our goals are twofold:

1. Our fifth-grade science class will learn about tornadoes.
2. We will provide a way to earn relief funds for rebuilding our school and our town.

   While the city and state governments will rebuild our school, there are many supplies and items that may not be immediately replaced (e.g., computers, software for instruction, books for the school library). Funds that we can generate will be provided to our principal to purchase those items.

   We will create a class wiki, complete with information about tornadoes in general and the tornado that destroyed our school. We will also generate a presentation that can be used by various organizations around the world in club meetings and so on that presents our needs after this story and provides a way for individuals worldwide to assist in helping in the recovery effort. Funds collected in this manner may be used either by our school's administration, or if members of the public choose, their donations will be provided to specific designated charities that are assisting in the rebuilding efforts in Birmingham.

Driving Questions

- What is a tornado?
- How does a tornado result in so much destruction?
- How can communities be better prepared for tornadoes?
- How can the public assist in the relief effort?

Resources:

Youtube.com/watch?v=DWSGJ-hG4RM

http://www.charitynavigator.org/index.cfm?bay=content.view&cpid=1004

http://bkig,ak,cin.spotnews/2011/04/street-by-street_search_effort.html

(Continued)

(Continued)

Required Activities

1. Learn about how a tornado works and what causes tornadoes, using the webquest developed for our class.

2. Learn about the system used to describe the strength of tornadoes (e.g., EF5 tornado).

3. Create a class wiki, as described above, for sharing information we find on this topic.

4. Review a minimum of three videos about the Birmingham tornado, and determine which video is most likely to elicit the support of your intended audience.

5. Develop a series of interview questions, and interview at least three individuals whose homes or businesses suffered damage during the storm and videotape those interviews.

6. Identify at least five ways that the public can contribute funds and/or support to those in the community.

7. Seek local news coverage of our project and our efforts to rebuild our school.

Our Culminating Project

We will develop a well-edited, finished video project presentation of 10 to 15 minutes on the Birmingham tornado. This presentation will be disseminated for use by the public at various public meetings, clubs, or other events to solicit funds for rebuilding our school. We intend to disseminate this presentation as widely as possible, including options such as YouTube and TeacherTube. The presentation will include

- video footage of the event;
- an explanation of what a tornado is and how it works;
- video footage of destruction of our school and community;
- testimony of those whose homes were destroyed; and
- suggested ways the public can contribute to the relief effort.

and excess water runoff), a science teacher in Indiana made the effort to introduce his students to a professional colleague who was headmaster of a school in Haiti, where tree-cutting had led to erosion and floodwater problems. The Indiana students explored how deforestation had led to flooding prior to the several hurricanes that hit Haiti in 2011. After those hurricanes hit, the Indiana students heard stories of school students clinging to rooftops and not getting food or clean drinking water for days.

One Indiana student then asked why her class couldn't do a lab to devise some way to obtain clean drinking water for their new friends in Haiti. That became the driving question for the project: How can we get these students some clean drinking water?

Students in the Indiana class began to generate questions on how to purify water, what made water unsafe, and so forth, and teams of students were formed to do research to answer those questions in the science class. Much of that research was done online with various search functions, and results were then reported back to the class. Students skilled in Internet usage can be vital for that type of task, and students with technology as a hobby tended to self-select for such tasks in differentiated PBL projects.

Another group of students, the "hands-on learners" in the class, chose to tinker with an actual water purification device (Boss, 2011). That group obtained a patented water purification device from a local retired engineer, which they immediately dismantled. They looked at its operation, testing the electrolysis device with various salts and different voltages (Boss, 2011). Rather than merely explain the device, the team sought ways to improve it, resulting in a very creative and active learning process.

Another team began to "invest" their community in the project. They didn't want to call their activities fund-raising, but rather "investing"! They wanted their community to care about water purification for Haiti. All of these student teams presented their work each Friday to each other, and within a year (and after the massive earthquake in Haiti struck), the whole school became involved in this exciting, authentic learning project. Ultimately eight students, selected competitively, and eight teachers used community-generated funds to travel to Haiti along with a number of water purification devices, which were then given to their new friends in Haiti.

Not every PBL project will involve the entire school, and certainly few projects actually involve international travel, but authentic learning of this nature provides a rich learning opportunity and excites students in a way that traditional learning will never do. In this project, as noted above, students self-selected into teams for different tasks that fit their preferred learning styles, and that is how PBL serves as an excellent model for differentiating instruction. In the final analysis, this instructional approach may be the ultimate form of differentiated instruction.

DIFFERENTIATED INSTRUCTION MODEL IV

The "Flipped" Classroom

The newest differentiated instruction model to be discussed in the literature involves "flipping" the curriculum, or turning the traditional lesson plan on its head! As seen in Box 2.1 in this chapter, the traditional whole-group lesson plan involved a number of sequenced steps or phases of instruction, and the orientation to the lesson and teacher-led, initial instruction phases always came prior to teacher guided practice or independent work on new content. Since this lesson plan model developed in the late 1960s and 1970s, teachers have taught in this fashion, and the assumption has traditionally been that teachers needed to deliver initial instruction prior to having students work with the new material.

However, the amazing array of information now available on the Internet has turned that assumption upside down. In fact, many students (and adults) seek information on the Internet today on many topics that they were not taught in school or were taught so long ago that they didn't retain the information. This has caused some teachers to "flip" the order of instructional activities such that students, working independently, use Internet content as initial instruction on a new topic, prior to any class time on initial instruction on that topic (Cook, 2011; Saltman, 2011; Sparks, 2011; Toppo, 2011). In this new order for learning, students work in a self-directed fashion using the curricula or videotaped instructional content on the Internet, and the first in-class learning experience on that particular topic then becomes a teacher-facilitated "lab" or "project application" type of learning experience.

This instructional innovation is quite recent (as the dates for the references above illustrate), and it is not now known if this instructional approach will be widely accepted or applied. However, many teachers around the nation are experimenting with this reordered type of instruction, and at the very least, we must note this innovative approach as a newly emerging option for differentiated instruction. Because this instructional model is heavily tied to technology, it will be described in much more detail in the next chapter.

CHOOSING YOUR DIFFERENTIATED INSTRUCTIONAL APPROACH

While these models of the new differentiated instruction paradigm do not represent all approaches to differentiation, they do represent the options that characterize the new differentiated instruction, ranging from simple modification of traditional lesson plans to PBL as the differentiated instructional approach to the flipped classroom. While learning centers (Model II) have been used more frequently to differentiate instruction in lower grades, both the modification of traditional lessons (Model I) and PBL (Model III) provide opportunities for differentiation in middle and high schools. Further, PBL has been applied across all grade levels as one engaging way to foster high levels of student involvement with the content. Finally, the examples of the flipped curriculum (Model IV) that are discussed in the literature as of 2011 are all in middle and high schools.

Of course, teachers wishing to investigate differentiated instruction should select the differentiated instructional approach they are most comfortable with. For example, many teachers in traditional primary and elementary classes have adopted learning centers, and beefing up the learning centers to foster increased differentiated instruction might be the best choice for some teachers. Other teachers who have frequently used projects as components of unit-based instruction may wish to explore using project-based learning as their unit of instruction and differentiated instructional model.

Regardless of the selections teachers may make, it is clear that differentiated instruction has matured past the modification of whole-group lessons as the only differentiation approach. Indeed, over the last decade many approaches have shown themselves to ultimately be differentiated instructional approaches. Further, as shown in the discussions of differentiation models above, modern technologies for the classroom tend to play a large role in how teachers differentiate their instruction today.

WHAT'S NEXT?

With these models of differentiated instruction in mind, other factors that have impacted differentiated instruction should be considered. The first of these factors is the dramatic innovations in the classroom made possible by newly emerging technologies. The next chapter explores technology in order to show how modern technology impacts differentiated instruction as never before.

Technology and the New Differentiated Instruction 3

TECHNOLOGY FOR 21ST CENTURY TEACHING

As this book was written in 2012, technology was in the process of drastically impacting instruction across the United States and around the world (Ferriter & Garry, 2010; Kay, 2010; Pemberton, 2011; Wilmarth, 2010). By 2012, many schools had already undertaken the goal of making Internet-based learning a primary feature in each classroom. While some schools have purchased laptops for all students, other schools are purchasing the less expensive iPads or other tablets (Pemberton, 2011). Still other schools are merely telling students to BYOD (bring your own device)! Schools that are not already wireless are struggling to become so, and almost all educators realize that technology-based instruction represents not only learning for the future, but a lifelong learning option for today's students (Bender & Waller, 2011a). Thus, there is a need to explore how technology-based instruction interfaces with the need to differentiate instruction for all students.

To be clear, this chapter focuses not on technology applications in education directly but rather on how modern instructional technology applications interface with and facilitate differentiated instruction in the classroom. Of course, some educators might suggest that students using a highly effective, computer-based software program might be experiencing highly differentiated instruction, since most modern instructional software programs such as Fast ForWord or Successmaker Reading and Successmaker Math are

1. Diagnostic in nature

2. Specifically targeted at students' exact instructional deficits

3. Adaptable in nature such that the software will adapt the lesson activities, based on an individual students' ongoing success

One might well argue that students' individual use of these software programs represents the epitome of differentiated instruction because in many such instructional programs the learning is self-directed and tied to the specific needs of the student. For that reason, Appendix A in this book presents some general information on various computer or web-based curricula that present totally individualized instruction, instruction that is directly targeted at students' needs.

> Modern instructional software is diagnostic in nature, specifically targeted at students' exact instructional deficits, and will adapt itself depending on the students' ongoing success, and it can be argued that this represents the epitome of differentiated instruction.

However, it is important to note that modern instructional technology can support differentiated instruction in many ways other than merely isolating students at computer terminals within a totally individualized reading or mathematics curriculum. In fact, the most recent technology applications tend to be highly communal in nature, involving social learning and the possibility of learning from one's peers (e.g., cloud computing via Google Apps, blogging, wikis, or using Twitter in the classroom).

Of course, many of these technology-based tools for instruction have been developed and/or adapted to the classroom within the last five years, and it is no exaggeration to suggest that a revolution has begun in technology for teaching. In fact, that revolution is providing many differentiated instructional options that could not have been envisioned only five years ago (Bender & Waller, 2011a; Pemberton, 2011; Richardson, 2010). Thus, certainly technology-based options for differentiating instruction could not, and were not, discussed within the differentiated instruction literature when differentiation was first conceptualized by Tomlinson in 1999. The new differentiated instruction is founded, in large measure, on technology developments that postdate the 1999–2007 time frame.

This chapter provides some introductory information on the ever-changing instructional technologies as well as on the use of these technologies for differentiating instruction in 21st century classrooms. First, a synopsis of where we are as this book was written in 2012 is presented. That is followed by specific recommendations on using a variety of modern instructional technologies to differentiate instruction in the general education classroom, but the emphasis will be on instructional practices rather than on specific curricula.

Technology in The 21st Century World

Modern technologies are drastically changing the world in which today's students live, and this will significantly impact 21st century classrooms (Bender & Waller, 2011a; Kay, 2010; Wilmarth, 2010). Modern technologies provide instructional and connectivity options today that were unrealized even as recently as 2008, and tools such as smartphones, iPads, and cloud computing have created a new world in education. Major shifts in instruction are predicted for the immediate future (Ferriter & Garry, 2010; Rushkoff & Dretzin, 2010; Pemberton, 2011; Wilmarth, 2010), and all teachers are well advised to get on board that technology train, as it has already left the station!

Here are the facts. Students text, on average, 3,000 times each month, and that has increased by 600% since 2008 (Feyerick, 2010). Many students today have a Facebook page, and many also use Twitter. In fact, some schools are using this very digital media to join in within the world of their students, and this tends to make the curriculum more relevant and much more interesting to 21st century students (Rapp, 2009). However, technologies for the classroom represent much more than merely instructional use of various social media options. Gaming is a multibillion-dollar-a-year industry in all economically developed countries, yet gaming for education is, by most accounts, still in its infancy. In developing a differentiated curriculum today, teachers must ask what options these instructional games may hold for the classroom. As all of these examples show, the educational power of the new communications technologies and social networking sites is nearly unlimited (Kay, 2010; Wilmarth, 2010).

> Today's smartphones and iPads, when coupled with modern educational software, educational gaming options, and the anytime, anywhere learning options on the Internet today, will ultimately lead to a revolution in education.

It is not an overstatement to say that today's mobile devices, such as smartphones and iPads, are creating a revolution in communications and that, when coupled with modern educational software, educational gaming options, and the anytime, anywhere learning options on the Internet today, will ultimately lead to a revolution in education (Ash, 2011; Bender & Waller, 2011a; Ferriter & Garry, 2010; Rushkoff & Dretzin, 2010; Partnership for 21st Century Skills, 2009; Pemberton, 2011; Wilmarth, 2010). Further, these technologies, as they are applied in various classrooms, will greatly enhance every teacher's opportunity to provide highly differentiated instruction for every student in the class. In short, 21st century students will be using these technologies to interact with their world, and educators would be remiss if we do not provide instruction within this framework as well as on appropriate uses for these tools.

Moreover, modern technologies should be seamlessly integrated into virtually every subject area class in order to prepare students for the environment they will face in their lifetimes (Ash, 2011; Ferriter & Garry, 2010). Rather than chain modern technologies to the outdated concept of school computer labs, every classroom should become a Wi-Fi environment, rich in technology for instruction. In today's media-rich, high-technology world, effective teachers simply must embrace these instructional innovations in order to both reach students today and provide the differentiated instruction that they need (Kay, 2010; Partnership for 21st Century Skills, 2009; Pemberton, 2011; Salend, 2009). Because so many students have extensive experience with these technologies in nonschool settings, schools must adapt by implementing instruction using these technologies as much as possible in order to hold the interests of today's preteens and adolescents. With the implementation of these new technologies, effective, highly differentiated instruction in the next decade will look drastically different from instruction only five years ago (Ferriter & Garry, 2010; Kay, 2010; Pemberton, 2011), and again, all teachers would be well advised to be prepared for these coming changes.

Teachers simply must embrace these instructional innovations in order to reach students today, and effective, highly differentiated instruction in the next decade will look drastically different from instruction only 10 years ago.

Of course, it is easy to be overwhelmed by the vast array of technologies today, and some teachers simply let the computer teacher or media person address the use of computers. Other teachers point out, quite reasonably, that it is impossible to teach with technology when no technology is available, or when schools themselves are not Wi-Fi–ready. How can a teacher use a webquest or wiki (as described below) when students do not have access to the Internet? However, one thing is clear. Our world is fast segregating itself into those that use these technologies daily for learning and those that don't. This is often referred to as the digital divide, and it is probably safe to say that no educator would wish to condemn his or her students to a life on the wrong side of that divide.

Our world is fast segregating itself into those that use these technologies daily and those that don't, and no educator would wish to condemn his or her students to a life on the wrong side of that digital divide.

To further emphasize how important the use of these technologies are in education, one need only consider that the Ministry of Education in the nation of India, in October 2011, developed a tablet (somewhat comparable to the early iPads) that can be sold to the general public for the equivalent of $39! What happens economically in our world if every student in the nation of India, the second most populous nation on the planet, becomes educated completely in the digital world while many students in the United States and other developed nations are not? Who then will be on the wrong side of the digital divide?

For these reasons, this chapter begins with relatively simple instructional tasks that facilitate differentiated instruction and that have been used by many teachers over the last decade or so, including webquests, blogging, wikis for the classroom, and modern instructional gaming. Toward the end of the chapter, some of the more recently developed instructional options are presented, including cloud computing, social learning via Google Apps, the Khan Academy, and the flipped curriculum as one option for differentiating instruction.

WEBQUESTS: THE FIRST TECH OPTION FOR DIFFERENTIATING INSTRUCTION

A webquest is a teacher-structured, highly focused research project completed in whole or in part using Internet resources. Webquests have been used in education since the mid-1990s and provide an exciting opportunity for students to research content online in a "guided tour" or perhaps a "scavenger hunt" type of format (Ferriter & Garry, 2010). In a webquest, students use prompts and links provided by the teacher to analyze and synthesize information from the Internet related to their topic of study. Students are able to sift through information on a particular topic, in a predictable order as predetermined by the teacher. In that sense, the teacher's development of the webquest, the questions to be addressed at each site or the activities to complete, represent the teacher's scaffolding of students' learning in order to build their comprehension of the topic as they progress through the webquest. A sample webquest is presented in Box 3.1 below.

BOX 3.1: A SAMPLE WEBQUEST

The purpose of this webquest is to gather information on tornados in general and the Birmingham, Alabama, tornado in particular. While all class members must complete the 10 questions in Section 1 of this webquest, some students will complete Section 2 activities also, while other students will complete Section 3 activities. The teacher may assign certain members of the PBL teams to work together on this webquest, and in those cases, students working together will receive the same grade. Again, all students must investigate all of the required sites in Section 1 and answer each of the 10 questions there with a written answer. Those answers may range in length from several words to nine sentences long.

Section 1 (Resource—http://www.pa.msu.edu/sciencet/ask_st/081397.html)

Questions:

1. What are the critical factors that cause a tornado?
2. Define the terms on the class wiki. If definitions are already provided, give examples and/or expand the definitions.

vortex	mesocyclone	rotating wall cloud
tornado warning	thunderstorm watch	severe thunderstorm warning
tornado watch	waterspout	weak tornado
strong tornado	violent tornado	

3. What wind speeds can be found inside tornadoes?
4. How many reach the United States each year?
5. What geographic features are associated with hurricanes?
6. Diagram in at least five phases how a tornado develops.

Resource—http://www.nssl.noaa.gove/edu/safety/tornadoguide.html

1. What time of day do tornadoes usually occur?
2. What should individuals do when a tornado is approaching?
3. How fast do tornadoes move across the ground?
4. What visible signs may indicate a tornado?

Section 2 (Resource—youtube.com/watch?v=DWSGJ-hG4RM)

1. What type of tornado was the Birmingham tornado?
2. How long did the tornado last?
3. What estimates of the costs of destruction are available?

Resource—http://bkig,ak,cin.spotnews/2011/04/street-by-street_search_effort.html

1. How many deaths were attributed to the tornado in Birmingham?
2. Why does the estimate of deaths vary from one news report to another?

(Continued)

(Continued)

Section 3 (Resource—Graph Master—www.mrnussbaum.com/graphmaster.htm)

Your goal is to develop a graph that will display the number of deaths in Alabama attributed to tornadoes in each year over a certain time frame. First, pick a time frame ranging from the last five years up to the last 20 years. Next, search the Internet in order to find data on the number of deaths attributed to tornadoes in Alabama in that time frame (or if necessary, use data on all tornadoes in the Southeast). Create an X/Y axis graph, as we learned in mathematics, using Graph Master, that relates data on the number of deaths to the specific years, and then write a one to two paragraph summary of those data.

> A webquest is a teacher-structured, highly focused research project completed in whole or in part using Internet resources.

As indicated in Box 3.1, webquests typically include a brief introduction, including in many cases an overall question, and they provide students with specific websites and instructions on what the students should accomplish at each location on the web. The introduction should be structured to motivate students and get them excited about the assignment. Students then use the links that have been previewed by the teacher, along with guiding questions associated with each link in order to work through information on the Internet in the selected resources section. Questions may be answered on a paper handout or actually answered in an online format (e.g., webquest journal).

While teacher-developed questions do enable students to select important information from a webquest site, websites that actually require students to *do something* typically elicit higher levels of student excitement. For example, on a science website, while teacher-developed questions might focus students' attention on specific content, having students complete an activity such as survey on the importance of a particular scientific discovery will usually energize students more. On some interactive websites, student responses are immediately merged with previous students' responses, and some type of data display may allow students to compare their personal answers with summarized information from others. Students are usually highly motivated by such activities, compared to merely answering content questions from the website.

Also, the most effective webquests encourage students to generate some type of product. In the example in Box 3.1, students are required to develop a graph that correlates tornado deaths with specific years in a multiyear time frame. In general, having students generate this type of content for the class or perhaps to be published via a class website or YouTube presentation can be highly motivating for many students. Also, in Box 3.1, note how the activities in the webquest progressed from collection of simple factual data at various websites to actual generation of new information in the third section of that assignment. Webquests should, in general, be structures more than merely "collect the answers from the web" type of activities, as demonstrated in Box 3.1.

There are numerous sites available online that can help teachers create their own webquest for any topic (two free websites are: http://www.kn.pacbell.com/wired/fil/ and http://www.zunal.com/). Also, several fee-based websites can assist teachers in developing a webquest (https://www.teachersfirst.com).

> In a webquest, students sift through information on the web in a predictable order, scaffolding their learning and building their conceptual understanding as they progress.

As described in Chapter 2, there are several models for providing differentiated instruction, and webquests can be components in any of those models. For example, the webquest in Box 3.1 would be a perfect fit within the broader project-based learning project that was described in Chapter 2 (see Box 2.5). Alternatively, webquests can function as stand-alone learning activities in a differentiated classroom that used a modified traditional lesson plan as described in Chapter 2. Further, a webquest can serve a number of functions, ranging from initial instruction to practice and reinforcement of knowledge. Also, as students become more proficient in technology and use of Internet resources, teachers may actually have students create their own webquests for later use by others.

While some webquests consist of searching on the web for answers to particular questions (see Sections 1 and 2 of the sample webquest in Box 3.1), others involve the creation and synthesis of information. For example, an additional assignment in Section 3 of the webquest above does not specify particular sites that provide the necessary data, and rather than merely answering specific questions, students are required to generate data on their own, in the form of a graph relating the frequency of tornadoes in Alabama to tornado deaths in Alabama over a five- to 20-year period. Webquest assignments of this nature clearly lend themselves to differentiating instruction, and the option of partnering certain students together for webquest activities presents an additional differentiation option.

Of course, webquests are highly effective teaching tools. Webquests allow students to discover information on their own or by working with partners or in small teams, and this can assist with motivational problems that are demonstrated by some students with learning disabilities. Instead of sitting in a lecture or class discussion, students can use the structured guidance within the webquest to explore content information directly, thus making the learning experience

> Webquests allow students to discover information on their own or by working with partners or in small teams, and this can assist with motivational problems that are demonstrated by some students with learning disabilities.

more interactive and much more personal. The links and questions developed by the teacher will serve to scaffold the information, and in order to further differentiate the assignment, teachers may assign all or one of the webquest assignments for particular students, as illustrated in the webquest in Box 3.1.

In order to explicitly state the expectations associated with a webquest, this type of assignment is typically graded via use of a rubric. Many sources provide information on the use of rubrics for evaluating webquests (Bender & Waller, 2011b; Boss & Krauss, 2007), and a sample rubric for use in this webquest is provided in Box 3.2.

BOX 3.2: RUBRIC FOR EVALUATION OF A WEBQUEST

Evaluation of Section 1

4. All questions were answered in some detail, all definitions were detailed, and numerous excellent guidelines were provided for responding to an approaching tornado.

3. All questions were answered in some detail, and all definitions were addressed. Only a few guidelines were provided on how to prepare for approaching tornadoes.

2. All questions were answered, more detail would be desirable. All definitions were addressed. Only a few guidelines were provided on how to prepare for approaching tornadoes.

1. Most of the questions were answered and definitions addressed, but more detail is necessary. Guidelines for preparing for tornadoes were lacking detail. This work will need to be redone.

0. The answers lacked detail and some of the questions were not addressed. This work will need to be redone.

Evaluation of Section 2

4. All factual questions were answered in some detail, and the question on variations of death estimates was addressed fully.

3. All factual questions were answered adequately, but the answer to the question on variations of death estimates lacked specificity.

2. All factual questions were answered, but more detail would be desirable. The answer on death estimates was minimally acceptable.

1. Most of the factual questions were answered, but more detail is necessary. The answer on death estimates was not acceptable. This work will need to be redone.

0. The answers lacked detail or questions were left unaddressed. This work will need to be redone.

Evaluation of Section 3

4. All required data were presented in a very neat chart over a multiyear period. The data were gleaned from a minimum of two sources that supported each other. The summary paragraph summarized the data and demonstrated excellent writing skills.

3. All required data were presented in a very neat chart over a multiyear period. The summary paragraph summarized the data and demonstrated acceptable writing skills.

2. All required data were presented in the chart, but neatness and readability of the chart should be improved. The data summary paragraph was adequate.

1. The chart did not present the data required, and the summary paragraphs were only minimally acceptable. This work will need to be redone.

0. The chart did not present the data required, and the summary paragraphs were not acceptable. This work will need to be redone.

(Continued)

(Continued)

Evaluation scores: Each student's score may range from 0 to 8. Every student should receive a grade on Section 1 above, and a grade on either Section 2 or Section 3, but no student should receive three scores. You should add your two scores together below to find your total score on this webquest. Totals scores of five and above are considered passing: 5 = D, 6 = C, 7 = B, and 8 = A.

My score: Section 1. _____
             Section 2. _____
             Section 3. _____
             My Total Score: _____

BLOGGING AS A DIFFERENTIATED TEACHING TOOL

A blog is an online journal in which both the teacher and the students in the class can create and share written content (Richardson, 2010; Waller, 2011). By offering a class blog in association with a particular topic of study, teachers are encouraging students to connect with each other in their discussions about class content and to ask questions of other students on important aspects of the topic under study. The ultimate result will be an increase in socially based learning among the students (Bender & Waller, 2011a; Ferriter & Garry, 2010, Richardson, 2010). Blog entries are typically categorized by date, and many blogs are structured so the teacher can see who makes any particular blog entry.

Also, all readers in the class are able to comment on postings by other students on a particular topic, making the class blog a highly interactive instructional tool. Also, when students realize that their written work will be read by their peers, they are quite likely to take more care in what they write, resulting in improved written work.

> A blog is an online journal in which both the teacher and the students in the class can create and share written content.

The popularity of social networking today demonstrates that most students enjoy social interaction, and educators can take advantage of that by using class blogs (Salend, 2009; Richardson, 2010; Waller, 2011). For these reasons, blogs are becoming increasingly popular in education, and like the webquests discussed above, even teachers who have not used technology a great deal in the classroom can initiate a class blog with relative ease. Teachers may wish to review a website on using blogs in the classroom (http://supportblogging.com/Links+to+School+Bloggers).

> The popularity of social networking today demonstrates that most students enjoy social interaction, and educators can take advantage of that by using class blogs.

There are many variations to consider in using class blogs, including student security, cost, and blog content. Like many things on the Internet, some blog sites for education are subscription based (fee based) while others are free. A password-protected blog provides teachers the option of limiting the blog to class members or class members and their parents. For example, http://www.classblogmeister.com/ is a free website that provides a template for teachers to

Figure 3.1

create their own password-protected classroom blogs. The website, www.gaggle.net, provides both a free or fee-based e-mail and blog tools for teachers and students. This site has numerous filters available that allow teachers to filter blog content for inappropriate words or images, and teachers likewise have control over who can post on the site. Also, http://www.21classes.com/ is another blog option for teachers that offers several layers of protection for students in the class, including password protection, and additional teacher controls.

Because students are creating their own content for the class blog, it is quite common for students to "differentiate" their own instruction in this format by virtue of the type of blog content they create. For example, students with linguistic skills are quite likely to post longer blog entries than other students, whereas students with a learning style based on bodily kinesthetic (motor) learning may be somewhat reluctant to create written entries. In such situations, the teacher might assist those students by suggesting that they work together to develop their postings. Learners who benefit from small-group work in mastering content might work as a small group and develop a dialogue or short scripted play for the class blog focused on the content under study. In that situation, the bodily kinesthetic learners may then be used to act out the script, while one or more spatial learners record the play digitally. In short, differentiation options based on learning style differences can easily be addressed in this framework.

> Because students are creating their own content for the class blog, it is quite common for students to "differentiate" their own instruction in this format by virtue of the type of blog content they create.

Blogs are particularly important for students with language-based learning disorders because these tools strengthen language and writing skills. Also, this form of communication is likely to characterize business communications for some time to come, and having students develop strengths as they practice these 21st century communication skills in the

> Blogs are particularly important for students with language-based learning disorders because these tools strengthen language and writing skills.

classroom will be critical to their long-term success, particularly for many students with learning disabilities.

To assist students with limited language skills, teachers might consider having several class blogs, with various class members working on each in order to differentiate the content. This would allow students with limited language skills to practice blogging in a relatively "safe" space along with other learners who are likewise challenged.

Finally, many students with limited verbal skills do not participate well in class discussions, and a class blog offers a "discussion" forum outside the context of spoken communication within the classroom. Discussion assignments using a class blog will help students who are not vocal in class express themselves in a less intimidating way. Blogs will also motivate students to publish work of a higher standard as they realize their work will be viewed by a much larger audience. The blog posting is likely to be read and reviewed by their peers and perhaps parents of others in the class, and this frequently results in more attention to the mechanics of writing and higher engagement overall with the assigned task. If the blog is public or if work is made public at the conclusion of the instructional unit, then the students' writing is available worldwide. This will further increase their desire to publish quality work.

WIKIS FOR DIFFERENTIATED INSTRUCTION

What Is a Wiki?

Wikis have been used in classrooms since about 1995 (Watters, 2011a; Richardson, 2010), though many teachers have yet to use this creative teaching idea because so many classrooms have limited technology and/or limited Wi-Fi availability. However, as schools increase Internet connectivity and more technology reaches the classroom, wikis are certainly a teaching tool that every teacher should consider (Richardson, 2010; Waller, 2011). Essentially, a wiki is an editable website that allows various users the ability to edit their own work and the work of others (Watters, 2011a). Whereas blogs offer the students the opportunity to comment on postings of other students, wikis actually allow students and teachers to directly edit content posted by others. Further, wikis are typically much more functional than class blogs because most wikis allow for the generation and publication of virtually any type of content, including discussion points, definitions, video demonstrations, photos, and other digitally generated media.

> A wiki is an editable website that allows various users the ability to edit their own work and the work of others.

Of course, the online encyclopedia Wikipedia is probably the most widely recognized of all wikis. However, there are many other wikis devoted to a wide range of topics (e.g., recipes, travel, famous quotes). As in all wikis, any user can add in their own favorite content (e.g., a recipe, their favorite famous quote, or a favorite hotel). Users can even edit someone else's recipe or hotel description. In that sense these collaboratively created wikis are usually self-correcting, and the use of wikis encourages individuals to publish their contributions and edit anyone else's content in a relatively ungoverned fashion. Over time, this leads to an online collaborative community of information providers, and most inaccuracies within the wikis are eventually corrected by later users.

Now, imagine the power of this collaboration in the classroom. Teaching students how to work together, sort through information, evaluate information using other sources, make contributions to the content on the wiki, and create newly synthesized information is clearly a set of skills that 21st century learners will need throughout life (Bender & Waller, 2011a; Waller, 2011). Because students today are inundated with information on a daily basis, it is the responsibility of teachers to teach students how to sift through information, evaluate its validity, determine the purpose of the author, and contribute their own findings and research in the digital world. Wikis provide the format to learn and apply these critical skills (Richardson, 2010).

> Wikis serve one function for teachers perhaps better than any other teaching tool; wikis are excellent for teaching subject area vocabulary.

Further, wikis serve one function for teachers perhaps somewhat better than any other teaching tool: wikis are excellent for teaching subject area vocabulary. Wouldn't it be nice to never have to spend time teaching vocabulary again but rather have the students pick up the necessary vocabulary terms for each instructional unit as they work through the wiki for that unit? This is what a wiki can do for virtually all elementary and middle school subject area classes. Note that, in the project-based learning project presented in Box 2.5 in Chapter 2, students were assigned to define the terms associated with a tornado, using the class wiki. By requiring that such work be completed on the class wiki, the teacher is requiring students to master that vocabulary in a manner similar to Wikipedia—either adding definitions on their own, or editing someone else's posted definition in assure accuracy. Most students enjoy this type of activity and will learn vocabulary terms based on this activity without the teacher having to take additional class time to teach content-specific vocabulary.

Using Wikis in the Classroom

Teachers who have never used a wiki previously can set up a wiki in approximately 30 to 45 minutes for use in their class. Further, the Internet provides many sites that will assist teachers in developing and using wikis. Regardless of the differentiated instructional approach teachers choose, teachers should begin to use wikis in virtually every instructional unit.

As one example, wikispaces (www.wikispaces.com) allows teachers in kindergarten through Grade 12 to set up a wiki at no cost, for use exclusively in his or her class. Various options allow for either closed wiki pages (where no edits are allowed) or open pages (wiki pages that anyone in the class can edit or add to). Also, most wikis allows teachers to track every posted entry to see who is making entries and who in the class is not. Wetpaint is another popular wiki site used by many teachers. At that site, teachers can choose from a variety of wikis related to grade level or subject (http://wikisineducation.wetpaint.com/page/Teacher+Peer+Wikis). Guidelines for setting up and using wikis in the classroom are presented in Teaching Tip 3.1.

Teaching Tip 3.1

While there are many places that offer templates for wiki creation, this step-by-step guide accompanies a wiki started at www.wikispaces.com. Wikispaces provides free, private wikis for educators.

1. To begin, access http://www.wikispaces.com/site/for/teachers. There is an option for teachers to create a free wiki for their class (toward the lower right of the wikispace homepage)

2. Once this site is accessed, teachers will need to select a username, password, and a wikispace name.

3. Teachers should initially create either a protected wiki (a wiki that everyone can view but only class members can edit) or a private wiki (only wiki members can view and edit). The private option is free for educators.

4. The wiki will have many pages. Typically, teachers should create a paragraph-long description of the wiki content and purpose, and on that page add a video or two related to the topic for increasing student interest. That homepage should then be "locked" so that no edits are possible on that page.

5. Next, teachers should set up a set of unlocked pages that students can edit. One of these should be a vocabulary page. There, teachers should add the vocabulary (but not definitions) of the terms in the unit of instruction. Students can then edit those, providing definitions and examples.

6. Once one or more pages are established, wikispaces will offer a wiki tutorial to help with setup. The teacher will use the "edit this page" tab to manipulate text, fonts, and spacing for each page.

7. Each time a new page is created, teachers should link to that page by highlighting the text and clicking the earth icon.

8. Images and files can be uploaded by clicking on the icon that looks like a tree in a box. Teachers can then invite students (perhaps parents also) to join the wiki using the User Creator feature.

Because using wikis is relatively simple, virtually every teacher in schools that have Wi-Fi capability should be encouraged to use wikis in the classroom today. Not only are wikis good tools for increasing student participation and creative activities centered on lesson content; they are also excellent for helping students use and understand 21st century technologies. In fact, many wikis are used today in the workplace when individuals from different locales are required to work together, as the editable function of wikis allows the ultimate wiki content to reflect the best thinking of all participants.

Further, when wikis are used in the classroom, students are not studying content in a passive fashion such as receiving information from a teacher's lecture or a textbook. Rather, in using wikis, students are creating informative content centered on the content under study. In using this teaching tactic, as well as many other 21st century classroom teaching tools, students become much more active in the learning process (Bender & Waller, 2011a).

> Not only are wikis good tools for increasing student participation and creative activities centered on lesson content, they are also excellent for helping students use and understand 21st century technologies.

Wikis for Differentiating Instruction

From the perspective of differentiated instruction, the use of wikis is, once again, a plus. Because wikis allow students to participate in their learning through creation of content for study, students will tend to segregate themselves somewhat, based on their learning strengths. For example, linguistically talented fifth-grade learners might work individually or together to develop a dialogue for a fictional debate to demonstrate the content of the lesson. For a lesson on the Civil War, as one example, students might develop a debate representing Generals Lee and Grant debating the importance of food and ammunition supplies at the Petersburg siege in Virginia in 1864 and 1865. However, learners who are more inclined to movement-based learning may wish to develop a month-by-month walk-through of the siege, demonstrating positions of the siege lines and major events during that siege. This could then be digitally videotaped and uploaded to the class wiki. As an enrichment activity, some of the more advanced fifth graders could develop a comparison poster that compares the Petersburg battle with the Battle of Verdun in World War I (another battle characterized by siege-line warfare). As these quick examples illustrate, students will have many options to exercise their learning strengths when wikis are offered as a differentiated instructional option within the class.

INSTRUCTIONAL GAMES FOR DIFFERENTIATING INSTRUCTION

Game-Based Learning Comes of Age

Instructional games in computerized form have been utilized in classrooms for several decades, and noncomputerized games are probably as old as education itself. However, with the advent of modern technologies as well as the popularity of games among today's youth and young adults, educators are taking a new look at the exciting possibility of educational games as critical instructional tools (Maton, 2011; Miller, 2011a; 2011b; Shah, 2012). For example, there are examples of teachers using a popular, widely played game called *Angry Birds* to teach physics principles, or using the popular commercial game, *SimCity*, to teach how complex systems interact (Sheehy, 2011). Of course, computer-based games such as the *Age of Empires* or *Civilization* have long taught players how civilizations come into existence, and the decades-old *Oregon Trail* did an admirable job teaching recent generations of Americans what the settlers of the western frontier faced as they traveled across the continent in the 1800s. Still, in 2012 as this book was written, much more attention is being given to games as a teacher tool, and game-based learning seems to be coming of age (Miller, 2011). Even students with learning disabilities and other special needs can benefit from these educational computer-based games (Pisha & Stahl, 2005; Shah, 2012), and these instructional tools can certainly provide many options for differentiating instruction.

Today, teachers from the primary grades through high school are using games for instruction. For example, a second-grade teacher, Joel Levin, used

> Teachers are using a popular, widely played game called *Angry Birds* to teach physics principles or a popular commercial game, *SimCity*, to teach how complex systems interact.

a popular game called *Minecraft* to teach students computer skills (Sheehy, 2011). After eliminating some content from the game (some monsters and other game elements would not have been appropriate in a second-grade class), Levin found his students responded very well to the game format as they learned computer skills, as well as online etiquette, Internet safety, and even conflict resolution in a gaming context (Sheehy, 2011).

Many modern games (if not most modern games) come complete with video examples of gaming scenarios, and these can be applied in many lesson formats. In that sense, games for education can be a very flexible instructional approach. In the game Minecraft for example (a game with over 15.5 million registered users worldwide), the players construct an imaginary world, including structuring their community and making decisions on their interactions with each other within the game (Sheehy, 2011). Of course, the main advantage of using games for education is obvious: By using instructional tools that students want to use, students' engagement as well as students' learning is likely to increase. Many teachers have anecdotally reported that their students enjoyed learning in technology-based gaming formats (Ash, 2011; Maton, 2011) and that they saw benefits from these games in terms of students' achievement overall.

Games and Simulations for Learning

Rather than retasking existing commercial games for educational purposes, many educators are devising games specifically for instruction. For example, educators can access a set of free educational games including *Pemdas Blaster* (order of operations) and *Algebra Meltdown.* These games are designed to teach a wide range of mathematics skills and are aligned with the Common Core State Standards in mathematics (see Mangahigh at www.mangahigh. com). These games have an objective or goal for students to achieve by repeatedly practicing the core learning concept. The games at this site are targeted for students ranging in age from 7 to 16, and teachers can receive their own login codes and passwords, allowing them to track the progress of their students.

BrainWare Safari is another example of using gaming for educational purposes. This educational software program, which may be used by teachers and home-schooling parents alike (Shah, 2012), is based in the emerging research from brain-compatible instruction as described in Chapter 1 to strengthen certain cognitive skills, including skills in the areas of attention, memory, visual and auditory processing, thinking, and sensory integration (http://www .mybrainware.com/how-it-works). The game is a cloud-based program (i.e., user performance data is stored on computers of the publisher) and operates like a video game. Over 20 different games are included, and each offers many levels of play and focuses on multiple skills. These games are sequenced and intended to help the student develop automaticity in the targeted cognitive skills. The developers recommend that students access the games three to five times weekly and spend 30 to 60 minutes on the game each time they play. In approximately 12 weeks, most users will complete all 168 levels.

Games such as these can benefit students with learning disabilities immensely by reinforcing content in a fun, motivating way. Teachers report anecdotally that students play these math games well into the night (see www.mangahigh.com

Games such as these can benefit students with learning disabilities immensely by reinforcing content in a fun, motivating way.

Rather than retasking existing commercial games for educational purposes, many educators are devising games specifically for instruction.

website for several teacher reviews). Thus, these teaching tools tend to keep even the most distractible students focused on the learning tasks within the game. Certainly any teacher of mathematics should take advantage of this website to access some educational games that will motivate most students, including students with learning disabilities or other learning challenges.

Perhaps an example would assist the reader in understanding the power of educational games and simulations for teaching important content. In a fifth-grade social studies class, when teaching about the antebellum period and the Underground Railroad, a teacher might have his or her students play a game called *Flight to Freedom,* a simulation game that was designed specifically for teaching that content. This simulation helps students experience the struggles of slaves in the antebellum South as they attempt to escape into freedom in Canada. For teachers who may not be experienced with educational games, it is well worth 15 to 20 minutes to go to the website below and actually play the game for a time (http://ssad.bowdoin.edu:9780/projects/flighttofreedom/intro.shtml).

This is a very simple computer-based game that was specifically constructed to teach about educational games, and like most such games, *Flight to Freedom,* can be played either individually or by small groups. It is intended for students from the mid elementary grades through high school grades. In this game, the player (or players) is presented the opportunity to choose one of nine historic characters from that antebellum period (e.g., Sojourner Truth, Frederick Douglass, Harriet Tubman, etc.). Players then read a brief biography of that character and use that character as an avatar or their character within the game itself.

The avatars are then randomly placed on a map somewhere in the southern states. The avatars each have a "status board" that described their circumstances (e.g., their overall health and financial resources). The game also presents a description of the situation in which they find themselves. Students then have to make choices as to what their avatars must do. Options include trying to escape from their current situations, remaining in place, or seeking information about family members. The overall goal of the game is for each character and their family to escape into Canada, and each decision students make holds consequences for the avatars in terms of costing money, damage to health (e.g., if sufficient food is not found), or being recaptured and taken back into slavery.

Game-based learning games are likely to result in much higher levels of engagement and, ultimately, higher mastery of the subject material.

Like most educational games, this game could be used as an adjunct to the class in order to help students sense the overwhelming odds against escaping slaves. While lectures, texts, and videos can be used to teach this same content, students are much more likely to sense what those enslaved persons actually felt—what they actually went through—when they are confronted with the same types of choices during their escape to

Canada. Clearly, this type of gaming scenario is likely to result in much higher levels of engagement and, ultimately, higher mastery of the subject material.

Alternate Reality Gaming

The latest trend in educational gaming involves alternate reality games (Maton, 2011) or ARGs. ARGs involve the creation of an alternative reality in which students play a role and learn academic content as they move through the game. These games are much more likely to be housed on the Internet than based on software that ties the game to a specific computer. This pro-

> Alternative reality games, or ARGs, involve the creation of an alternative reality in which characters play a role, and learn academic content during the game.

vides the advantage of anytime, anywhere learning. Today, most ARGs may be played using computers at school or home or even on smartphones or tablets such as the iPad or Kindle Fire. If a student can access the Internet, he or she can play an ARG. As in the games discussed previously, students typically take on the role of a character and complete assigned tasks that involve the content under study by making choices within the alternative reality of the game, working either individually or in teams. Most ARGs are highly interactive games that require students to engage in various activities in the real world, the alternative reality world, or both in order to compete with each other. As in more traditional games, students playing ARGs receive clues for the activity and other instructions, as well as feedback, during the gaming activity itself.

Here's an example. Kevin Ballestrini, a classroom teacher teaching Latin, developed an ARG that placed students' characters in ancient Rome in order to teach them Latin (Maton, 2011).The student must work online, wandering the streets of Rome, interacting with others and directing their character in Latin, in order to plan, act, create, and write like a Roman citizen. During the game the characters help to rebuild the city of Pompeii. Students seek inscriptions on stones and solve mysteries during that process, learning the language and applying it in ways not possible in a more standard Latin classroom. That ARG is now being used experimentally in 30 classrooms across the United States, and the latest version can even be played using Internet-capable cell phones!

The current technology for ARGs is only in its infancy, but educators are beginning to experiment with ARGs in the classroom. ARGs weave together real-world information and artifacts, using clues and puzzles hidden within alternate reality and using any form of digital media available. This may include documents from any online library, photos from museums, or a wide range of content from various websites. Using these resources, and/or other resources, players meet and talk in the ARG environment and jointly use various online resources to complete the puzzle or task as they learn about the topical content.

An ARG called *Pheon* (www.pheon.org) was recently developed by the Smithsonian American Art Museum and launched in the fall of 2010. *Pheon* uses the traditional "capture-the-flag" format as teams of students compete to gather information on various online exhibits related to American art. *Pheon* has a real-world component and can be played in the real world at the museum itself by students living near the museum. Alternatively, it can be

The ARG *Pheon* uses the traditional "capture-the-flag" format as teams of students compete to gather information on various online exhibits related to American art.

played entirely online, using online photos of museum resources. However, the ARG involves more than merely acquiring information from these sources. One activity in the game requires students to complete tasks such as taking pictures of specific artifacts that in turn will help them solve puzzles and thus complete their missions. In that context, they will be learning about the art as they explore the Smithsonian collection online.

Another activity in *Pheon* requires players to take a digital picture of their favorite tree (or other living objects) and post that to the *Pheon* website. In that way, students are actively contributing information to the museum. To be specific, those pictures and information are ultimately included in a massive online catalogue of biological species worldwide, called the Encyclopedia of Life, a multi-institutional project intended to create a digital archive of every species on earth (Strange, 2010). By participating in this ARG, students are not learning exclusively in a passive, receptive fashion any longer. Rather, in this context, students are also actively contributing to online content, a process referred to as "crowdsourcing." Students are usually highly motivated to complete this type of work, and even students with learning disabilities and other learning disorders typically find this type of activity highly motivating.

One ARG that can be freely explored by teachers (or anyone) is *Second Life* (www.secondlife.com/secondlife). *Second Life* is an alternative reality that anyone can join, and in this game individuals are encouraged to create any universe (or island) they like. For those interested in history, *Second Life* includes a plethora of environments to explore, ranging from an 1879 mining camp in Idaho to ancient Greece to the country of Coventry—a medieval simulation set in the 1400s in England. In many of these environments, students can actually experience life in these historic periods as their character explores this ARG.

However, because ARGs such as *Second Life* are generally uncontrolled, teachers using this for instruction must carefully monitor their class. Most of the other avatars in the ARG are, in reality, being controlled by real individuals worldwide, and virtually anyone can create an avatar in this environment. While learning can take place in *Second Life*, many of the various environments are devoted to fantasy, and in general, the entire world of *Second Life*, is regulated. Teachers should be extremely cautious in using this instructional option.

With that caution noted, *Second Life* does provide an excellent opportunity for educators to experience an alternative reality. Further, various educational communities are being established within *Second Life*. Both Harvard University and Ohio State University have now created islands within *Second Life* and offer some courses (for auditing) in this alternative reality. Teachers from Grade 3 and up should explore the use of *Second Life*, and in most subject areas, a wide array of educational content is already available in that context. Moreover, a wiki on *Second Life* is available and can help teachers explore this ARG world (http://wiki.secondlife.com/wiki/Education).

Accessing Games and Simulations for the Classroom

Many simulations games are available for every grade level in virtually any subject area. Some are free and others may be accessed for a fee. The Techtrekers website (www.techtrekers.com/sim/htm) presents a catalog of hundreds of teaching games and simulations that teachers can use immediately in the classroom in virtually every curricular area. While most of these are focused on middle and high school grades and relate to content areas in mathematics and science, many social studies games and simulations are also included as are games in a variety of other content areas and at virtually any grade level. Teachers should spend some time checking on the links at this site, since many of those simulations can be used within ongoing instructional units.

Game-Based Learning and Differentiated Instruction

From the perspective of differentiated instruction, both educational games and ARGs present many differentiation options. In these environments, students are forced to act more independently than in a traditional classroom environment, and they are typically much more active in the learning process. Again, students tend to differentiate themselves within these gaming scenarios as linguistically talented learners tend to select game activities that focus on language-based content, whereas students with a visual learning strength would tend to select more visual activities.

> In gaming environments, students are forced to act more independently than in a traditional classroom environment, and thus, they are typically much more active in the learning process.

Depending on the game, many differentiation options abound including the activities within the game, the level of play selected for and by various students, and many other factors. However, regardless of what choices are made as the gaming scenario is developed for a particular class, one thing is certain: Students are almost always highly motivated to participate in this type of learning activities, and with increased academic engagement, student achievement is also likely to increase. Teaching Tip 3.2 presents some general guidelines for using games and ARGs in the classroom.

Teaching Tip 3.2

Games and ARGs in the Classroom

Select games that teach! While gaming is a great activity and students will enjoy it, teachers must carefully select games in order to maximize the educational potential of the gaming activity. Some games have much richer content than others, and knowing if the goal of the game is initial instruction or practice of previously learned content is critical in making gaming selections. This is also a great way to use games in differentiated instructional activities. Simply put, some students need more practice than others, and teachers can use games to provide extended practice for some students and, alternatively, gaming activities to provide new instruction for others.

Preview the game/site. Teachers must preview any game or ARG selected for classroom use. This will allow the teacher to determine possible uses of the game and, in many cases, set up the game for students at various levels. While simple math or science games are relatively straightforward, a preview is always recommended, and once a teacher begins to know and trust the games available at a given site, he or she should use other resources from that same location.

Be careful of fee-based games/sites. While many such sites are frequently used by teachers, such costs can quickly mount. Fee-based sites for games that involve a set monthly access fee or a per student fee that is set for the year are the best locations for teachers to use as the costs can be predicted in advance.

Consider Common Core standards and game objectives. One problem in using games in the classroom has traditionally been fitting them into and within the curriculum. Understanding how a game will assist with specific standards from the Common Core State Standards and/or other standards is critical, and teachers must seek direct connections between the content to be mastered by the students and the content taught by the game. Further, making this connection might be easier in some areas (e.g., learning linear equations in mathematics) than in others (exploring the relationship between religion and politics during the Tudor dynasty in England).

Be careful of unregulated gaming sites. Many gaming websites are ungoverned, and caution must be exercised. In Second Life, as one example, teachers might preview a specific location that teaches about history or science and then have student access that location only in class when the teacher can directly supervise their learning.

Teach cyber safety. Use gaming websites to teach students about their own personal cyber safety. Second Life, like many locations on the Internet, involves others from around the world, so teacher supervision of activities in that environment is critical. Further, teachers should advise their students to never access that environment at home and to never provide any personal information in that context.

SOCIAL NETWORKING FOR INSTRUCTION

By 2012, as this book was being written, both students and adults have amply and conclusively demonstrated their desire to socially network using modern communications technologies. The dramatic increase in the use of such popular social networks as Facebook and Twitter is reported on nearly every week in the national media. Somewhat less well known are networking options that lend themselves more readily to classroom use, such as *Ning*, or sites devoted to education, such as Edmodo. Because of the popularity of this modern communications trend, many educators are investigating how social networking might be used in the classroom to increase engagement and develop deeper conceptual understanding of the academic content under study (Ferriter, 2011; Richardson & Mancabelli, 2011; Stansbury, 2011; Waller, 2011; Watters, 2011c).

The dramatic increase in the use of social networks such as Facebook and Twitter is reported on nearly every week.

As Richardson and Mancabelli (2011) point out, computer-facilitated learning networks, which are primarily used for learning academic content, are somewhat different from social networks, which tend to be used for social exchange between family and friends. While the host network may be the same for both social networks and learning networks and some teachers are using Twitter or Facebook in their classes for instructional purposes (Ferriter, 2011), the reason for the use of these networks is different.

Clearly, establishing a network for content instruction is different from a family-and-friends communication tool, and as teachers become fluent in using these network tools themselves, they will become much more effective at recognizing these differences. Those teachers can then identify ways to use the power of social networking for academic instruction while still taking advantage of the power and excitement within such networking. Again, today's students have demonstrated through their constant practice of social networking that they enjoy social exchange, and educators in today's classrooms would be remiss not to harness that energy for instruction (Richardson & Mancabelli, 2011).

Facebook in the Classroom

Over the last decade, over 750 million individuals worldwide have chosen to present information about themselves via Facebook (Watters, 2011c; Wilmarth, 2010). On Facebook, individuals can establish an individual web page, post pictures of themselves, list their hobbies and interests, and post an entry about their daily (or hourly) activities that anyone else on Facebook can read. Typically, Facebook participants develop a network of "followers" who access the information and can post back to others' Facebook pages. Postings may include text, photos, or brief videos, and again, the vast majority of *Facebook* users use it for socially networking with friends or family.

However, some teachers have begun to set up Facebook pages for their classes (Ferriter, 2011; Watters, 2011c). In one example, a teacher in an Atlanta, Georgia, high school established a Facebook page related to her class, specifically at the request of her students! That teacher had previously encouraged students to use her cell phone number (on a very limited basis) to call her on the night before a unit test with any questions they had. She received no calls about the content before the first three units. When she asked why the students had not reached out to her with their questions as they studied the academic content before the quiz, they replied, "We are all on Facebook. Can you set up a Facebook page and let us contact you there?"

This example, which was shared directly to this author by the teacher, demands a bit of a reality check for educators: When our students specifically request content-related communications via a specific communications option, shouldn't we, as educators, set up that communication tool?

Because so many students are using Facebook, it is advisable to consider that as one instructional option. Of course, any communications between teachers and students should be limited to content-related issues, as it is clearly inappropriate for teachers to "socialize" with students on Facebook or using any other tool. Further, when teachers choose to use Facebook for teaching the content in their class, they should always include an administrator from

> When our students specifically request content-related communications via a specific communications option, shouldn't we, as educators, set up that communication tool?

the school as a participant. In that fashion, virtually all communications can be monitored, and both the teacher and the students are protected.

Once a Facebook page is established for a fourth-grade science class, as one example, the teacher can post interesting things there for students to explore or make notes for them to review. News items that might relate to the science class can be noted with a suggestion from the teacher that students follow a particular news item online. Because so many students enjoy Facebook, and participate on Facebook for many hours weekly, it is likely that a Facebook presence for a particular class will increase interest and engagement with the content of that class (Watters, 2011c).

Recently an educational application has been devised for Facebook, called Hoot.me (http://hoot.me/about/), that effectively connects students from the same school or class that happen to be studying the same content on a given evening (Watters, 2011c). When a student gets online via Facebook, rather than ask the usual question, "What's on your mind?" the new application prompts the student with the question, "What are you working on?" When students answer that question, they might be presented with the option to join a study session with others on that topic. Also, the application will seek out other students with a Facebook account from the same school or class who are likewise working on that topic (Watters, 2011c), and then the hoot .me application suggests that those students chat with each other about that content. Thus, the application is effectively linking students for joint study opportunities!

Twitter as a Teaching Tool

Twitter (www.twitter.com) is a micro-blogging service that is being used in many classrooms today (Ferriter, 2011). It allows users to send and read brief blog-like messages, with each message limited to only 140 characters. These posts are called "tweets" and are posted on the author's Twitter page, as well as on the pages of anyone in his or her social network. Twitter has been one of the fastest growing social networks since 2008 (Richardson & Mancabelli, 2011; Waller, 2011).

Once a student has established a Twitter account, he or she can sign up to "follow" friends, teachers, political candidates, various famous persons, or others. As an example, once you establish a Twitter account, you can sign up to follow this author if you like (at Twitter.com/williambender1). I use that account as a way to share information for educators, and I typically post two or three times each week, focusing mostly on educational items that teachers would be interested in, such as notices of good teaching ideas or technology articles that might be of interest to other educators. Teachers can even use Twitter and sign up to follow tweets from professional development organizations such as the Partnership for 21st Century Learning (www.p21.0rg).

Teachers have begun to use Twitter in a variety of ways in the classroom (Cole, 2009; Ferriter, 2011). Because the length of each tweet is quite limited, this is not a place to put up lengthy assignments, content discussions, lists of readings, or digital videos. A class blog, discussed previously, would be more appropriate for those types of postings. However, teachers can use Twitter to remind students of class activities ("Remember, the quiz tomorrow on the solar system! Study up!"), or teachers can highlight news stories related to class content. Teachers can also encourage parents to sign up to follow them on Twitter, and when some parents get a reminder (see above) about a class quiz, they might be prompted to remind their kids to study for that quiz.

Twitter can also be used as a classroom teaching tool to make classes much more interactive (Ferriter, 2011; Richardson & Mancabelli, 2011). In one example, a teacher in California had students using laptops and/or smartphones during class discussions, along with their Twitter accounts. Students were asked to use Twitter to "tweet" their thoughts during the discussion to the teacher's Twitter account. At that point, the teacher could access those tweets, using the teacher's computer, and send all of the tweets directly to the interactive whiteboard in the class. Thus, during the class discussion itself, the teacher and all class members could see the tweets (i.e., the thoughts) of all other members of the class during that class discussion. Further, the teacher could see who was and who was not tweeting relative to the class content and then prompt those students to participate more actively. Needless to say, the students in that school considered those class discussions to be among the most interesting activities during their entire school day!

> Twitter can also be used as a classroom teaching tool to make classes much more interactive.

Differentiated Instruction and Social Learning Networks

Social networking in teaching involves a combination of advantages. First, students enjoy social networking and using these tools for education taps into that desire for socialization. Next, personal tweeting or personalized Facebook interactions with the teacher and/or other students tends to address individual learning needs of each student quite specifically as these are, in almost all instances, one-to-one communications. Finally, students are demonstrating their desire to participate in these activities, and that provides perhaps the most powerful advantage of using these tools in education. For teachers who choose to use these tools, there is likely to be higher student participation, even from students who would not normally complete their class or homework assignments (Wilmarth, 2010). These advantages make social networking for learning a powerful teaching tool, a tool that easily lends itself to differentiated instruction.

One decision a teacher must make involves which tool to use. Not every teacher should take advantage of all of these newly developed technology tools since merely keeping up with these options can seem like a full time job. Rather, teachers should pick one social networking tool and perhaps one or two other technology-based teaching ideas (e.g., gaming, wikis, blogging, or webquests, etc.) and practice with those teaching ideas, at least initially. Further, there are social networking options that are more limited than the worldwide networking tools such as Facebook or Twitter. Several of these are presented in Box 3.3.

BOX 3.3: OTHER SOCIAL NETWORKING SITES FOR TEACHERS

Edmodo

Edmodo is a free social networking option for teachers and students to share content in a Facebook- or Twitter-type fashion (http://www.edmodo.com). Links to websites, digital files, assignments, and class calendars can be shared, and teachers and students alike can create and respond to posts of others. Initially, teachers create a free account and then invite their students to join. Students then sign up using a teacher-generated code. Teachers can post to their class or privately to students (e.g., for awarding grades), and there is even a set of reinforcement badges teachers can award.

Ning

Ning is a fee-based service and is the world's largest platform for creating social networks (http://www.ning.com). This networking option was originally designed for business but has been used by many teachers to set up networking functions for their classroom. It includes all of the functions described previously. In particular, Ning Mini is a simple option for small social networks, such as an individual teacher's class, and costs $2.95 monthly.

> Teachers should pick one social networking tool and one or two other technology-based teaching ideas and practice with those teaching ideas initially.

> Cloud computing means that, rather than house learning software and students' work on a single computer at the school, the software and students' work are housed on a server outside of the school.

CLOUD COMPUTING AND GOOGLE APPS

In the 2010 to 2012 time frame, the term "cloud computing" became popular. Cloud computing simply means that, rather than house learning software and students' work on a single computer at the school, the software and students' work within that software would be housed on servers outside of the school (Richardson & Mancabelli, 2011). While teachers and students would use the same learning programs or educational games, they would get online to run them, and any work they did within that software would be stored on servers outside the school.

While this distinction may sound somewhat trivial, it is not. By using the "cloud" teachers and students can access their software as well as their own work within that software, whenever and wherever they access the Internet. For example, imagine a fourth-grade student who is working through a guided reading story independently on the computer. That student may have finished the reading of the story but completed only five of the 10 comprehension questions associated with the story. Using traditional software, that student would have to wait to return to school the next day to complete the other comprehension questions, but using cloud computing, he or she could go home, use a password to get online, and then complete the remaining questions as homework. The work from the class would have been stored on servers maintained outside the school, and thus, the work would be immediately available online, including the answers to questions that the student had previously completed in class.

Google Docs

Perhaps the greatest news related to cloud computing is that many of the programs we need in education are free of charge! For example, word processing and spreadsheets are two of the most basic needs in education of the 21st century, and the program Google Docs offers them to students for free! Google Docs is a resource for creating, editing, and sharing written content online, either individually or as a collaborative effort. Google Docs supports Word documents, spreadsheets, and PowerPoint presentation software, and all work is stored on a Google server and protected by a login procedure and password (Bender & Waller, 2011a; Richardson & Mancabelli, 2011). Thus, cloud computing is free for all educators and students!

Perhaps the greatest news related to cloud computing is that many of the programs we need in education are free of charge.

To use Google Docs, teachers simply create a free Google account and an account for each student. Next, the teacher or a student creates a new document, saves it, and sends it to other students for them to review and edit. Any of the students or the teacher can edit the document at any time. All of the revisions are archived (again, on servers at Google), and previous revisions of the document can be opened and explored as necessary. On collaborative assignments, the teacher can use this function to see which student made specific contributions to a document and if necessary revert back to a previous edition of the document.

Google Apps

While many teachers have explored Google Docs over the last five years, Google has now developed a more comprehensive set of programs for education that many school districts are beginning to use (Owen, 2011). This is referred to as Google Apps (http://www.google.com/apps/intl/en/edu/). All Google Docs functions are included in this new suite of free programs, and Google Apps, like Google Docs, uses servers at Google, thus again taking advantage of cloud computing. However, many other desirable options are included in Google Apps, including free e-mail services for all students, blogging options, and wikis that are hosted "on the cloud," as well as photo and video hosting (Richardson & Mancabelli, 2011). Only a few districts have begun using Google Apps, but as early as 2010, 50 of the 197 school districts in Oregon had signed up to use this new educational tool (Owen, 2011), and other districts were exploring this application.

Cloud Computing and Differentiating Instruction

Other commercial companies are likewise making cloud computing and various educational programs freely available for teachers and students. For example, both Microsoft Live@edu and OpenOffice (OpenOffice.org) provide many of the same cloud computing services as Google Apps, and any of these may be used free by educators. Further, there are many ways to use any of the free document development and sharing tools in the classroom, and consideration of these instructional options clearly delineate the difference between 20th century learning and the new differentiated instruction of the 21st century. Here's an example.

Imagine a fifth-grade teacher teaching science in 1993, focusing on the topic invertebrates and vertebrates in the Jurassic Period. That teacher might have identified several small groups of students based on similar interests and learning styles and then required each group to develop a research paper on one or two specific animals from that period. Those students would have used encyclopedias, their text, and other resources from the media center to find information and pictures of animals for their report. They would then have written the report, and in that process, one student would have done some of the writing and then hand-delivered those pages to other students for editing. Ultimately, those students would probably have had to recopy or retype that report several times, through several different edits, prior to handing the assignment in to the teacher. That was the model for group-work report writing in the 20th century classroom.

Now consider the same assignment housed on the cloud (e.g., using an application such as OpenOffice, Microsoft Live, or Google Apps). In today's classroom, the assignment and the entire teaching and learning process become vastly different, much more communal in nature, and generally more interesting because of the collaboration options within cloud computing. First, the assignment would not be a static, written report to be handed in on lined paper or typed sheets. Rather, the assignment might be the production of a wiki on the topic or perhaps development of an edited, content-rich videotape presentation on the topic.

Initially, one student from each group might go to the Internet to seek pictures or brief video segments that illustrate a vertebrate or invertebrate life while another two or three students in the same group would prepare a video script of information on each animal. They would use the word processing functions within these cloud-based computerized instructional programs, and thus, the script would not have to be handed from one student to another prior to editing. In fact, any student in the group could help edit that script online, as necessary, with many working on it at the same time. Another student might be preparing to digitally record one or two group members delivering the scripted statements about each animal, and that student would digitally overlay that scripted segment with pictures of each animal. In that manner, a two- to 10-minute video report could be developed, housed on the cloud, and/or published worldwide.

> The entire teaching and learning process becomes vastly different, much more communal in nature, and generally more interesting using cloud computing.

With that example noted, educators can clearly see that the 21st century version of the assignment is much better preparation for the types of tasks that students will be expected to do over the next decades than is the 20th century assignment. Indeed, and inability to use these tech-based teaching and learning tools (e.g., wikis, digital media editing, cloud computing, collaborative product development) is likely to handicap students in a manner that no teacher would find acceptable.

As discussed previously in this chapter, students have demonstrated that they enjoy socializing in online networks, and implementation of Google Apps, Microsoft Live, or OpenOffice in the classroom will certainly facilitate that. In fact, students have anecdotally reported that they are more likely to complete homework when it is collaborative in nature through these online programs, and they indicate that being able to write and edit the same document is "cool!" (Owen, 2011).

One important aspect of differentiated instruction has always been the fact that students, working in differentiated small groups, can and do learn from each other. In other words, in differentiated groups where group membership is based on the same general learning styles and preferences, students will be able to instruct each other, and are likely to motivate each other toward mastery of the learning content. Clearly the types of collaborative work that can be fostered within these cloud-based document creation and sharing programs will facilitate that critical aspect of differentiation.

THE KHAN ACADEMY, THE FLIPPED LESSON, AND DIFFERENTIATION

As described in Chapter 2, many teachers are reversing the traditional order of instruction, as one differentiated instructional option. In the "flipped classroom" differentiated instructional approach, students are required to undertake initial instruction in a new topic on their own as a self-guided phase of learning, using Internet-based instructional resources (Cook, 2011; Maton, 2011). Again, the advent of cloud computing makes such instruction possible in that students can access instructional content information at home as well as they can at school. Further, if teachers have students access the right Internet locations, the results can be quite remarkable.

However, one major reason for this trend toward flipped classrooms is the development the Khan Academy (www.khanacademy.org). The Khan Academy is a free online curriculum that is housed on the cloud. It was developed by Mr. Sal Khan and structured as a nonprofit organization. The curriculum exercises range across grade levels from kindergarten up through high school and into college. While most of the focus has been in mathematics, curriculum content ranges across many subject areas and is constantly expanding in areas such as history, astronomy, biology, and earth sciences.

> The Khan Academy curriculum originally focused on mathematics, but now curriculum content ranges across many subject areas and is constantly expanding in areas such as history, astronomy, biology, and earth sciences.

Because the Khan Academy is cloud based, it represents an anytime, anywhere learning tool that is intended to freely educate anyone, worldwide (Sparks, 2011; Toppo, 2011; Watters, 2011b). It is self-directed such that students can study this curricular content alone, but many teachers from Grade 1 up are beginning to use Khan Academy in some fashion in their classrooms. Because of the anytime, anywhere learning goal of Khan Academy, this organization received significant funding from the Bill and Melinda Gates Foundation and other foundations over the years to ramp up its service capabilities. While many curriculum areas are now included, the Khan Academy content was originally focused more heavily in mathematics, so we'll use examples from that curricular area below.

Using Khan Academy in the Classroom

The Khan Academy website presents many tools for teachers. The website features specific exercises for virtually any type of mathematics problem that might be covered in the Common Core State Standards, ranging from one-plus-one up through calculus. As well as the online practice exercises, the website also offers video demonstrations of how to do many of those math problems. In those videos, students see an interactive whiteboard where the various steps of the problem appear as a "voice" (the voice is done by Mr. Khan himself in many of the original videos) explains the steps in the problem (for example, Level 1 linear equations such as $4x + 6 = 22$). The steps are discussed leading to problem completion along with the reasons for various steps and mathematics operations. Thus, this curriculum can function, for many students, as initial instruction on that type of mathematics problem!

Over 3,200 videos are presented as demonstrations of particular problems or issues in the content areas. Each video is a "digestible chunk" of information, and these are not over 10 minutes in length. Students who access the website try some practice problems and then, if necessary, watch a video describing a particular type of problem. Again, in the flipped classroom, this serves as the "initial instruction" phase of learning that, in more traditional classes, has always been undertaken in class with the teacher demonstrating the problem on the board (Toppo, 2011; Watters, 2011b).

Working at home, students then use the gaming feature to practice that particular type of problem. Each problem in the game-based practice sessions can be broken down into simple step-by-step instructions provided as immediate feedback should any student experience difficulty with a particular type of problem. Several guidelines on how to begin using the Khan Academy in the classroom are presented in Teaching Tip 3.3 below.

Teaching Tip 3.3

Guidelines for Beginning Khan Academy

1. *Explore Khan Academy.* Prior to using this in the classroom, teachers should explore Khan Academy content themselves, just as they would any new teaching curriculum or approach. Take care to investigate the fit between Khan Academy coverage of content and terminology and the terminology used in your curriculum. Also consider the knowledge map and possible use of that in your class.

2. *Look at permissions and the sign-in process.* Carefully investigate how teachers sign students into Khan Academy. Ultimately, teachers should register their entire class, including students who have no computer or Internet access at home. Prior to any wholesale signup, teachers should obtain permission from their administration and each student's parents.

3. *Begin using this as a reference tool.* While the Khan Academy is structured as a stand-alone teaching tool, teachers wishing to use it in conjunction

with the classroom may find it beneficial to teach students how to use it. In short, use Khan Academy as a reference tool at first until students get used to it. When students ask a question on a mathematics process, teachers might assign them a partner and have that pair of students look for the answer on Khan Academy. Once they go through one of the videos, those students can explain that process to the class.

4. *Encourage students to bring their own devices.* After discussing the issue with your administrators, teachers might encourage students with cell iPads, other tablets, or even Internet-capable cell phones to use them in class to access Khan Academy. The goal is to get students used to seeking and using answers on how to do math (or answer questions in other subject areas) as a self-directed activity, and nothing can foster that as well as using devices that students already have.

5. *Have students use the knowledge map.* The knowledge map within Khan Academy is the structuring tool for students to know what they should study next. As they demonstrate their ability in certain content, the knowledge map and curriculum itself award them a "badge" and suggest the next area for them to study. Some students have moved far beyond their own grade placement in various subject areas, and getting these rewards is quite motivating for some. One occasionally hears of a fifth-grade student who completes high school algebra because he or she wanted the badges and wanted to be the first fifth grader to get there. For students who do excel, additional classroom or school recognition is always recommended!

6. *Assign Khan Academy as a preinstructional unit homework assignment.* At some point, after students have demonstrated their ability to use Khan Academy in the classroom, you should begin to assign homework in the curriculum. Of course, many students can begin with Khan Academy with no in-class practice (indeed, it is intended to be used in that fashion), but others will need some help initially. However, move all students in the direction of using Khan Academy content as a stand-alone learning tool.

7. *Encourage note taking.* Many teachers, as they begin having students use this content, have chosen to have students make notes on the Khan Academy content as they practice a particular problem or watch a demo video. By checking on those notes when students return to class, teachers get a good sense of who accomplished what the night before and ultimately who did their assigned work in the content.

8. *Try a flipped lesson.* Once students are used to using Khan Academy content in the above fashion, your class is ready to try the "flip" to a flipped lesson on new content. Even if some reluctant students are still having difficulty in the curriculum, teachers can assign content as a homework assignment that has not been taught at all in class and then conduct the following class as a "practice the content class," a project-oriented class, or a math-lab type of class. Each teacher's ultimate goal should be instilling in every student the belief that they can seek out, find, and master difficult academic content on their own, with no teacher to teach them—this is truly the goal of anytime, anywhere learning.

Tracking Students' Progress in Khan Academy

Within the curriculum, teachers can set up student accounts for every student in the class. Students' work in the academy is then saved (again, via cloud computing), and teachers can see the data representing each student's progress. Other documentation is also available. For example, a class profile lets teachers glance at the dashboard, which is a summary of the class's performance, and quickly determine what content to emphasize in the math lab class the following day. Because the overall goal of Khan Academy is independent, undirected learning, Khan Academy itself refers to teachers as coaches (coaches may be teachers, parents, or peers),

Students' performance data are presented as an X/Y axis chart showing individual student growth over time. Using these documentation tools, teachers or coaches will know immediately if a particular student is having difficulty with any particular content, and they can then assign video demonstrations on that content to help. Further, all of these data are saved over time, such that teachers can review students' progress and make determinations about students' rates of progress relative to stated goals.

> The knowledge map is an individualized teaching tool that tracks each student's progress, and students typically find the knowledge map of their progress quite motivating.

The knowledge map within Khan Academy is an individualized teaching tool that tracks each individual student's progress, and students typically find the knowledge map of their progress quite motivating. Students (or coaches) can determine from the knowledge map what the student has completed, what concepts have been mastered, and what the student's next emphasis needs to be. The knowledge map will also remind students when they might need a review.

Throughout the exercises, students are highly motivated by the gaming basis of this curricular support program, but the program also provides the opportunity to earn badges, which are displayed on each student's knowledge map to show that student his or her own progress. As soon as students begin their work, they will begin to earn these badges and points for learning specific content. The more students challenge themselves, the more they achieve, and the more badges they earn; thus, the more bragging rights they get! While some badges can be earned by successful completion of one or two exercises, other badges take many months or even years to earn.

Differentiated Instruction in Khan Academy

Educators should understand that Khan Academy is truly a game changer in education! It is a totally new type of tool that has only become possible within the last decade with the advent of the Internet and cloud computing. Students worldwide are now free to seek and master nearly any content they choose, and this can be truly empowering. One might well imagine a student in South America or Africa seeking Internet access through a government-sponsored library and mastering rigorous content in history, political science, or higher mathematics! That is exactly the vision of the founders and promoters of Khan

Academy (see www.khanacademy.org for more on the goals of this group), and that is a powerful vision indeed. Teaching students to seek information and ultimately become lifelong learners is ultimately a goal that educators worldwide should embrace.

Of course, many students with learning problems have difficulty using this tool, and guidance of the teacher or "coach" will be critical for many. Still, having this tool available does change the landscape of education, and one viable goal for educators today must be to prepare students to self-direct their learning in this fashion. This is, perhaps, the most important of the 21st century skills our students will need.

> Khan Academy is a game changer in education.

Khan Academy is a game changer in education. It is hard to overstate the degree to which this free curriculum changes the learning process, as discussed in Box 3.4 below. This curriculum, available via cloud computing worldwide, will most certainly impact education rather drastically in the next few years. Teachers are well advised to consider the implications of this instructional option.

In terms of the new differentiated instruction, this tool allows instruction to be totally self-directed. Within such a curriculum, students will seek out content they are interested in and motivated to learn, and they will learn it using learning styles and preferences that are their choice. When students experience a problem in class, rather than the teacher having to make time to provide an explanation there and then, the teacher can refer that student to Khan Academy for help and instructional assistance, and thus, empower that student. In fact, Khan Academy, and the flipped lesson concept represent not only the newest option for differentiated instruction, but also the option in which classroom learning most parallels lifelong learning skills in the 21st century. Again, this author recommends that every teacher today explore the use of Khan Academy in his or her class.

BOX 3.4: IMPACT OF KHAN ACADEMY

Khan Academy is a game changer in education. We've all often heard the goal if not the mantra of teachers worldwide:

Give me a fish, I eat for a day.

Teach me to fish, I eat for a lifetime.

Khan Academy now allows us to modify that statement for the next century.

Teach me content, I will learn that content.

Teach me how to seek out and master new content on my own, and I will then master new learning on my own for my entire life!

THE NEW DIFFERENTIATION: CHANGING THE TEACHING AND LEARNING PROCESS

> Not only does technology impact differentiated instruction in many fundamental ways, it likewise changes the very fabric of the teaching learning process itself.

If this chapter begins to sound like a whole new world for differentiated instruction, that is not far from the reality. Not only does technology impact differentiated instruction in many fundamental ways, it likewise changes the very fabric of the teaching-learning process itself (Wilmarth, 2010). For example, the type of interactive Google Docs assignments described above represents the fundamental change in what students will learn as well as how they learn it. In the 21st century differentiated classroom, students will learn to collaborate in a whole new manner as they master content working intimately together and actually create content in a more interactive and less passive fashion (Bender & Waller, 2011a; Wilmarth, 2010). Using this and several of the other technology tools described here, students work together, create content together, review and critique each other's work. Thus, the learning process itself becomes something of a peer-mediated instructional process.

No longer will students be passive recipients of knowledge delivered via textbooks, teachers, videos, or even via the Internet. Now, students are content creators of presentations, projects, and reports that engage and excite them, as described earlier in this chapter and in the section on project-based learning in Chapter 2. Those products are then published worldwide using tools such as the web or YouTube (Bender & Waller, 2011a; Ferriter & Garry, 2010). This collaborative, self-correcting, creation-of-knowledge process represents a fundamental change in learning, and many students find this much more interesting and exciting because of the "connectedness" with other students and the use of 21st century communications tools (Wilmarth, 2010).

WHAT'S NEXT?

This chapter has focused on how technology-based instructional practices present new opportunities for differentiating instruction. However, differentiated instruction impacts more than instructional practices in the classroom. Both lesson planning (as discussed in Chapters 1 and 2) and student assessment are components of differentiated instruction, and several factors have refocused assessment in the classroom within the last five years.

First, the response-to-intervention process has provided a tool for all educators to focus intervention and assessment efforts on students who are struggling in the curriculum, using both universal screening assessments and progress-monitoring assessments that are built into rigorous intervention processes. Next, a wide variety of alternative assessment options have been recommended within the general education classroom for all students. These factors together are generating a movement towards differentiated assessment in all grades.

The next chapter will present ideas for differentiating assessment in general education classes. This will include whole-class differentiated-assessment options, as well as progress-monitoring assessment options for students needing additional supplemental intervention instruction in Tiers 2 and 3 of a response-to-intervention procedure.

Response to Intervention and Differentiated Assessment Strategies

4

RESPONSE TO INTERVENTION IN THE DIFFERENTIATED CLASSROOM

Perhaps no area of education is changing today as rapidly as assessment strategies for formative assessment in the classroom (Chapman & King, 2005; Guskey, 2011; Niguidula, 2010; Reeves, 2010, 2011). To be specific, as recently as the 2006–2007 school year, most primary and elementary teachers were not individually screening all students in reading and mathematics multiple times each year (Bender & Waller, 2011b). They were not benchmarking students relative to overall achievement, Common Core standards, or even in relation to the curricular standards in their state. However, because of the response to intervention initiative (RTI), since that time, universal screening in the primary and elementary grades, undertaken two or three times each year, is the rule rather than the exception. Further, students thus identified then receive supplemental instruction complemented by extensive progress monitoring assessments weekly or every other week in most elementary general education classrooms (Bender & Waller, 2011b).

Independent of the Response to Intervention (RTI) initiative, other factors in education have increased the level of and visibility of formative assessment. Many educators are currently arguing for improved formative assessments in the classroom in order to enhance learning for all students in general education (Sousa & Tomlinson, 2011; Wiliam, 2011). Others recommend specific types of assessment within certain school reform initiatives, such as the authentic assessments recommended within the context

> Because of the response to intervention initiative (RTI), universal screening in the primary and elementary grades, typically undertaken two or three times each year, is the rule rather than the exception today.

of project-based learning or to facilitate instruction in 21st century skills (Bender, 2012a; Reeves, 2010).

Given this increasing emphasis on formative, classroom-based assessment, we must note that large-scale normative assessments have also been implemented in every state (Connor & Lagares, 2007). Further, the recent adoption of the Common Core State Standards (www.commoncore.org/the-standards) is likely to result in changes in statewide assessment practices over the next few years. While these assessment results, so frequently discussed in the national press, suggest that students' performance is a critical concern for teachers, the formative assessments that teachers perform in their classrooms are much more likely to yield information on students' performance that can actually be used to plan instruction in the classroom (Niguidula, 2011; Sousa & Tomlinson, 2011). This is another reason that formative assessment is increasingly emphasized.

A number of writers have described the impact of various assessment strategies within the differentiated instructional approach (Chapman & King, 2005; Sousa & Tomlinson, 2011). Further, a wide variety of assessment strategies have been recommended as methods whereby assessment may be differentiated in general education classrooms. However, the impact of the three catalysts for change described previously in this book (RTI, differentiation, and technologies in the classroom) on formative assessment in the classroom, can only now be intelligently discussed, as these factors are impacting each other in ways unforeseen previously (Bender & Waller, 2011a).

The purpose of this chapter is to present practical assessment strategies for conducting differentiated assessments in the classroom, within the context of the recent RTI initiative. Initially, an overall discussion of assessment modifications for use in the differentiated general education class is presented. Next, RTI is discussed, since that factor is driving many of the assessment transformations that teachers are experiencing daily. Next, several additional differentiated assessment options are presented for Tier 1, general curriculum assessment, including universal screening procedures in reading and mathematics, digital portfolio assessment, and authentic assessment. Next, assessment procedures that facilitate frequent progress monitoring in Tier 2 and Tier 3 interventions are presented, including criterion-referenced assessment and curriculum-based assessment. Next, a complete RTI procedure is presented in order to highlight how formative assessment drives the RTI process and the interventions presented in every phase of that process within the differentiated classroom. Finally, a discussion of grading options within the differentiated general education class is presented.

ASSESSMENT MODIFICATIONS FOR DIFFERENTIATED CLASSES

In almost all classes, teachers are called upon to implement group-administered assessments as unit tests, or at the end of each grading period. Likewise, statewide achievement tests are typically administered in the spring for many grade levels. Obviously, these assessments can be daunting challenges to many students with learning disabilities. For this reason, teachers may need to consider other differentiated assessment strategies for some of those assessments as well as ways to modify more traditional tests in order to accommodate the needs of students with learning disabilities and/or other academic challenges, and there are a variety of assessment modifications that can be considered (Bender, 2008; Chapman & King, 2005; Salend, 2005).

For example, in the differentiated class, where students are exposed to different learning activities based on their learning strengths, teachers may wish to consider differentiating the assessment strategies for those students along the same lines. While this type of differentiated assessment would not be allowed or practical on statewide or district-wide achievement assessments, such modifications would be very appropriate for unit tests and/or end of grading period tests. Here is an example.

Imagine a classroom in Grade 6 that is focusing a unit of instruction on the settlement of the "Wild West." If one group of students, who each demonstrate a visual/spatial learning strength, have participated in an art project to draw a group picture of a frontier fort, the teacher may assess those students by having them each draw a version of that fort, label the buildings, discuss the function of each building, its necessity, and the types of construction materials used. Those students would, via their drawings, demonstrate the understanding of those forts. In fact, while Hollywood always depicts "Indian" forts as wooden palisade constructions, many historic forts on the plains were earthworks, since trees and lumber were very hard to find in that region. The students' drawings would, presumably, show that understanding, and such an assessment would be more representative of students' knowledge than would their performance on a traditional paper-and-pencil test.

In addition to these individualized assessment practices, teachers may be called on to modify group-administered assessments and should be prepared with an array of strategies that will allow for accommodation for students with learning disabilities and other academic deficits. The sample strategies below will assist in that regard (Chapman & King, 2005; Salend, 2005), and of course, rather than merely selecting one group of these tactics, teachers should individually tailor their accommodations to the particular needs of each student.

Omit Complex Multiple-Choice Questions: Unlike simple multiple-choice questions that include a question stem and a selections of three to five answer choices, complex multiple-choice questions provide an "answer set" and the actual answer selections involve combinations of the answers from the answer set (e.g., a. Answers 1 and 2; b. Answers 1 and 3; c. Answer 3 only). These are very difficult for many students with learning difficulties and generally should be avoided. In most cases, the same information on a student's understanding can be obtained via traditional multiple-choice formats.

Use Technology: Judicious use of grammar checks, spell checkers, or calculators will assist many students with learning disabilities in essay types of answers. Further, use of these 21st century technologies more closely approximates how individuals function in the working world than do written assignments where these technologies are not allowed.

Extend the Testing Time: Extending time may be necessary to obtain a clear picture of how well students with learning disabilities understand the information. When extended time is allowed, it should be an option, and use of extended time should be noted on the assessment report.

Allow Alternative Response Modes or Alternative Locations: Paper-and-pencil tests are scary challenges for many students, and providing the same test verbally may obtain a better picture of the child's performance. On essay questions, some students perform much better when the writing requirement is eliminated. Thus, allowing those students to audiotape their essay answers can enhance their performance. Also, allowing students to take tests with a paraprofessional or special educator teaching in another room will sometimes help relax the student, resulting in a more accurate picture of his or her academic performance.

Present Fewer Test Items: Presenting fewer items can alleviate test anxiety for many students. Another option may involve presenting a more limited set of questions for some students.

Present Fewer Items at a Time: While some teachers present fewer test items overall for particular students, another option is presenting only one-half or one-third of the test questions at a time. For students with text anxiety, this can be as effective as shortening the test, and this option results in the student actually taking the same test as all of the other students.

Provide Individual Directions: Students with learning disabilities often are challenged by directions associated with an assessment, so providing directions individually can result in an improved opportunity for those students to respond more completely. Also, for some students, teachers should consider requiring that the child repeat the directions back to the teacher prior to beginning the assessment.

Offer Extra Credit: Extra credit (in some cases, the mere opportunity to earn extra credit) can alleviate test anxiety and result in a more accurate measure of the student's understanding. One or two optional questions at the end of the test allow students to "show their comprehension" more completely. Also, allowing the students some choice in which questions to answer has the same effect.

RESPONSE TO INTERVENTION: THE DRIVING FORCE FOR IN-CLASS ASSESSMENT

> Response to Intervention is nothing less than an effort to change a student's life!

RTI in the broadest sense is nothing less than an effort to change a student's life! That is, RTI should be undertaken with the goal of changing a student's trajectory of learning in either reading or mathematics from a trajectory that leads to failure to a trajectory that leads to success (Bender & Waller, 2011a). With that lofty goal in mind, it is easy to see that RTI will involve almost all aspects of instruction, including assessment of students' performance.

The reauthorization of the Individuals with Disabilities Education Act in 2004 presented the option of using assessments of how students respond to particular highly targeted research-based interventions as one basis for determining eligibility for special education (Bender & Shores, 2007; Bender & Crane, 2011). The set of procedures used for documenting how students respond to instruction came to be known as "response to intervention" or RTI.

In that legislation, the issue of determining eligibility for learning disabilities services was addressed by allowing schools to use measures of student performance on well-designed, scientifically based interventions as one option for determining the existence of a learning disability. This logic suggests that if students were exposed to a series of well-designed instructional interventions and their performance did not improve, the lack of improvement would provide some evidence of a learning disability (Bender & Waller, 2011b). Clearly, with this new emphasis on RTI and the increased emphasis on monitoring of student performance on all educational endeavors, teachers had to quickly become fluent in these newly developing assessment/progress monitoring tactics.

Differentiated Assessment Within RTI

In particular, the initial research descriptions of the RTI process presented two purposes for formative assessments that are now undertaken by all primary and elementary general education teachers (Bender & Shores, 2007; Bender & Waller, 2011b). These do not represent all of the assessment needs within a differentiated classroom, but they do represent the recent influence of the RTI initiation on differentiated instruction. These include

Universal Screening—defined as screening every child in the general education class on an individually administered screening assessment two or three times each year in order to document whether or not each individual student was meeting benchmarks in the reading or mathematics curriculum. This level of assessment might be referred to as "benchmarking" in some states. These universal screening data are used to determine if students need supplemental instructional interventions on particular skills in reading or mathematics.

Progress Monitoring—defined as frequent repeated assessments, typically completed each week or every other week, during supplemental RTI interventions in order to document the impact of the intervention and to assist in planning the student's ongoing educational intervention program.

Teachers should understand the relationship between RTI and previously discussed innovations in assessment because assessments within RTI draw on a long tradition of formative assessment for instruction. In fact, RTI has its roots in a variety of innovation practices such as curriculum-based assessment, criterion-referenced testing, and more general performance monitoring initiatives (Deno, 2003; Koellner, Colsman, & Risley, 2011). In this and the more recent assessment literature, differentiated assessment is seen as a tool to enable the teacher and student, working in concert, to specifically target the student's weaknesses and design instruction to address those specific weaknesses (Chapman & King, 2005; Niguidula, 2011; Sousa & Tomlinson, 2011). Thus, assessment and instruction are not seen as separated endeavors but rather as techniques that are mutually supportive.

As the RTI initiative continues to grow, it is important that teachers understand the relationship of RTI to other assessment practices in the classroom. In the simplest terms, universal screening is a Tier 1 function, because it applies to every student in the school, whereas progress monitoring is a function of Tier 2 and Tier 3 RTI procedures. Further, while some commonly used assessment practices in most classrooms may serve as universal screening procedures, many states have required specific assessments for universal screening within the RTI paradigm (Bender, 2012b). Each of these issues is discussed below.

The Three-Tier RTI Model

While most educators in primary and elementary grades are now familiar with the RTI pyramid model, understanding how various assessment tools fit within the model in order to foster differentiated instruction may be new to some. Because 73% of school districts in various states indicated that they implemented a three-tier RTI model (Spectrum K12/CASE, 2008), that will serve as the RTI example in this book. The three-tier pyramid model itself is presented in Figure 4.1.

Differentiated Instruction and Assessment Options

In this model, Tier 1 represents all the instructional activities that are provided for students in general education. Within this model, the figure 80% indicates that approximately 80% of students have their instruction needs met at the Tier 1 level, and those students do not progress higher in the model. Since most of the students have their educational needs met in Tier 1, that is presented as the largest section at the base of the pyramid (Bender & Shores, 2007; Bender & Waller, 2011a).

Of course, this pyramid also indicates that perhaps as many as 20% of students will require some supplemental intensive instruction in order to master the reading

Figure 4.1   The Three-Tier RTI Pyramid

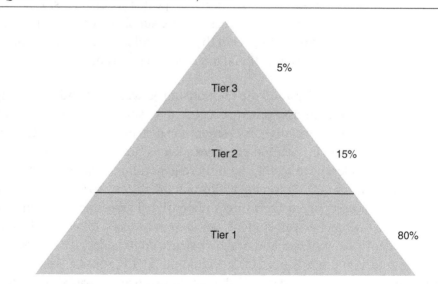

From *The Teaching Revolution: RTI, Technology, and Differentiation Transform Teaching for the 21st Century* by William N. Bender. Thousand Oaks, CA: Corwin, 2011. Used with permission.

or mathematics skills. Universal screening assessments are used to delineate which students need more intensive intervention instruction at the Tier 2 or Tier 3 level.

A recent review of RTI plans from the 50 states showed that virtually all states specifically indicated that differentiated instruction should take place in all or most general education classes as a primary component of Tier 1 instruction (Berkeley, Bender, Peaster, & Saunders, 2009). Thus, any assessment activities used in the classroom represent Tier 1 assessment options within the RTI model.

> A review of RTI plans from the 50 states showed that virtually all states specifically indicated that differentiated instruction should take place in all or most general education classes, as a primary component for Tier 1 instruction.

In addition to the usual classroom assessment tools, the RTI literature presents the expectation that primary- and elementary-level general education teachers will use universal screening assessments three times each year in reading and mathematics in order to identify those students who need a more intensive supplemental intervention at the Tier 2 level (Bender & Waller, 2011a). Thus, universal screening is an assessment function that is largely associated with Tier 1 instruction.

These universal screening assessments are typically administered individually to each student by the general education teacher in the primary and elementary grades. Thus, the general education teacher is the first person to collect hard data on students' performance within the RTI procedure. In middle and high schools, because students change classes frequently, this screening function is often undertaken in different ways that may involve a targeted screening for lower achieving students, and/or use of existing student performance measures rather than individual assessments (see Bender, 2012b, for a discussion of how RTI is implemented differently in middle and high schools).

> Universal screening is an assessment function that is largely associated with Tier 1 instruction.

Tier 2 and Tier 3 Instructional and Assessment Options

As indicated in the RTI model, universal screening data in general indicate that 20% of students are not succeeding in Tier 1 instruction (Bender & Shores, 2007; Bender & Waller, 2011b). Those students will require a supplemental intervention in order to attain mastery of the content. Further, the growing data on RTI implementation indicates that while 20% of students generally require a supplemental intervention at the Tier 2 level, approximately 15% of those students will have their instructional needs met at that level and therefore will progress no further up the pyramid (Bender & Shores, 2007). Tier 3 in this model suggests that perhaps as many as 5% of all students might require a very intensive intervention to have their instructional needs met.

In most primary and elementary classes, it is expected that the general education teacher takes responsibility for Tiers 1 and 2 of the RTI procedure but not Tier 3 interventions. Thus, in most cases the general education teacher will not only teach all students using differentiated instruction for most general education activities (the Tier 1 level of instruction) but will likewise deliver intensive Tier 2 instruction for the 20% to 30% of the class needing it.

Typically, this might involve 20 to 25 minutes of small-group instruction each day in the core subjects of reading and mathematics (Bender & Shores, 2007).

Again, in middle and high schools, these procedures are a bit different (Bender, 2012b). In those grade levels, the screening procedures used to identify students for Tier 2 interventions, the Tier 2 interventions themselves, and the Tier 3 assessment and interventions are directed by someone other than the general education teacher. For example, many students require Tier 2 instruction in Algebra 1, which is typically taught in either Grade 8 or Grade 9. Because the algebra class itself may be only 45 to 55 minutes long, it is not a realistic expectation that the algebra teacher undertake a Tier 2 intervention for 20 to 25 minutes daily. Rather, general education teachers other than the algebra teacher would, in most cases, undertake the Tier 2 intervention instruction during a supplementary mathematics period as well as completing any screening procedures that might be necessary to place students in such Tier 2 instruction (Bender, 2012b; Gibbs, 2009).

Further, the research literature on effective Tier 2 interventions stresses a number of additional requirements that tend to assure the efficacy of such interventions at the Tier 2 or Tier 3 level (see Bender, 2012b, or Bender & Waller, 2011b, for review of that literature). First, Tier 2 and Tier 3 interventions must be specifically targeted to individual students' academic deficits rather than be merely an "extra" mathematics or reading remedial class. While using a "math lab" or "reading lab" type of instructional period can often meet the requirement for a Tier 2 or Tier 3 intervention, it is not appropriate to merely place students in an extra math class in which whole-group instruction is provided and consider that class as their Tier 2 or Tier 3 intervention. Rather, interventions at the Tier 2 and Tier 3 level, in order to be appropriately considered RTI interventions, must be targeted to each individual student's needs. This is because targeted interventions are much more likely to assure that the intervention has significant positive results over the long term for each student. In short, targeted, highly focused interventions do change student's lives, whereas merely an extra math or reading instructional period is much less likely to do so.

> Tier 2 and Tier 3 interventions must be specifically targeted to individual students' academic deficits rather than merely an "extra" mathematics or reading period.

Next, within each Tier 2 and Tier 3 intervention, each individual student's academic progress must be repeatedly monitored; typically, this is done every week or every two weeks (Bender & Shores, 2007). Within most of the RTI literature, the term "progress monitoring" is used to represent this level of assessment of a student's performance during intensive, supplement instruction at the Tier 2 and Tier 3 level. Therefore, the term progress monitoring refers to assessments that are typically undertaken only for students in Tier 2 and/or Tier 3 interventions. While a variety of assessments can be used for this, curriculum-based assessments, as described later in this chapter, are particularly useful for specifically targeting a student's deficits, and for following an individual student's progress related to those deficits over time.

> The term progress monitoring refers to assessments that are typically undertaken only for students in Tier 2 and/or Tier 3 interventions.

Tier 3 Interventions and Assessment Options

Many aspects of the intervention and assessment options for Tier 3 have been described above because they are similar to Tier 2 options. However, the assumption behind Tier 3 interventions is that these interventions are extremely intensive and may involve supplementary instruction for 30 to 60 minutes daily. In all grade levels, Tier 3 interventions are typically undertaken by general education persons other than the student's main general education teacher, such as mathematics or reading coaches, mentor teachers, or reading/math lab teachers (Bender, 2012b; Bender & Waller, 2011b). This is because, in most cases, general education teachers with 20 to 35 students in the general education class are finding it quite challenging to undertake all Tier 1 instruction for all students and also conduct universal screenings, as well as deliver the necessary Tier 2 interventions. Thus, in virtually every case, Tier 3 interventions and progress monitoring for them is typically done by someone other than the general education teacher (Bender & Waller, 2011b).

DIFFERENTIATED ASSESSMENT PRACTICES FOR TIER 1 INSTRUCTION

Within this recent RTI initiative, it is important to understand various differentiated assessment options for the general education class. In general education classrooms in the United States, Canada, and around the world, teachers are finding various options by which they can differentiate the assessments that they undertake with particular students (Bender, 2008; Chapman & King, 2003, 2005). While the initial literature on differentiated instruction did not emphasize differentiated assessments a great deal (Tomlinson, 1999), more recently there has been an increased emphasis on finding the right assessment for particular students with varied learning styles and preferences, and thus differentiated assessments are critically important for all general education teachers today (Bender, 2008; Chapman & King, 2005; Sousa & Tomlinson, 2011).

Assessment innovations such as authentic assessment, portfolio assessment, and digital portfolio assessment have received increasing emphasis as assessment paradigms that provide a clearer picture of what students have mastered in the general education class at the Tier 1 level (Bender, 2012b; Chapman & King, 2005; Larmer & Mergendoller, 2010; Niguidula, 2011). These all represent assessments for the 21st century that should be used in virtually all general education classes at the Tier 1 instructional level. Further, in some cases, some of these assessments may meet the requirements for universal screening within the RTI paradigm.

Authentic Assessment in the Differentiated Classroom

Authentic assessment—which is occasionally referred to as performance assessment—is based on the concept that students should produce actual products that are similar to products that would be produced in the "real world." In this approach, evaluation of the students' conceptual understanding should be based on those products or their performance in producing those products

(Bender, 2012a; Boss & Krauss, 2007; Larmer & Mergendoller, 2010). Because of the recent resurgence of interest in project-based learning, there has been an increased emphasis on authentic assessment in the last decade and in the PBL framework as discussed in Chapter 2 (recall that products are referred to as artifacts in project-based learning).

Authentic tasks require that the student perform tasks in as realistic a fashion as possible, based on the context of the real world (Larmer & Mergendoller, 2010). Further, some authentic tasks may be quite extensive and involve participation of groups of students rather than merely an individual student. Box 4.1 presents several examples of authentic assessments that have been used in various schools.

As these projects suggest, the list of performance assessment projects is virtually endless and the only limit is the creative imagination of the teacher. However, brainstorming various projects is merely the first step in authentic assessment. Teachers must also plan carefully what constitutes a final product or performance and how those authentic assessments may be evaluated (Bender, 2012a). Typically, in evaluating projects of this nature, a rubric, such as that described in Chapter 2, is used. These rubrics may be as extensive as necessary but should stipulate the specific components of the performance assessment project as well as the relative grading "weight" for each required assignment or artifact. In that fashion, students quickly realize what aspects of the project to emphasize (Bender, 2012a).

Portfolio Assessment

The concept of portfolio assessment, collecting a portfolio of a student's work over time, has been discussed for several decades (Bender, 2008). A portfolio is an indexed compilation of selected work by the student that demonstrates the academic growth of the student over time and provides evidence of student accomplishment on particular skills. Portfolios encourage student ownership of the responsibility for the work and make the teacher and the student joint collaborators in the student's academic progress.

The portfolio should include work that the teacher and the student believe reflects the student's accomplishments most accurately. Students may

BOX 4.1: EXAMPLES OF AUTHENTIC ASSESSMENT PROJECTS

Write a song or poem of a particular period	Develop a digital journal
Draw a picture of a historical scene	Develop a multimedia report
Develop a model (e.g., toothpicks and glue)	Illustrate a story
Teach a 15-minute period of class	Write a one-act play
Write an article for school/local paper	Write government officials about an issue

include work that they are particularly proud of, work that represents their most challenging task, or work that represents ongoing studies in progress. Also, each portfolio should include an index prepared by the student as well as a reflective essay or other written document describing why the student believes that the selected work represents his or her most important efforts. That reflective essay should show the relationship between the work projects in the portfolio and describe that relationship in terms of student growth over time. The portfolio index may even be developed as an ongoing project within the portfolio itself. However, the reflective essay should be completed prior to grading the entire portfolio.

Finally, the portfolio should include work from a student over a period of time. In some cases, work will be from the first of the academic year compared directly with work from the end of the year, though other portfolios are completed in more limited time frames (e.g., a single grading period). All of the portfolio materials should be gathered and placed in some type of folder, and while some teachers use an actual portfolio folder—hence the name—others may use small boxes or other containers to keep the work together and organized. Like the authentic assessments described above, rubrics are often used in portfolio assessment for both development and evaluation of specific work within the portfolio as well as overall portfolio evaluation. The overall rubric should be developed with detailed indications of the level and scope of the work to be included within the portfolio and should stipulate the grading criteria to be used in the final grading process.

Digital Portfolios

With the increased use of digital media, educators now recommend digital portfolios as a differentiated assessment tool in general education classes (Niguidula, 2011; Stiggins, 2005). In digital portfolios, work is developed, presented, and stored digitally, and in most cases, the index for the work in the portfolio is likewise digital in nature. Niguidula (2011) recommends structuring the index for a student's digital portfolio, around the Common Core State Standards for student performance. In that sense, when a student, the student's parent, or a teacher wishes to show that the student demonstrated competence relative to a specific standard, that teacher could get into the student's digital portfolio, select a specific standard, and the portfolio itself would present work completed by the student that demonstrated the student's competence relative to that standard (Niguidula, 2011).

Both the content of the portfolio and the hard-copy reports developed by students can, with today's technology, be scanned into digital form, and any presentations or digital photo/video products may likewise be put into digital portfolios. While digital portfolios were originally housed on school computers (Niguidula, 2011), technology applications such as Google Apps (described in Chapter 3) now present the option of housing digital portfolios "on the cloud," thus making these portfolios of student work available to the students worldwide for many years to come.

Portfolios for Universal Screening in RTI

As one example of portfolios in general education, imagine a teacher in Grade 4 using portfolio assessment to target students' weaknesses and strengths in reading comprehension. That teacher would probably collect each student's responses to comprehension questions on grade-level stories across six or 10 short stories over a period of time. Clearly, such portfolios would indicate which students were on benchmark levels in reading comprehension, and they could identify students that were not meeting benchmark expectations. Thus, those portfolios could provide assessment evidence that any given student might need supplemental Tier 2 intervention support in reading comprehension. In that case, work within a portfolio might serve as one option for universal screening.

Recall that one purpose of universal screening was to target specific skill deficits for remediation in Tier 2 interventions. Both portfolios and digital portfolios, as described here, could help the teacher accomplish that task of targeting specific deficits for individual students. In most portfolios, a great deal of student work is showcased, offering the option for teachers to do additional analysis of errors. In this scenario, such an analysis might suggest that a particular student did acceptably well on factual comprehension questions but demonstrated considerable difficulty in questions that required drawing a conclusion from the content or drawing inferences from the reading sample. Thus, the portfolio data could be used not only to indicate that a persistent problem in reading comprehension existed that was not adequately addressed by the Tier 1 instruction but also identify or target specific types of comprehension deficits. In turn, those targeted deficits would become the basis for a subsequent Tier 2 intervention.

In this example, portfolio assessment in the general education class would clearly represent one assessment option that might be used as a universal screening procedure at the Tier 1 level for all students. Of course, unit tests, analysis of work samples, student presentations, and many other activities can likewise be used as assessment options in differentiated classes, though not all assessments in general education can serve as universal screening assessments. An assessment tool can serve as a universal screening instrument if it meets the expectations as delineated above for universal screening. They must be universal (all students assessed), delivered multiple times each year, and able to specifically target a student's deficit areas.

COMMONLY USED UNIVERSAL SCREENING TOOLS

In some states, Ohio and West Virginia are examples, specific assessment instruments are identified as the universal screening assessments for Tier 1 assessment within the RTI process. While most states leave selection of the universal screening instruments to the teachers and/or the school districts, the wide acceptance and application of various universal screening devices suggests that teachers should have some familiarity with them. All of these assessment tools have strengths and weaknesses, but at a minimum, teachers should know what these tools are, and how they may be used for universal screening.

Of course, this section of text could be extended indefinitely as many assessment tools have been developed for universal screening in reading and mathematics. These specific assessments are described here because they are either very widely used or only recently available. Further, some of these assessment tools are appropriate not only for both universal screening but also for progress monitoring in Tier 2 and 3 interventions.

That type of dual-use assessment tool is one reason for the considerable confusion among educators today relative to the terms universal screening and progress monitoring. Again universal screening is a function of Tier 1 instruction and is undertaken for all students in general education (hence the "universal" term), whereas progress monitoring is undertaken only for students in Tiers 2 and 3 of the RTI pyramid.

DIBELS

More so than any other assessment tool, the early implementation of RTI was associated with the use of an assessment of early reading literacy skills, called DIBELS, or Dynamic Indicators of Basic Early Literacy Skills (www.sopr
iswest.com). The most recent edition of this assessment is referred to as DIBELS Next, and many states have identified this or earlier versions of DIBELS as the universal screening assessment for reading in the primary and elementary grades.

> More so than any other assessment tool, the early implementation of RTI was associated with the use of an assessment of early literacy skills, called DIBELS.

DIBELS was developed by Roland Good and Ruth Kaminski (2002), two reading researchers with an emphasis on benchmarking early literacy and reading development. This assessment tool measures literacy skill in several different areas: phonemic awareness, phonics, reading fluency, vocabulary, and text comprehension. The seven subtests may be used from kindergarten up through Grade 6. The instrument can be administered quickly since not all subtests are administered to any single student; rather, only the subtests that apply for a particular student's grade and skill level are used, and this assessment will identify not only students needing remedial reading assistance through targeted interventions but will also identify specific skill deficits to emphasize in those interventions. Thus, it is very useful in identifying students for Tier 2 instructional support.

AIMSWeb

AIMSWeb is an integrated assessment and data aggregation software system instrument that allows teachers and school administrators to input data from a wide variety of assessments in order to compare each student's achievement with that of other students (www.AimsWeb.com). Also, a variety of academic probes in reading and mathematics are built into the AIMSWeb program. These include assessments in early reading, reading fluency (words read correctly per minute), and comprehension, as well as mathematics assessments in early numerosity, operations, spelling, and other areas. These probes are frequently used as universal screening assessments in both reading and mathematics. Further, this system allows and facilitates assessment data presentation at three levels: benchmarking Tier 1 skills for universal screening, strategic progress monitoring in Tiers 2 and

3 for individual students, and comparison of student data within or across classrooms. Because of these functions, many schools have chosen to base their RTI reading interventions on this DIBELS assessment system.

ASPENS

With the widespread application of the DIBELS assessment, it should be no surprise that the same company, Sopris West, worked diligently to provide a universal screening and progress-monitoring tool in early mathematics. ASPENS stands for Assessing Student Proficiency in Early Number Sense (www.sopriswest.com). ASPENS is a series of one- to two-minute timed probes that may be used in kindergarten and Grade 1 to assess early mathematics skills, and target specific deficits for Tier 2 intervention.

This mathematics assessment allows educators to identify students who are at risk in mathematics, provide targeted interventions, track student progress, and monitor student growth, as well as evaluate the effectiveness of the intervention program in mathematics. ASPENS was in development for a number of years and only became available in 2011. However, the widespread success of DIBELS, an assessment published by this same company, will in all probability assure a great deal of attention to this assessment tool in mathematics as both a universal screening instrument and a progress-monitoring assessment tool.

PROGRESS MONITORING IN TIERS 2 AND 3

As indicated above, progress monitoring is undertaken in Tiers 2 and 3 of an RTI intervention procedure, and in many cases, the same assessment tool may be used for both universal screening in Tier 1 and for progress monitoring in Tiers 2 and 3 of the RTI process. Within Tiers 2 and 3, progress monitoring procedures are intended to both document a student's progress overall and indicate what instructional practices may need to change in order to facilitate academic growth. Of course, these two needs have been obvious in education for several decades prior to the recent RTI initiative, and progress monitoring today has roots in both criterion-referenced assessment and curriculum-based measurement (Bender & Shores, 2007; Deno, 2003). These assessment emphases are described below.

Criterion-Referenced Assessment

While most statewide assessments compare a student's performance with the academic performances of his or her peers (this is often referred to as norm-based assessment), criterion-referenced assessment essentially assesses a student relative to a specific list of educational standards. These may be Common Core State Standards in reading and mathematics or other state-specific standards (e.g., both Texas and Alaska

> While most statewide assessments compare a student's performance with his or her peers, criterion-referenced assessment essentially assesses a student relative to a specific list of educational standards.

have chosen not to adopt the Common Core State Standards but rather to retain their own standards). Over the years, criterion-referenced assessment has served as the basis for or components of many other types of assessment, such as curriculum-based assessment and portfolio assessment, each of which is described in this chapter (Bender, 2008; Jones, 2001).

In simpler terms, a criterion-referenced assessment typically involves a list of sequenced skills (the education standards) in a particular area and items for each of those skills. Thus, the student's performance references how well that student does only on those skills. As one example, consider the sequenced skills involved in whole-number addition. A test including the specific types of problems associated with each individual skill in this area would involve some problems such as those presented in Box 4.2. In this example, the list of specific objectives (i.e., targeted skills) associated with each type of problem is presented in Box 4.3. Note that each row of problems in Box 4.2 represents a different type of mathematics problem as described in the objectives in Box 4.3.

BOX 4.2: CRT ASSESSMENT FOR WHOLE-NUMBER ADDITION

1. $\quad$ 5 $\quad\quad$ 7 $\quad\quad$ 4 $\quad\quad$ 2 $\quad\quad$ 8
    $\quad$ +2 $\quad$ +2 $\quad$ +4 $\quad$ +6 $\quad$ +2 $\quad\quad$ Percentage Score _____

2. $\quad$ 6 $\quad\quad$ 3 $\quad\quad$ 8 $\quad\quad$ 2 $\quad\quad$ 9
    $\quad$ +8 $\quad$ +9 $\quad$ +4 $\quad$ +4 $\quad$ +2 $\quad\quad$ Percentage Score _____

3. $\quad$ 35 $\quad\quad$ 47 $\quad\quad$ 54 $\quad\quad$ 25 $\quad\quad$ 83
    $\quad$ + 42 $\quad$ + 32 $\quad$ + 24 $\quad$ + 13 $\quad$ + 22 $\quad\quad$ Percentage Score _____

4. $\quad$ 27 $\quad\quad$ 27 $\quad\quad$ 37 $\quad\quad$ 28 $\quad\quad$ 69
    $\quad$ + 46 $\quad$ + 25 $\quad$ + 34 $\quad$ + 13 $\quad$ + 22 $\quad\quad$ Percentage Score _____

5. $\quad$ 64 $\quad\quad$ 87 $\quad\quad$ 98 $\quad\quad$ 79 $\quad\quad$ 78
    $\quad$ + 36 $\quad$ + 35 $\quad$ + 24 $\quad$ + 14 $\quad$ + 22 $\quad\quad$ Percentage Score _____

6. $\quad$ 73 $\quad\quad$ 87 $\quad\quad$ 98 $\quad\quad$ 76 $\quad\quad$ 81
    $\quad$ + 36 $\quad$ + 35 $\quad$ + 21 $\quad$ + 13 $\quad$ + 22 $\quad\quad$ Percentage Score _____

From *Differentiating Instruction for Students With Learning Disabilities: Best Teaching Practices for General and Special Educators*, Second Edition, by William N. Bender. Thousand Oaks, CA: Corwin, 2008. Used with permission.

BOX 4.3: OBJECTIVES FOR CRT ASSESSMENT FOR WHOLE-NUMBER ADDITION

1. When presented with a series of five whole-number single-digit addition problems involving math facts that sum to less than 10, the student will complete the problems with 100% accuracy.

2. When presented with a series of five whole-number single-digit addition problems involving math facts that sum to 10 or more, with regrouping in the *1s* place, the student will complete the problems with 100% accuracy.

3. When presented with a series of five whole-number double-digit addition problems involving no regrouping, the student will complete the problems with 100% accuracy.

4. When presented with a series of five whole-number double-digit addition problems involving regrouping in the *1s* place, the student will complete the problems with 100% accuracy.

5. When presented with a series of five whole-number double-digit addition problems involving regrouping in the *1s* place and the *10s* place, the student will complete the problems with 100% accuracy.

6. When presented with a series of five whole-number double-digit addition problems involving regrouping in the *1s* place, the *10s* place, or both, the student will complete the problems with 100% accuracy.

From *Differentiating Instruction for Students With Learning Disabilities: Best Teaching Practices for General and Special Educators*, Second Edition, by William N. Bender. Thousand Oaks, CA: Corwin, 2008. Used with permission.

With a criterion-referenced assessment along these lines in hand, it is relatively easy to determine the specific skills that have not been mastered by a student with a learning disability or other academic deficit. Using this assessment, the teacher can determine exactly what instruction to offer. For example, if a student completed the first three rows of problems at 90% or 100% accuracy, and then achieved only 20% accuracy on the fourth row of problems, the student clearly has mastered single-digit addition with regrouping in the *10s* place, and double-digit addition without regrouping. However, based on those data, the teacher could be fairly certain that the student was having difficulty understanding the concept of regrouping in general or place value in double-digit operations because that is the exact difference between the problems completed successfully and those that were not completed successfully. That student would require intensive instruction on place value and regrouping, and intensive instruction would begin with the problems involving double-digit addition with regrouping in the *10s* and *100s* place.

This type of assessment in many ways provides the basis for much of the universal screening and progress monitoring assessments that are required in the RTI process. As described previously, one requirement of effective RTI interventions (a requirement that is obvious within the extensive literature on reading and mathematics RTI procedures; Bender & Waller, 2011b) is that the intensive interventions in Tiers 2 and 3 should specifically target discrete skills on which a student is having difficulty.

Curriculum-Based Measurement

Curriculum-based measurement (CBM) may be considered as an example of criterion-referenced assessment. Like criterion-referenced assessment, CBM involves specifically targeted skills from the curriculum and focuses on how well an individual student does on those skills (Deno, 2003). However, most of the recent literature on CBM has focused on using CBM as a progress monitoring tool within the RTI process (Koellner et al., 2011).

Historically, traditional assessments sometimes emphasized measurement of cognitive ability deficits such as auditory perception, visual memory, or other cognitive skills that might hamper learning (Deno, 2003; Jones, 2001). In contrast, many educators in the 1980s and 1990s began to stress academic performance measures that involve direct assessment of specific academic skills within the curriculum. Thus, curriculum-based measurements, or CBM, evolved over recent decades as one progress monitoring system that allows teachers to focus specifically on highly discrete skills in the curriculum and to differentiate their instruction to emphasize the specific skills a child has not mastered (Deno, 2003; Fuchs & Fuchs, 2005; Jones, 2001; Koellner et al., 2011).

> CBM evolved over recent decades as a performance monitoring system that allows teachers to focus specifically on highly discrete skills and to differentiate their instruction to emphasize the specific skills a child has not mastered.

Scholars agree that through repeatedly measuring a child's progress on a particular set of academic skills, teachers can obtain information that is highly useful for planning the next instructional task for that child (Deno, 2003; Fuchs & Fuchs, 2005; McMaster, Du, & Petursdottir, 2009). For this reason, assessment based directly on the skills in the child's curriculum, measured on a repeated and frequent basis, seems to be the option of choice for differentiating instruction at the Tier 1 level for all students within general education classes.

However, scholars disagree on the frequency with which a child's behavior should be assessed in curriculum-based assessment models. For example, some theorists argue that a teacher-made assessment administered weekly may be sufficient (Fuchs & Fuchs, 2005), whereas others have suggested that student progress should be assessed every day in the RTI process (see Bender & Shores, 2007, for a review). Despite these differences of opinion, the components of curriculum-based assessment are fairly widely accepted and complement nicely the requirements of RTI. These include the following:

- that assessment for educational planning should be based only on the skills listed in the child's curriculum;
- that assessment should be repeated regularly and frequently; and
- that these repeated assessments should be used as the basis for educational decision making.

A CBM Example

An example using CBM may be helpful. Imagine a teacher in a third-grade basic skills class who introduces two-digit multiplication on a Monday. After teaching for two weeks through examples on the dry-erase board, seat-work, and homework, she tests her students on the second Friday. To her surprise, she determines that half her class has not mastered this skill. Furthermore (although she may not realize it), several members of the class had mastered that new skill by the second day of the two-week lesson and did not really need to spend any additional time on that skill. Thus, their participation over that two weeks was, essentially, wasted time. Clearly, this was not effective instruction for many students in that class.

Suppose, however, that the same teacher had used the daily worksheets as a continuing CBM assessment and required that each student chart his or her progress after each day's lesson. After only one or two days, she would have discovered that some students had already mastered this skill because their data would show 90% to 100% correct each day. In contrast, other students whose daily work indicated problems with comprehension of this task might have been offered different instructional examples after only a few days or perhaps received some additional instruction on a one-on-one basis until they mastered the work. Obviously, repeated assessment on specific curriculum skills, even when it is as informal as worksheets done in class, can be a very effective tool for instructional planning and in differentiating the instruction within the class. Furthermore, the more frequent the assessment, the more responsive the instruction can be.

Finally, if CBM assessment data are summarized in some readily interpretable form, such as X/Y axis charts of individual students' performance, this information is even more useful. In this example, the daily CBM data could easily serve as either universal screening data from Tier 1 or as progress monitoring data in a subsequent Tier 2 intervention. In particular, if the teacher in this

> If CBM assessment data are summarized in some readily interpretable form, such as charts of individual students' performance, this information is even more useful as this can serve as universal screening data and/or progress monitoring data in a Tier 2 intervention.

example had not required that the students chart their own progress, he or she would have to look through all of the worksheets for each child and compare that work with the work of others to determine that a specific child's progress was not commensurate with his or her peers, However, as described in the example here, the data charted by each student could not only target a student for supplemental Tier 2 intervention but would also specifically target discrete academic skills for emphasis within that intervention. Clearly CBM assessment represents the best possible example of assessment for instruction throughout the general education class, as well as all of the RTI intervention tiers.

COMMONLY USED CBM MEASURES

With the advent of RTI, many assessments have become frequent that were not traditionally measured on classroom assessments or statewide assessments only a decade ago. Use of some of these measures stems from research that has shown these measures to be effective benchmark measures in either early reading or mathematics (Bender & Crane, 2011; Good & Kaminski, 2002; McMaster et al., 2009). Further, early research likewise indicated that remediation interventions targeted at these specific skills were likely to increase students' long-term achievement overall (Good & Kaminski, 2002). For these reasons, these assessment measures have received increased emphasis over the last five years.

Words per Minute (WPM) for Assessing Reading Fluency

While some measures of reading skill have long been emphasized in education, reading fluency was not one of them. However, as research indicated that the number of words a student could read per minute was an effective predictor of early reading success (Good & Kaminski, 2002; Pierce, McMaster, & Deno, 2010), teachers began to use this as an indication of students who might need a supplemental (i.e., Tier 2) reading intervention within the RTI process (Bender & Waller, 2011b). Today, many assessments include a measure of words read correctly per minute (sometimes abbreviated as WPM), including DIBELS Next and AIMSWeb, which were described above. Further, specific interventions have been developed that target this specific skill. For example, the Read Naturally curriculum (http://readnaturally.com/index .htm) focuses on increasing a student's reading fluency (see Bender & Waller, 2011b, Appendix A, and the research at the website above).

Maze Procedures for Assessing Reading Comprehension

Rather than placing reading comprehension problems at the end of a reading text, many progress monitoring tools today measure reading comprehension using a Maze procedure (Fuchs, & Fuchs, 2005; Gibbs, 2009; Good & Kaminski, 2002; Pierce et al., 2010). A Maze procedure is a multiple-choice cloze procedure (essentially a fill-in-the-blank reading exercise) that a student completes while he or she is reading the reading selection (Bender, 2011b). In a Maze procedure, every seventh word is replaced by a blank, followed by a choice of three different words in parentheses. The student must select the correct term based on his or her comprehension of the rest of the sentence and/or reading passage.

Maze procedures provide an accurate measure of reading comprehension. For this reason, several authors have recommended Maze procedures for assessing comprehension both in reading curricula and in subject areas texts from the elementary grades up through high school (Gibbs, 2009; Bender & Waller, 2011b; Pierce et al., 2010). Also, Maze measures are used in AIMSWeb and many of the other assessments currently used for progress monitoring in RTI.

Mathematics Fluency

For assessing a student's fluency in math facts, a skill that is sometimes referred to as automaticity, many mathematics teachers use a procedure similar to the WPM assessment procedure above (Fuchs & Fuchs, 2005). They present a worksheet of math facts and time the student to generate a score on problems done correctly within a minute. This procedure may also be used as an assessment of student performance on simple mathematics operations such as double-digit addition, with or without regrouping.

EasyCBM

EasyCBM is a CBM-based assessment tool in reading and mathematics, and many of these resources are free for teachers in Grades K–8.

Because these CBM measures have received increasing attention within the RTI literature, several websites have been developed to assist teachers in generating these measures for use in progress monitoring during RTI procedures. As one example, easyCBM (http://easycbm.com), presents a set of CBM-based assessment tools in reading and mathematics, and many of these resources are free for teachers in Grades K–8. Each of the individual measures described (WPM, Maze, and automaticity in math operations) may be found at this site. Teachers are required to establish an account and must log in to use these resources, but the resources can be invaluable. Various tools are available at this website that allow teachers to construct assessments as they need them, including WPM assessment and progress monitoring tools, Maze reading procedures, and mathematics fluency measures. Both the reading and mathematics assessments are based on recommendations of professional groups in each respective area.

Developed by researchers at the University of Oregon, easyCBM is intended to be used at all three tiers for progress monitoring during the RTI process. It includes a variety of reporting and progress monitoring options. Those range broadly, from allowing a teacher to follow an individual student's progress through class, school, or district-wide reports on academic progress. All records of progress are stored so that student records are maintained from year to year. This includes both online student tests and paper-and-pencil assessment tools.

Intervention Central

Another CBM assessment and intervention resource for RTI is Intervention Central. This website also provides teachers with free assessment resources (http://www.interventioncentral.org). This resource was developed by Dr. Jim Wright, an author and expert in RTI. Both assessment tools and intervention tools may be located here, so the partnering of curriculum and assessment that is so essential to CBM is emphasized. Teachers, after they log in, can access tools that help them generate the exact worksheets or assessment tools they need during the progress monitoring process. Resources include a behavior report card maker, a reading fluency generator, an early math fluency generator, a math worksheet generator, a math fluency generator for WPM assessments, a Maze passage generator, and many other tools. Using this resource, teachers essentially generate their own intervention and/or assessment worksheets that exactly fit the targeted skill for monitoring progress of particular children during the RTI process.

ASSESSMENTS WITHIN A SAMPLE RTI PROCEDURE

With this plethora of assessment options available for universal screening and progress monitoring during Tiers 2 and 3 of the RTI process and in the differentiated classroom at the Tier 1 level, it can become somewhat confusing as to what assessments might be most beneficial for a given student. One guiding principle in all assessment endeavors can help clarify the matter; assessment tools in the differentiated class should be selected by the teacher to specifically target discrete skills on which a student is struggling. Subsequently, interventions should be provided to alleviate those difficulties, based on solid data from the assessment tools used. Perhaps an example will help.

Case Study: RTI Assessment and Intervention

Imagine that Chris is in the first grade and has not been doing well in his reading assignments. The teacher, Ms. Snyder, noticed during the first couple of weeks of school that Chris was struggling in reading. He didn't seem to be learning new vocabulary words as quickly as he should and had difficulty decoding single syllable words with regular consonant and vowel sounds. When Ms. Snyder checked Chris's reading screening score from the previous year, she verified that Chris was in the lower 25% of kindergarten students. Further, Ms. Snyder had used the DIBELS Next assessment described previously (and that measure includes a measure of WPM) as the universal screening assessment in her class, and those data, likewise, indicated that Chris was behind on several benchmarks including word fluency. Based on those data, Ms. Snyder decided to implement a Tier 2 intervention with Chris and five other students in her classroom. She decided to work with these students at least three times weekly for the next nine-week grading period, and in each session, she worked exclusively with those students for 25 minutes.

> Assessment tools in the differentiated class should be selected by the teacher to specifically target discrete skills on which a student is struggling, and interventions should be provided to alleviate those difficulties, based on solid data from the assessment tools used.

In undertaking this Tier 2 RTI procedure, Ms. Snyder was differentiating the instruction for Chris since she would, from that point on, be providing supplemental instruction for Chris and the other Tier 2 students daily, as well as monitoring Chris's performance more closely than some other class members' (Bender & Shores, 2007). Ms. Snyder had access to the SRA Reading Mastery curriculum, which is a scientifically validated curriculum, and each lesson in that curriculum focused on phonemic skills and word attack skills. While decoding words is not synonymous with quickly reading words in a fluent manner, Chris did have difficulty in both skills, and Ms. Snyder felt that this curriculum would fit nicely with Chris's target skill of increasing WPM. While Reading Mastery has a number of built-in assessment options, Ms. Snyder also planned to use a WPM measure, which was described earlier in this chapter, as the primary progress monitoring measure for Chris. Thus, her Tier 2 intervention was sound and related directly to the academic problem experienced by Chris—reading decoding and fluency.

Ms. Snyder also developed a chart as a performance monitoring tool to graphically display Chris's individual progress. For many students with learning problems, charting their performance is one of the most effective motivational tools teachers can employ since a simple, clearly interpretable data chart can be shared with the student and may enhance the student's desire to achieve, as well as the student's academic self-concept. The data in Figure 4.2 represent weekly progress monitoring for Chris in his WPM score on first-grade vocabulary words. In order to generate these data, Chris was presented with a brief reading selection at the first-grade reading level and asked to read those terms at the end of each week. Ms. Snyder counted the number of words read correctly per minute from that reading text. For Grade 1, Chris would normally be expected to read 20 to 40 words correctly in one minute, but any student who could not read 15 words correctly in one minute would be judged to have a significant reading difficulty.

One question that frequently arises when schools implement RTI involves the frequency of progress monitoring in Tiers 2 and 3. Daily progress monitoring offers the teacher the option of checking a student's progress each day, and this is best practice for instruction (Bender & Waller, 2011b) since daily progress monitoring in Tier 2 and 3 interventions allows a teacher to be highly responsive to the progress or lack of progress shown by the student. However, daily progress monitoring does take time, and weekly progress monitoring, or every-other-week progress monitoring is also effective, as shown within the RTI literature (Bender & Shores, 2007; Deno, 2003; Fuchs & Fuchs, 2005). Of course, many scientifically validated curricula that are currently on the market present the option for daily monitoring of pupil progress, and teachers should

Figure 4.2   Tier 2 Intervention Data for Chris

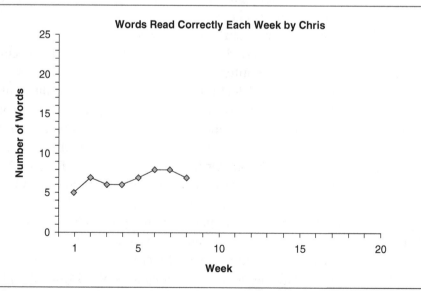

avail themselves of that opportunity, if they are using such a curriculum. At the very least, teachers should plan on monitoring progress every two weeks, and if the curriculum provides an easy option, perhaps more frequently. In this example, Ms. Snyder decided to monitor Chris's performance every week.

As shown by the data, Chris was not progressing in the second tier of this RTI process. In short, Chris should have responded to that intervention, but the data show that he did not. However, two questions must be addressed in order to assure that the child in any Tier 2 intervention has received a fair chance at improvement.

1. Did the child have the opportunity to learn from a scientifically validated program?

2. Did the teacher teach the program as recommended by the instructor's manual?

These questions must be addressed in the RTI process in order to assure that children like Chris are not moved quickly through the entire RTI process and then inappropriately placed in a special education program (Bender & Shores, 2007). In that sense, these questions are considered in order to protect students from incorrect placement.

Of course, the use of scientifically validated curriculum should be the goal of every teacher for every student. However, the second question—was the curriculum used appropriately—deals directly and more substantively with the child's opportunity to respond favorably to the intervention. This second question is commonly referred to by the term "treatment fidelity" or "instructional fidelity" in the RTI literature (Bender & Waller, 2011b).

Fortunately, these issues can be dealt with rather easily by having an outside observer come into the classroom and observe a lesson delivered by Ms. Snyder that includes Chris. Bender and Shores (2007) recommended a simple observation to address the two questions above. Thus, another teacher (or administrator) might enter the classroom and observe as Chris receives his Tier 2 instruction on one day, making notes on Chris's participation, and noting that the teacher followed the lesson protocol as outlined in the instructor's manual. Those notes should then be dated by the observer and placed into the student's IEP or RTI file.

Perhaps at this point, it would be beneficial to explicitly state several of the guidelines mentioned above in this case study. Teaching Tip 4.1 below presents guidelines for teachers in consideration of how to implement Tier 1 screening and Tier 2 and 3 assessments and instruction (Bender & Shores, 2007).

Once the child has not responded favorably to this Tier 2 instruction, the RTI process requires children to be provided a more intensive intervention, typically referred to as a Tier 3 intervention (Bender & Waller, 2011b; Bender & Shores, 2007). The Tier 3 intervention involves a more intensive instructional program for an additional period of time. Bender and Shores (2007) recommend that the planning and preparation of the Tier 3 intervention be a team-based planning procedure and involve the special education teacher as one of the support persons for the general education teacher. Others may likewise become involved in

Guidelines for RTI Assessments and Interventions

Guidelines for Tier 1 and Tier 2 Assessment and Instruction

1. When a teacher suspects a problem, he or she must obtain an appropriate score on a universal screening measure (typically in either reading or math), in order to get a general picture of the child's academic ability in comparison with other children.

2. When the universal screening score indicates an academic score in the bottom 20% to 25% of the population, a Tier 2 intervention must be initiated (Fuchs & Fuchs, 2005). Tier 2 interventions are undertaken in the general education classroom and are typically the responsibility of the general education teacher. These interventions should directly address the specifically targeted academic skills identified by the teacher and the universal screening assessment.

3. Tier 2 interventions typically involve educational curricula and procedures that the teacher has implemented for the entire class or for a subgroup of students within the class.

4. Tier 2 interventions may be implemented by the general education teacher without consultation as these are a function of the general education classroom. However, consultation with the principal and/or the student support team chairperson is certainly recommended.

5. During the Tier 2 intervention, another educator (i.e., the reading teacher, or school administrator) should observe the teacher and should prepare a set of notes from that observation attesting to the implementation of the curriculum in a manner commensurate with the recommended teaching procedures.

6. Because Tier 2 interventions are a function of the general education classroom, these interventions do not require specific notification of parents, though teachers would typically be expected to communicate with all parents regarding general progress of their children.

7. Tier 2 interventions are typically conducted for a period of six to nine weeks and should result in a minimum of six data points or six assessments of academic progress since those data points serve as the basis for the next instructional decisions for that student. These interventions should include progress monitoring assessment each week or every other week.

Tier Three Implementation Guidelines

1. When the Tier 2 intervention is deemed unsuccessful, the special and general education teachers should briefly discuss the student's problem and select an intensive tier three intervention that addresses specific targeted academic skills.

2. These individuals should likewise make a determination as to who should implement this intensive instruction and how often.

3. Tier 3 interventions are typically undertaken by someone other than the general education teacher. Of course, interventions that involve the child's placement into another class must involve parental notification, parental permission, and hopefully parental participation and support.

4. Tier 3 interventions must be intensive interventions that are clearly more intensive than Tier 2 interventions. These should involve a teacher and a very small group of students. Typically, Tier 3 interventions are offered each day in order to assure intensity.

5. During the Tier 3 instructional lesson, the reading teacher or school administrator should again observe the lesson and, again, prepare a set of notes from that observation attesting to the implementation of the intervention in a manner commensurate with the recommended teaching procedures.

6. If a tier three intervention is less than successful, the student support team should forward the data from that intervention and previous interventions to the child study team, and that child study team should then begin their deliberations relative to the existence of a learning disability.

planning and implementing this more intensive Tier 3 intervention, including principals, reading specialists, or school psychologists. In many states (Georgia, Montana, Texas, and North Carolina are examples) this team-based decision is undertaken by the student support team or the student assistance team. While consultation for the Tier 2 and 3 interventions is not mandatory in federal law, it is advisable and should involve a variety of concerned educators.

The Tier 3 Intervention

To return to our example, Ms. Snyder would probably consult with the principal and perhaps the special education teacher or reading intervention teacher in the school, using the Tier 2 data to suggest a Tier 3 intervention. Because the Tier 2 intervention did not result in increased reading scores for Chris, a Tier 3 intervention would then be planned. In this example, Ms. Snyder is pleased to find that the reading teacher can add Chris to a reading group for some more intensive, small-group instruction for 30 to 45 minutes daily for a period of several weeks. This would provide a wonderful opportunity for a Tier 3 intervention since a scientifically validated curriculum is utilized in that reading class, and Chris would receive intensive small-group instruction.

For the Tier 3 intervention in this example, based on discussions with the reading teacher, the team decided to let Chris participate with the reading teacher, who was using the Fast ForWord Program as described in Appendix A. That program has been scientifically validated in a repeated series of studies (see Appendix A). Thus, as a Tier 3 intervention, Chris received intensive reading instruction for 35 minutes each day in a small group, and his progress was monitored both within the Fast ForWord program itself and via Ms. Snyder's continued weekly monitoring of WPM. In this example, that Tier 3 data are directly comparable to Tier 2 data for Chris. Figure 4.3 presents a chart of weekly performance of Chris's progress in reading first-grade words in a one-minute time period for his Tier 3 intervention.

Figure 4.3   Tier 3 Intervention Data for Chris

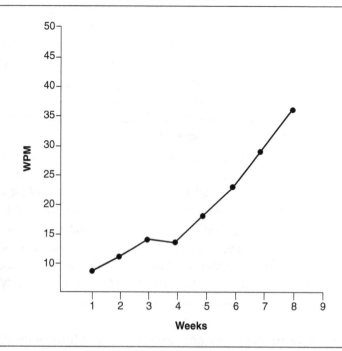

From *Differentiating Instruction for Students With Learning Disabilities: Best Teaching Practices for General and Special Educators, Second Edition, by William N. Bender.* Thousand Oaks, CA: Corwin, 2008. Used with permission.

In many states, when a student does not succeed in either the Tier 2 or Tier 3 interventions, that student is then considered for special education services for learning disabilities. Of course, prior to placement within those services, other assessments must be conducted and all the protections of special education law must be addressed. Thus, the data from Tiers 1, 2, and 3 would be handed to the child study team for consideration of the possibility of a learning disability.

The data in Figure 4.3 present a picture that is typical in RTI; this is a successful intervention that does *not* result in a student managing to catch up to his grade-level peers. As the data indicate, the Tier 3 intervention was successful in this example, and Chris responded quite positively to the intervention. The data show that his scores were increasing rather dramatically, and that is clear evidence that he does not have a learning disability. However, because he was not yet functioning at his grade placement, the RTI team decided to continue the Tier 3 intervention for the next grading period. This is a fairly frequent occurrence in RTI procedures, and student support teams should expect to see this result quite often.

Seamless Assessment and Interventions

Several aspects of RTI assessment in this case study should be noted. First, the assessments and instruction within the RTI process in this example are relatively seamless. In RTI assessments, there should be a consistency or a fairly obvious flow of similar information from the assessments since comparable data will better inform the instructional decisions for a given student. That seamlessness, in this example, is clear from the Tier 1 universal screening in the differentiated class, through the Tier 2 and Tier 3 assessments. In this example, a specific, discrete skill was tentatively identified by Ms. Snyder in Tier 1 instruction—reading fluency as measured by WPM—and that measure was carried throughout the RTI process for Chris.

Of course, Ms. Snyder had the option of using other assessments, and in this case an assessment of reading decoding would have clearly been very appropriate since both Fast ForWord and the Reading Mastery Curriculum emphasize that skill and have such assessments built into the curriculum. Still, reading decoding is highly related to reading fluency, and Ms. Snyder and her colleagues chose to use the WPM measure as their primary progress monitoring tool throughout this RTI procedure. As this indicates, teachers should target a specific, discrete skill or set of skills and focus the entire RTI intervention and assessment process on those.

Next, as this process indicates, decisions relative to Chris's intervention were data driven. From the universal screening using the WPM measure within the DIBELS Next assessment, all the way through the Tier 3 instructional process, the focus was on assessment data, and those data were used repeatedly to make important instructional decisions to assist Chris in his reading progress. Data-driven decision making is critically important for all assessments within the RTI process, as well as within assessments for all students in the differentiated classroom.

Next, one question that often comes up relative to RTI is the use of RTI procedures for students who are already identified with a learning disability. Because the RTI process was initially implemented to assist with eligibility decisions, some educators have assumed that RTI might not be applicable to students who are already identified. In contrast, other teachers have chosen to view RTI supports as options for all students in the inclusive class, and thus, even students currently identified for special education services may be placed in Tier 2 or Tier 3 interventions. While this question involves available resources that may be used for struggling students, educators should consider each case individually and make decisions that best serve the needs of each individual student. In most cases, that will result in students who are already identified as having a learning disability being placed in some Tier 2 interventions in the school in either reading or mathematics.

Finally, this example illustrates how differentiated instruction and RTI work together in 21st century instruction. One could view differentiated instruction as the first tier of the RTI process, or in contrast, one can argue that RTI is merely the continuation of the differentiated instructional effort for those students who may be struggling academically. Clearly these initiatives do go hand in hand, and RTI clearly fits well with the differentiation of instruction paradigm. RTI allows teachers to precisely pinpoint academic problems and differentiate their instruction to remediate them, and that represents differentiated instruction's most lofty goal.

DIFFERENTIATED GRADING

No discussion of classroom assessment in differentiated classes is complete unless one major concern of many teachers is addressed: How do teachers award a grade in a differentiated classroom? This question, of course, stems from the fact that in differentiated lessons, not all students complete exactly the same instructional activities. This is because activities will be differentiated at many points within a single grading period, and not all students will complete all of the same tasks. In short, how can one grade students fairly when not all students have done the same activities?

The Reason and Rationale for Grading

However, the issues with grading today run much deeper than merely how teachers should grade in a differentiated class (Kohn, 2011; Chapman & King, 2005; Guskey, 2011; Reeves, 2011). In fact, how can one possibly differentiate grading at all, if the purpose of grades is to compare students' performance with each other on the same general scale of performance? For some educators, the very concept of differentiated grading seems to be nonsense. Traditionally, the very essence of awarding grades involves comparing one student's performance to other students', using students of the same general age and in the same grade as the comparison group.

Recently, various authors have raised objections relative to this traditional view of grading, and few discussions among educators elicit more intense emotions (Kohn, 2011; Marzano & Heflebower, 2011; O'Connor & Wormeli, 2011). Reeves (2011), for example, indicated that any changes in grading policy can elicit a firestorm from the community since many parents as well as many educators have this traditional view of what grading should mean. However, some educators recommend a different view of grading. For example, Guskey (2011) identified this concept, grading based on one's standing when compared with one's classmates, as a barrier to effective grading. Some suggest that grading should be structured to reward a student's individual progress and not make comparisons between students (Reeves, 2011). Clearly, if this traditional view represents a teacher's perspective on what grades should be, how can that teacher differentiate the grading process and still make meaningful comparisons between students?

The answer is, of course, one cannot—not if grading is defined as awarding a letter or numeric grade that directly compares a student's performance with that of his or her grade and/or age-mate peers within the class. To make grading matters more problematic, there may be legal or school district policy requirements that mandate that any grade awarded be based on "expected" performance for students in a certain grade. This has occurred for two reasons:

1. Grades have historically been awarded in that fashion.

2. Parents or other community members may insist on grades that let them know where their child stands with other age or grade mates as a comparison.

In such cases, teachers are left with few options and must award an omnibus grade based on summative assessments that are founded on grade-level academic skills. Of course, for students who are average and above average, this process presents no concrete problems. However, for students who are desperately trying to master the curriculum but whose academic skills may be well below grade level, such rigid grading policies are unfair and in many cases meaningless (Reeves, 2011). Imagine, for example, a student struggling in Grade 5 because he is reading at a Grade 3.0 level. If that student receives a strong daily supplemental intervention in reading (i.e., a Tier 2 reading intervention using a research-supported reading curriculum) his reading is likely to improve considerably over one or two grading periods. Thus, by the end of an 18-week intervention, that student might be reading at a 4.1 reading level. Those data document that the student made essentially a year's worth of reading gain, in just one half of an academic year.

Of course, demonstrating more than a one-year jump in reading achievement documents hard work on the part of any student. Most educators would suggest that, in all fairness, such a student should receive an excellent grade in reading—perhaps even an A! In fact, the literature on RTI interventions is literally filled with students who, when presented with an excellent Tier 2 intervention, do make such leaps in achievement in relatively short time frames (Bender & Shores, 2007; Bender & Waller, 2011b). However, note that in this instance the student is still achieving below his grade level. In this case, if a traditional, rigid grading policy is in place, this student would be denied a grade of A because, even with his success in the Tier 2 intervention, he would still probably not compare well to other fifth-grade students. While this may seem a rather obscure case, this issue is likely to arise in most schools as educators increasingly implement effective RTI procedures for struggling students.

Grading Options in Differentiated Classes

Many educators have a more open view of grading today. In this view, grading should be not only an indication of student progress but also, in the best of circumstances, a celebration of student success. With that goal in mind, various options for grading students in the differentiated class can be considered. Of course, grading remains a hotly debated topic in education (Guskey, 2011; Reeves, 2011), and while this author cannot answer this question to everyone's satisfaction, several options can be presented. Clearly, the first step is to determine the grading requirements in your school district. If a mandate is in place that all report card grades must reflect a student's performance related to an omnibus grade on specified grade-level criteria, then such grades must be awarded. However, even in those circumstances, Marzano and Heflebower (2011) recommend that teachers also award additional grades that more accurately reflect and celebrate a student's progress. That additional grading procedure should be documented and explained for the student's parents, as well as documented in the student's RTI file and/or in the student's IEP process, if the student is receiving either RTI or IEP supports. This represents one option for teachers to consider.

> Grading should be not only an indication of student progress but also, in the best of circumstances, a celebration of student success.

Other options involve variations in the assessment strategy used to derive the grades (Chapman & King, 2005; Marzano & Heflebower, 2011) or encouraging retakes of assessments that allow students to redo earlier assessments, including assessments from units of instruction that have been completed (Marzano & Heflebower, 2011; O'Connor & Wormeli, 2011). In using these strategies, students would be encouraged to demonstrate their knowledge without fear of an omnibus grade with the understanding that they can redo the assessment at a later point and hopefully raise the grade.

> Many educators today recommend standards-based grading that effectively compares a student's performance to the Common Core State Standards for that student's grade level.

Of course, most districts are not quite so rigid in their grading policy, and even in districts that are, several additional options may exist for students with learning disabilities and other academic deficits. Many educators today recommend standards-based grading (Marzano & Heflebower, 2011), which effectively compares a student's performance to the Common Core State Standards for that student's grade level. As indicated in the discussion of criterion-referenced assessment above, standards-based grading defines the student's performance based on a variety of standards that he or she is required to master, thus eliminating the omnibus grade since students would get report cards that document their performance on a variety of specific standards.

For example, teachers may have the option of awarding a letter grade in their subject or of delineating specific standards and skills that the student has mastered and those which he or she has yet to master. Further, this report to parents may even be accompanied by a portfolio of successful work from the student, which would include data showing what the student has accomplished as well as what the student needs to accomplish in the future, coupled with comments celebrating and praising the student's successes.

Other districts may allow for differentiated grading based on a student's documented learning struggles. In those states and/or districts, for example, students with a previously documented learning disability or other learning difficulties may have the option of being graded based on their level of achievement gain over time. For many struggling students, grading reports based on that option would tend to be much more positive than more traditional normative grading reports. Further, for students who may not have an identified learning disability or other disability but who are participating in Tier 2 or Tier 3 interventions, grades might be assigned based on improved performance in those interventions.

Finally, we should point out that virtually all of the assessment options discussed previously in this chapter (e.g., digital portfolio assessment, authentic assessment, CBM-based assessment) can easily provide the basis for a written evaluation of a student's progress. Again, district and/or state grading policy must be respected, but in the end, effective grading practices must be a celebration of student achievement. In that regard, all options should be considered in terms of student motivation and the individual student's overall academic achievement.

WHAT'S NEXT

As this chapter has indicated, assessment in the differentiated class is a bit more complicated than merely averaging grades. The RTI process, in particular, has drastically impacted assessment in general education classes, and discussions of grading options are found everywhere in the educational literature today (Guskey, 2011; Reeves, 2011). While universal screenings represent one of the most effective ways of monitoring instructional efficacy for all general education students, students with learning disabilities and/or other academic deficits may require much more in-depth progress monitoring, particularly if they are placed in supplemental Tier 2 or Tier 3 interventions. Further, the RTI procedure, as well as other performance monitoring procedures described herein, will enable the student with a learning disability or other academic deficits to see his or her performance in relation to previous efforts and to celebrate his or her growth toward mastery of specific standards. As indicated previously, for many students with learning disabilities, charting their performance is one of the most effective motivational tools teachers can employ and may enhance the student's academic self-concept.

This chapter has reviewed a variety of assessment strategies that are founded on this need for universal screening and, for many students, increased progress monitoring. Strategies such as CBM, CRA, portfolio assessment, and/or authentic assessment are being utilized much more frequently today than they were only a decade ago, prior to the RTI initiative. Although there is considerable overlap between some of these strategies, application of any of these assessment or progress monitoring systems is likely to increase the academic growth of all students who are struggling with academics as well as most students with learning disabilities.

The next chapter focuses on intervention options for differentiated classrooms. Many of the instructional and assessment innovations described previously will be discussed in the context of various reading or mathematics interventions, with an emphasis on practical strategies that can be incorporated into almost every differentiated general education classroom.

Instructional Support Strategies for Differentiated Instruction

5

THE NEED FOR INSTRUCTIONAL SUPPORTS

Students with learning disabilities and other struggling students typically require various supporting instructional strategies in their differentiated general education classes in order to succeed. These supports may be considered to be part of the Tier 1 instruction provided for all students in general education. A wide array of instructional support strategies have been developed in recent years, some of which assist students by scaffolding the content to be mastered, while others enhance the instructional content under study. The term *content enhancement* has been used over the last decade to delineate many of these instructional supports (Bulgren, Deshler, & Lenz, 2007; Gajria, Jitendra, Sood, & Sacks, 2007). Other types of instructional support may involve strategies that use the peers in the class as reciprocal tutors or for reciprocal teaching in the general education classroom.

This chapter presents information on a variety of these instructional supports in a variety of areas. These include scaffolded instruction and content enhancement techniques such as story maps, study guides, and graphic organizers. Also, instructional supports using peer tutoring and reciprocal teaching are described. While many other instructional strategies could have been discussed in this context, these strategies and techniques provide the general flavor of the types of supports that are frequently offered in the differentiated class at the Tier 1 level.

SCAFFOLDED INSTRUCTION

The concept of scaffolded instruction developed over the past two decades as an important component of instruction for struggling students in the differentiated class (Larkin, 2001; McEwan-Adkins, 2010). Scaffolded instruction may best be understood as a sequence of prompted content, materials, and/or teacher or

> Scaffolded instruction may best be understood as a sequence of prompted content, materials, and/or and teacher or peer support to facilitate learning.

peer support to facilitate learning (Fisher, Frey, & Lapp, 2012; Jitendra, Hoppes, & Yen, 2000; Larkin, 2001). The emphasis is placed on the adult assisting the student in the learning process with individual prompting and guidance that connects new knowledge with what the student knows already, and is tailored to the specific needs of the individual student in order to offer just enough support (i.e., a scaffold) for that student.

In scaffolded instruction, the student is initially considered an apprentice in the learning effort; thus, too little support leaves the student stranded and unable to comprehend the assigned work and complete the task, whereas too much support would prohibit the student from independently mastering the task (Stone, 1998). Therefore, the level of support must be specifically tailored to the student's ever-changing understanding of the problem. Further, in scaffolded instruction, the instructional supports would gradually be withdrawn, allowing the student to eventually "own" the task performance. Research has shown scaffolded instruction to be highly effective for students with an array of learning challenges, and several authors have presented suggestions for teachers that will facilitate successful scaffolding (Fisher, Frey, & Lapp, 2001; Larkin, 2001; Stone, 1998), and these are summarized in Box 5.1.

As these features of scaffolded instruction indicate, a critical component of scaffolding is the sensitivity of the adult who is supporting the student in the learning process. Teachers must closely observe each student in order to provide the necessary support and to withdraw the supports as the student's mastery of the content grow. As this indicates, scaffolded instruction is an instructional strategy that facilitates high levels of differentiated instruction

BOX 5.1: KEY FEATURES OF SCAFFOLDED INSTRUCTION

In order to scaffold a learning experience, teachers should

- Identify content the student needs to know
- Solicit the student's involvement in learning that content
- Begin with content the student knows already, what the student can already do
- Stretch that task to include some new information and set up quick success for the student using the old and new information
- Provide a range of supports for the student including direct tutoring by the teacher, graphic organizers, guides, and so on
- Carefully observe student progress in grasping the new content by constantly assessing the student's understanding
- Use only the supports that the student actually needs to achieve success
- Begin to withdraw instructional supports as student mastery of the content increases
- Ultimately withdraw all supports as students reach mastery

(See Bender, 2008; Larkin, 2001; and Stone, 1998).

since teachers will need an in-depth understanding of what a student knows prior to initiating the scaffolded lesson. Also, when working with students in the type of one-to-one or small-group work that scaffolding typically requires, teachers are in a better position to provide scaffolded instructional activities that are based, in part, on the students' preferred learning styles. Finally, scaffolded instruction assists students with learning disabilities and other learning challenges because with this instructional technique, they are likely to receive exactly the level of support they require. Thus, scaffolded instruction is recommended for all general education classes.

CONTENT ENHANCEMENTS

In addition to direct scaffolded instruction provided by the teacher, a variety of other structured learning supports may be considered "scaffolds" on which a student may depend in the learning process. Strategies such as questioning techniques that cause the student to probe more deeply into the content, prediction of the content points, and/or summarization of content are excellent learning supports, and will be discussed later in the chapter. Also, various charts and/or graphics that assist in the learning process can be considered scaffolds that the student, with initial adult supervision, could use to master newly presented subject matter. Many of these instructional supports may be considered as enhancements to the text or content under study, and the term content enhancement is used to represent these instructional supports (Bulgren, Deshler, & Lenz, 2007; Mason & Hedin, 2011).

Content enhancements (sometimes referred to as text enhancements, or content enhancement routines) are routines or strategies that assist with the organization of the content to facilitate students' ability to identify, organize, and comprehend the information (Mason & Hedin, 2011). While the term content enhancement is relatively new, the body of research that serves as a basis for these instructional strategies has been ongoing for at least four decades, and that research has repeatedly shown that these instructional tactics are effective with learners at all levels (Bulgren, Deshler, & Lenz, 2007; Gajria, Jitendra, Sood, & Sacks, 2007; Mason & Hedin, 2011).

> Content enhancements are routines or strategies that assist with the organization of the content to facilitate students' ability to identify, organize, and comprehend the information.

The Story Map and Text Structure

One example of a content enhancement that is frequently used in differentiated classes is the story map. As noted throughout this text, many students with learning disabilities have difficulties organizing their thoughts during learning tasks, and this is equally true in their efforts to comprehend content material or stories. These students do not understand that, in many reading passages, there is an underlying structure, and as a result they miss the opportunity to use the story structure to enhance their comprehension of the reading passage. For this reason, a number of researchers have encouraged specific instruction in story structure using story maps for students with learning disabilities (Swanson & De La Paz, 1998). Thus, this story map instructional tool may be considered as a content enhancement, since it provides a scaffold on which students may explore and comprehend new stories.

Content of the story map depends on the story structure components teachers wish to emphasize. Specifically, most stories at the primary and elementary levels will include the following:

- Information on the story setting
- Information on several primary characters
- An initiating event or problem for one of the main characters
- A sequence of actions to solve the problem
- A climax describing when and how the main character successfully deals with the problem, and
- A conclusion or resolution of the problem.

These rather predictable story components may be formulated into a story map that will assist the student with a learning disability or other learning difficulty to organize his or her thoughts. Thus, when a student with a learning challenge reads a story silently in the general education classroom, he or she should simultaneously complete a story map as a scaffold on which to build understanding of that story. A sample story map is present in Box 5.2

This story map activity is also very effective when completed as a "buddy" activity in the general education class. In that instance, two or three students may partner together to complete the map. Furthermore, these story maps can be used as teaching tools beyond the reading setting. For example, a completed story map should be reviewed in class as a post-reading activity to check for accuracy and for comprehension of the reading material. Finally, the story map can subsequently be used as a study guide for any future tests on that content. In fact, a wide variety of instructional activities can be built around the story map concept, and teachers in inclusive general education classes can greatly enhance the likelihood of reading success for students with learning challenges by simply using a story map as a scaffold for virtually every reading assignment in the differentiated class.

Although reading expository text in subject area classes does not usually involve the same components as a story narrative, teachers may use the content structure as a content enhancement to assist students with learning disabilities while they are also reading in content areas by developing maps that focus on the structure of the content in the expository text (Lenz, Adams, Bulgren, Pouliot, & Laraux, 2007; Mason & Hedin, 2011). For example, the structure of expository text in content areas typically includes one or several of the structure elements listed below, though these may not be present in every reading selection:

- Descriptive texts on specific concepts and examples of each concept
- Discussions of persons involved in the content under study
- Cause/effect relationships that help to analyze the content

BOX 5.2: A STORY MAP

Name _____

Date _____

Story Title _____

The story setting was _____
_____

The main character was _____
_____

Other characters were _____
_____
_____
_____

The problem began when _____
_____
_____
_____

Then several important things happened _____
_____
_____
_____

After that, _____
_____
_____
_____

Next, _____
_____
_____
_____

The problem came to a head when _____
_____

The story ended when _____
_____
_____
_____

From *Differentiating Instruction for Students With Learning Disabilities: Best Teaching Practices for General and Special Educators*, Second Edition, by William N. Bender. Thousand Oaks, CA: Corwin, 2008. Used with permission.

- Sequences of events, including specific timelines that summarize content
- Persuasive or argumentative text advocating positions of specific beliefs
- Technical texts describing machines, processes and so on

Teaching these text structures to students can enhance their understanding of expository texts, and this is likely to increase students' achievement. In fact, Williams, Nubla-Kung, Pollini, Stafford, Garcia, and Snyder (2007) presented evidence that teaching text structure to students as young as second grade will enhance their understanding of expository text in social studies. Clearly, general education teachers in the differentiated class, from Grade 2 and up, should be using some type of text structure instruction to enable all students to benefit from the instruction provided in each general education class.

This concept of text structure has now been expanded to a broader level than merely the structure within an expository text. For older students with learning difficulties, Lenz and his coauthors (2007), advocate use of a curriculum map, an organizer that shows the organizational structure or relationship of the content in relation to the previous unit of study and the rest of the curriculum. Thus, a curriculum map shows students the overall structure not of a particular section of text but of the curriculum as a whole (Lenz, Adams, Bulgren, Pouliot & Laraux, 2007). In that fashion, students with learning challenges might be better prepared to undertake more serious study of the content to be mastered. Of course, different teachers may choose to emphasize merely text structure and not overall curriculum structure, but virtually all teachers should consider teaching some aspect of text structure in order to support students with learning difficulties.

> Older students should use a curriculum map, an organizer that shows the organizational structure of the content in relation to the previous units of study and the rest of the curriculum.

ADVANCE AND PARTICIPATORY ORGANIZERS

Another content enhancement option is the use of "advance organizers" and/or "participatory organizers." These enable students to comprehend the basic organization of the material to be learned prior to actually studying the material. This term "advance organizer" was originally introduced by Ausubel and Robinson in 1969, but today, many types of organizers exist, including some which may be used during readings and content discussions rather than prior to them. Of course, many of these terms overlap in the education literature (i.e., the story map previously described may well be considered an advance organizer), and different educational theorists may use slightly different terminology. Some may even argue that these terms represent different instructional ideas, but essentially all of these ideas may be considered content enhancements and content organizers. Some of the commonly used terms include

concept maps	semantic webs	thinking webs
anticipatory organizers	graphic organizers	study guides
semantic maps	environmental visual aids	

Essentially, these devices present conceptual information in a way that illuminates content and connects new information with previously learned information (Dexter, Park, & Hughes, 2011; Mason & Hedin, 2011). The presentation of this type of material allows the student to mentally organize the conceptual content within his or her studies and represents one way to "hook" or "ground" new knowledge within existing knowledge. As examples of these organizers, the discussion below presents both graphic organizers, study guides, prediction/summarization strategies, text lookback organizers and verbal retelling for improving reading comprehension.

Graphic Organizers

Graphic organizers (GOs) are advance organizers that present information in a spatially relevant and significant form. Though some teachers may confuse graphic organizers with use of any visual aids in the classroom, GOs should be more than merely pretty pictures; they should display in some fashion the relationships between conceptual items under study and represent as much of the content as possible (Rock, 2004). When that requirement is met, research has shown that graphic organizers are powerful learning tools that will enhance both memory and comprehension for the content under study among students with learning difficulties as well as normally achieving children in the class (Dexter, Park & Hughes, 2011; Lenz et al., 2007; McEwan-Adkins, 2010).

> In graphic organizers, the graphic displays should display in some fashion the relationships between conceptual items under study and represent as much of the content as possible.

GOs can assist students in a variety of comprehension tasks, including assignments involving both reading and writing about topical content. GOs have also been effective instructional tools for science, mathematics, Spanish, and social studies (Institute for the Advancement of Research in Education, 2003). Because of the efficacy of GOs, many core curriculum texts today present these as teaching tools in instructor's manuals. A sample GO is presented in Figure 5.1 (see page 130).

Note that in this GO, both a timeline and sequence of important events is presented graphically with earlier events at the top of the page and others listed later. Thus, the very structure of this GO presents information that visually oriented students are more likely to recall.

As indicated previously, technology is playing a larger role in classrooms today, and several software programs are available that facilitate students' development and use of graphic organizers by helping them design their own GOs. The Inspiration software (intended for Grades 6–12) and Kidspiration software (intended for Grades K–5) are perhaps the most frequently used software for developing GOs. These are sold on a "fee per school" basis, and are widely used in classrooms today (http://k12software.com/view_details.php?PHPSESS ID=0214de944916000d2571036206bec337&ID=4142).

These programs provide a variety of tools for student use, such that as students develop plans for a written assignment on particular content, they can select an appropriate GO format and develop a GO for that content themselves rather than having teachers develop the GOs in every instance. Research has shown the efficacy of this software for students with learning disabilities (Sturm, & Rankin-Erickson, 2002), and these tools should certainly be considered for use with those students and others in the differentiated class.

Figure 5.1   Sample GO: The American Revolution

Student Directions: List 2 or more events/items in each box, and note the boxes generally represent both a timeline and a cause/result.
(Note: Student's contributions are presented in cursive)

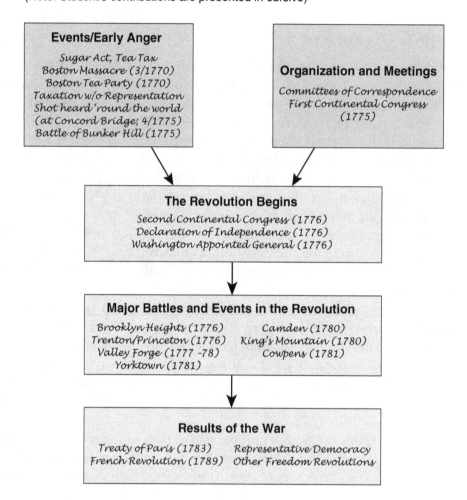

From *Differentiating Instruction for Students With Learning Disabilities: Best Teaching Practices for General and Special Educators*, Second Edition, by William N. Bender. Thousand Oaks, CA: Corwin, 2008. Used with permission.

Of course, once a GO is developed, it may be used to differentiate the activities in the classroom in a variety of ways, including

- Present labeled or unlabeled graphic organizers to various class members, depending on their skill level
- Provide GOs for some students while having others develop their own, either with or without software
- Have students predict the types of information that may be used to complete the GO prior to the activity
- Have students complete the organizer as the activity in the class progresses, either individually or using a buddy system
- Use the GO as a discussion tool among pairs of students in order to review the content of the daily lesson

Several theorists have provided various other guidelines for the use of GO (Foil & Alber, 2002; Rock, 2004). These are summarized Teaching Tip 5.1.

Study Guides

In contrast to a graphic organizer, a study guide typically presents content information that is organized in some type of linguistic form, either as an outline or a sequenced list of study points (Lovitt & Horton, 1994). Such study guides can provide an effective instructional support for students with learning difficulties. An elementary-level study guide for the Revolutionary War is presented in Box 5.3.

Research has shown the positive impact of study guides. For example, Lovitt, Rudsit, Jenkins, Pious, and Benedetti (1985) provided evidence for use of study guides in a science lesson. In that study, students were taught some science content using traditional instruction, and subsequently, they were taught other content using traditional instruction coupled with study guides. The results indicated

Teaching Tip 5.1

Guidelines for Using GOs

- Research has shown that GOs, as well as most content enhancements, should be specifically taught to students. Whenever possible, teachers should indicate and discuss the structure of the GO in an instructional unit and how that structure represents the content independent of the actual words or labels on the GO.
- Structure a specific time for GOs in each unit of instruction and repeatedly refer to the organizers at various points in each lesson. Repetitive use of organizers will enhance the effectiveness of this technique as a memory aid.
- As a differentiated lesson activity, you may increase student involvement in use of the organizers by having various groups of students develop or modify the organizers. You should stress the variety of different, yet appropriate, ways content may be structured for learning while relating that to the various and learning styles of the students in the class.
- Scaffold the instruction in the organizer by modeling the use of the organizer, practicing in a large group and then having students do it in pairs. Next, each individual student should complete the GO under teacher supervision.
- Explore the use of technology applications that will facilitate the development and use of GOs in the classroom. Again, this might be either an individual assignment or a partner activity.
- Teach a brainstorming idea such as "list/label" in which a category is listed as the central theme of the organizer and other related, yet subordinate, concepts are listed around the broader label. Have groups of students work together to formulate a rationale for why some concepts are subordinate to others.
- Publish the completed GOs either through class display or (after a complete checking of the content) digitally on the class wiki or perhaps, the school's website. If GOs developed by students are published in digital form accessible to parents, it is always advisable to let parents know they can review some of their child's work on the wiki or website.

BOX 5.3: REVOLUTIONARY WAR STUDY GUIDE

Name _____

Date _____

Riots and other events predated the outbreak of the Revolutionary War. These include (list at least 3)

_____

Colonists were angry because of

_____

_____

Several important meetings were (list documents arising from these meetings)

_____

_____

The first shots were fired at

_____

The main leaders for each army were

_____

The major battles and events were (describe at least four)

_____

_____

_____

_____

The final battle was

_____

The results and important outcomes of that war were

_____

_____

_____

_____

that provision of a study guide for junior high school science students resulted in greater gains in achievement than did the traditional instructional option.

These authors also reported that the students had become more involved in the lesson in order to complete the study guide (Lovitt et al., 1985). The positive results of using a study guide were demonstrated for several different groups of students including high-achieving, normally achieving, and low-achieving students, as well as for students with learning disabilities. Clearly, provision of study guides facilitates increases in achievement for all students, particularly for students with learning disabilities, and thus, use of this type of instructional support should characterize the differentiated classroom at all grade levels.

> The positive results of using study guides have been demonstrated for several different groups of students including high-achieving, normally achieving, and low-achieving students, as well as for students with learning disabilities.

As a variation, general education teachers might develop a study guide for use as both an advance organizer and subsequently as a participatory organizer. In using the same study guide as both an advance organizer and a participatory organizer, the teacher may have to reproduce the study guide several times. However, students should be encouraged to save each completed version of the study guide, as those earlier study guides may help students reflect on information they knew at the outset of the unit compared with information they learned later. Study guides completed later should show increased detail and more extensive descriptions when compared with study guides completed earlier in the lesson or instructional unit.

Note that research had demonstrated the effectiveness of using study guides not only for students with learning disabilities, but also for other students in the class (Lovitt & Horton, 1994; Lovitt et al., 1985). Of course, this last point cannot be overemphasized. All students benefit from the use of study guides—not merely students who are struggling with the content. This research indicates that study guides are an effective instructional support strategy for virtually all general education classrooms. Further, teachers should never view preparation of study guides as additional work that benefits only students with learning challenges; rather, study guides will enhance learning for all students.

Prediction/Summarization Participatory Organizer

Students with learning challenges often approach reading differently than do normally achieving readers because reading difficulties have negatively impacted their reading skills for so long. Many challenged readers approach a reading task with some fear or uneasiness, particularly if oral reading before their classmates is on the agenda. In such cases, they may fear embarrassment, so they may approach the reading assignment without thinking or predicting what the content might be. Further, after completing the reading, they do not rethink the content and summarize it in any form. Of course, predicting and summarizing are things that effective readers do without really thinking of it (Mason & Hedin, 2011; Ward-Lonergan, Lies, & Anderson, 1999). Once an average achieving student reads the title to a story or a chapter in a content text, that student typically considers any prior knowledge they have on that subject and predicts what the chapter might say, and during the subsequent reading, they recheck their own predictions.

> Average students consider their prior knowledge as they read, predict what the chapter might say next, and later, they recheck their own predictions.

Also, after reading a section of text, experienced readers summarize the text briefly for themselves, prior to reading the next section. That summarization might also provide the basis for predicting the contents of the next reading selection. In order to increase the likelihood that challenged students will practice these effective reading skills, general education teachers from the primary years up through middle school should foster both text prediction and text summarization skills, since research has shown that use of these tactics will improve reading comprehension (Mason & Hedin, 2011). Often this can be accomplished by providing a learning support organizer that includes both prediction and text summarization activities. These can be easily created by teachers for almost any reading content, and an example is presented in Box 5.4.

BOX 5.4: A PREDICTION/SUMMARIZATION ACTIVITY

A Prediction/Summarization Tactic

Before Reading

What is the story title?

What content predictions can I make based on that?

Are there pictures that suggest the topic?

What do I want to learn about that topic?

During Reading

What is the main idea or problem?

How was the problem managed?

After Reading

Was the problem successfully dealt with?

What is the main story or lesson?

What did I learn?

From *Differentiating Instruction for Students With Learning Disabilities: Best Teaching Practices for General and Special Educators*, Second Edition, by William N. Bender. Thousand Oaks, CA: Corwin, 2008. Used with permission.

A TEXT LOOKBACK INSTRUCTIONAL SUPPORT

Another instructional support that will assist older students with learning disabilities and other learning challenges in their reading summarization skills is instruction in "text lookbacks" (Swanson & De La Paz, 1998). In using a text lookback tactic, teachers should directly teach the skills involved in looking back over a text chapter or assigned reading to find specific information. When provided with a set of specific comprehension questions, the ability to look back in the text to find answers to the questions will greatly assist students with reading problems in comprehension of the assigned reading material.

> The ability to look back in the text to find answers to the questions will greatly assist students with reading problems in comprehension of the assigned reading material.

Some general education teachers may assume that telling students with reading difficulties to "look back over the chapter and find the answer" is sufficient for those students. However, the fact is that there are a number of different skills involved in looking back through a chapter for specific information, and many students with learning disabilities and other reading comprehension difficulties in the elementary and middle grades do not know how to search for answers to questions in the textbook. At a minimum, these text lookback skills would involve the following:

- Remembering when certain information was covered—early or late in the chapter
- Using headings to find the right section of text
- Reading topic sentences under the appropriate heading
- Identifying a specific paragraph where the answer might be
- Finding the answer in that chapter or continuing the search

Swanson and De La Paz (1998) encouraged teachers to directly model this text lookback strategy for their students while verbally rehearsing the skills. In modeling text lookback skills, the teacher would look for information in text while he or she "thinks aloud" about the text (Swanson & De La Paz, 1998). Box 5.5 presents a sample dialogue for such a modeling lesson.

BOX 5.5: MODELING A TEXT LOOKBACK STRATEGY

I've read about the Apache Indians and how they lost their land and their forced removal from the plains. The question is asking me to name the most important treaty that resulted in the removal of these Native Americans from their homeland. First, I'll skim the chapter to see if I see a heading about Indians losing land or Indian removal. The first section heading in the chapter deals with the need of settlers for land of their own and how most immigrants wanted their own farms. The answer wouldn't be there. The next section is titled "Moving Into New Lands." The answer may be in that section, so I'll look a bit more closely here. I see one side heading that mentions "Conflict Over Land." A picture above that section shows Native Americans at war with settlers in a wagon train. This is where I'll find the answer. I'll read this paragraph carefully, and look for the mention of any words like "treaties" that might be a clue to the answer."

THE VERBAL RETELLING TACTIC

Many strategies for increasing comprehension today emphasize the students' ability to retell what they have read (Ward-Lonergan et al., 1999). In fact, verbally retelling the information from a story, a reading passage, or even a lecture in a subject content area has been shown to increase comprehension among students with learning reading problems in the elementary and middle grades (Ward-Lonergan et al., 1999). Verbally retelling the main information helps a student focus on the important aspects of the information presented and thus represents one method by which a student may summarize the information in the text.

For this reason, teachers in differentiated classes in the general education classroom should frequently require students to retell information that has just been read or otherwise presented in class. When a selection is read, either silently or orally in the class, the teacher may invite students to retell the important aspects of the reading selection by saying something like the following:

> Now we're going to work together to retell the information we just read. You may refer to your books as you need to. I'd like for someone to tell me the names of the persons we just read about, and then I'll call on someone else to tell me the first thing that happened.

With this type of "team" approach, it will be easier to get students with learning challenges to participate in retelling a part of the reading passage. Also, teachers can strengthen this activity by having another student summarize the main points of the passage on the dry-erase board in outline form. Subsequent to the retelling, teachers may call on yet another student with a learning disability or reading problem to review that outline for the class and add to it as necessary.

Technology for Content Enhancements

While all of the ideas above have been shown to increase achievement for struggling students, modern technology presents an array of options based on the same research, for streamlining the use of these content enhancement ideas. The use of software to facilitate student development of GOs was discussed previously, but in addition to that technology option, instructional technology options today provide a much wider array of content enhancement options (Berkeley & Lindstrom, 2011; Pemberton, 2011). Further, by using these content enhancement instructional technologies, teachers are providing increased differentiation for many students in their classes (Pemberton, 2011). While this text cannot present all of these options, an example or two will suffice to show how technology can greatly enrich student understandings by providing for a variety of content enhancements.

Imagine a student reading an expository text section from the science textbook and encountering an unknown vocabulary term. In many cases, the student with learning challenges might merely skip or "read over" that term, and continue his or her reading. In some cases, the student can use the context to establish the meaning of the skipped term, but skipping too many vocabulary terms might restrict the student's understanding of the expository text. When the same text is read in a digital format, however, a wide variety of content enhancements are typically offered. When a student encounters an unknown term in a computerized reading lesson, many software programs allow the student to click on the unknown term, and a definition for that term immediately pops up. In other programs, by clicking on the term, the student not only sees a definition of it, but the computer pronounces the term for the student. Other computerized programs facilitate the highlighting of main ideas in the text, or present critical questions as pop-ups, while students read the text. Many of the text enhancements have been shown to positively impact learning for struggling students (McArthur, & Haynes, 1995).

In fact, teachers may already have access to some of these content enhancement technologies without even realizing it! Berkeley and Lindstrom (2011) point out that Microsoft Word, a software program that is already available on many computers in schools today, includes a feature called AutoSummarize. Using the AutoSummarize function in combination with text that

> Teachers already have access to some of these content enhancement technologies without even realizing it!

is in digital format, teachers or students can have the software highlight key points in the text or create a "summary" that is 10%, 20%, or even 50% of the length of the original text. While both features can assist struggling readers, the highlight feature, in particular, can help a student identify and learn key components in the enhanced text.

In addition, text-to-speech features are likewise available at no cost for teachers in programs such as Microsoft Word, Adobe Read Out Loud, and Internet Explorer. Information on these text enhancement features is available at the websites below (Berkeley & Lindstrom, 2011). Taking advantage of these free, immediately available content enhancements should be a priority of every teacher.

Microsoft Word: http://support.microsoft.com/kb/306902

Adobe Reader: http://www.adobe.com/enterprise/accessibility/reader6/sec2.html

Internet Explorer: http://support.microsoft.com/kb/306902

Again, many technologies of this nature are available, and some of these are free (Berkeley & Lindstrom, 2011). This is one of the reasons that research continues to show increased student achievement as associated with increased computer availability in the classroom (Barsenghian, 2011; Digital Trends, 2011; McArthur & Haynes, 1995). Teachers in general education are well advised to take advantage of every technology option available in order to provide content text enhancements for students with learning disabilities and other learning challenges.

Differentiating Instruction With Content Enhancements

As noted previously, advance organizers come in many other formats beyond text structure curriculum maps, GOs, and study guides, and the term content enhancements includes many other instructional techniques. These may include teaching tactics such as prediction of lesson content, summarization, questioning techniques, and so on, and all of the instructional supports do enhance the learning for struggling students in Tier 1. However, GOs and study guides were selected for discussion in this context for a specific reason; the contrast between GOs and study guides can enlighten teachers concerning implementation of differentiated instruction. Like all of these organizers, graphic organizers and study guides represent adapted content enhancements that can help focus students with learning disabilities and other learning difficulties on the assigned task (Dexter et al., 2011; Rock, 2004).

However, from the perspective of differentiating instruction, graphic organizers may be more effective for use with students who demonstrate a spatial learning preference, since these are graphic in nature. In contrast, study guides, which tend to be linguistically formatted, may work better with students who have a linguistic or analytic learning style. Thus, when a teacher considers using a study guide, that teacher is well advised to develop a GO that covers similar information and present both options to the students. In that fashion, students are free to choose an organizer that fits their own learning style. Further, as the examples in this chapter indicate, it is relatively easy to formulate both a GO and a study guide that present similar information on the Revolutionary War. Using this idea, it is relatively easy to differentiate the instruction by providing GOs for the learners with a spatial learning style and study guides for learners with a linguistic learning style.

PEER TUTORING IN DIFFERENTIATED CLASSES

Classwide Peer Tutoring

Peer tutoring is one of the most effective tactics available to assist students with learning disabilities and other students who struggle in the differentiated classroom (Greenwood, Tapia, Abbott, & Walton, 2003; Mortweet et al., 1999; Utley, Mortweet, & Greenwood, 1997). This instructional support can increase both the quality and the amount of instruction that students with learning problems receive, because this tactic provides tutoring support as well as some cooperative instructional support for learning the instructional content.

> Peer tutoring is one of the most effective tactics available to assist students with learning disabilities and other students who struggle in the differentiated classroom.

This is an excellent strategy for the general education classroom, since this strategy results in students getting tutorial assistance at exactly the level they need, without taking undue time from the teacher. Further, several of the peer-tutoring approaches involve cooperative learning since, in some peer-tutoring examples, rewards are shared among the group; thus, it is in everyone's best interest that all students do well in peer-tutoring situations.

The first of these peer-tutoring systems to be developed was classwide peer tutoring (CWPT), which was developed in the 1980s by Charles Greenwood and his coworkers (Greenwood et al., 2003; Mortweet et al., 1999; Utley et al., 1997). The program has been used successfully as an integration strategy for children with a range of disabilities and learning problems as well as with high-risk students and students with learning disabilities. Further, the program works very well in the differentiated classroom, since the content under study in CWPT is determined for each student individually. CWPT may be used in many content subjects such as reading, vocabulary, spelling, and mathematics, and this versatility suggests that CWPT should be considered as one strategy for every differentiated class (Burks, 2004; Greenwood et al., 2003). Burks (2004) provided an example of CWPT in a spelling lesson in a general education classroom as described in Box 5.6.

Research has been strongly supportive of peer tutoring in terms of positive academic results for both tutors and tutees (Burks, 2004; Greenwood et al., 2003; Mortweet et al., 1999; Utley et al., 1997). Clearly, this is certainly a strategy that is appropriate for virtually every primary and elementary differentiated classroom. However, as the Burks (2004) study suggests, this strategy could well serve as a Tier 2 intervention for students with learning challenges and/or special needs. While that particular study predated the national emphasis on RTI, it still demonstrates how instructional tactics in general education can result in targeted instruction for specific students and increased progress monitoring for those students. When a general education teacher conducts a CWPT instructional process for all students in the class (which would be considered Tier 1 instruction), the target skills would have

BOX 5.6: CWPT IN A SPELLING LESSON

Burks (2004) implemented a classwide peer-tutoring project to enhance spelling for three students with learning disabilities in elementary school. Using a baseline and intervention design, the target behavior was identified as spelling accuracy on weekly spelling tests. During baseline, each of the three students participated in traditional spelling lessons, but during a seven-week intervention, peer tutoring was implemented once per week for 20 minutes. During the CWPT, students worked in pairs. One student would call out words to his or her partner for 10 minutes, and when the tutee wrote a word, the tutor would check it for accuracy. If a word was spelled incorrectly, the tutee was required to write the word two times correctly. Each pair received 2 points for each word spelled correctly and 1 point for corrected words. After 10 minutes, the pair was reversed with the tutor becoming the tutee and the other student (the original tutee) calling out words for the next 10 minutes. Spelling words for each student were changed each week. Results of this tutoring experience indicated that all of the target students improved their word accuracy in spelling, and the intervention condition spelling scores were much higher than the baseline scores.

The peer-tutoring strategy could well serve as a Tier 2 intervention for students with learning challenges and/or special needs.

CWPT is reciprocal in nature; every student engaged in CWPT serves as both tutor and tutee.

already been determined for each individual student as required by the CWPT process. Further, by merely adding a progress-monitoring measure for the target students, as exemplified by Burks (2004), the teacher would have a very effective Tier 2 intervention for selected students who might be struggling with the curriculum.

Note that CWPT is reciprocal in nature; every student engaged in CWPT serves as both tutor and tutee. This is another strength of this tactic for differentiated classes. During the CWPT sessions, all students are paired with a partner and each student pair is assigned to one of two competing teams. One student, serving initially as the tutor, will use preselected materials and call out problems to the tutee. Halfway through each tutoring session—after approximately 10 minutes—the teacher signals the students to change roles. The tutors then become tutees and vice versa.

As shown in the example above, the tutees earn points for their team by correctly responding to specific content questions or problems that are presented to them by the tutor (Utley et al., 1997), and the team with the most points wins. The winning team can be determined daily or weekly and is based on each team's total points. Another strength of this program is that the tutor and tutee roles are highly structured to ensure that tutees receive questions or problems rapidly and in a consistent format, and the content varies from one student to another such that every student receives instruction at exactly the level he or she needs. In many ways, this CWPT tactic represents differentiated instruction at its best.

Further, CWPT results in increased time-on-task for the tutees and makes this strategy particularly effective as a differentiated instruction strategy for students with learning challenges. Implementation requires that all students be trained during this process to become effective tutors, and the structure of the tutoring sessions ensures consistency of instruction (Greenwood et al., 2003; Mortweet et al., 1999).

The Teacher's Role

While students are effectively serving as tutors for each other in CWPT, the teacher's role is still critical. Prior to initiating CWPT, the teacher organizes the content of the course material into daily and weekly lessons, and then formats the materials to be used by the students. Instruction in this system must be planned individually, and each student is assigned spelling, reading, math, or language arts work at his or her instructional level. Needless to say, this may take some time because many of the students will have different instructional needs, but this organization of the curricula content also allows the teacher to specifically differentiate the instruction based on the needs and learning styles of the particular learners.

Once the material is organized, training for the tutoring occurs simultaneously for all tutor-tutee pairs involving the entire class at the same time

(Arreaga-Mayer, 1998; Mortweet et al., 1999). This training regimen is a major advantage of this method for general education teachers; as students take on increased instructional tutoring responsibilities, more teacher time is free for other class activities, such as undertaking Tier 2 interventions with small groups of students. Alternatively, the teacher may wish to supervise and monitor all students' responses during the tutoring sessions. The training strategies for CWPT are described in Teaching Tip 5.2.

After the training phase, during the actual CWPT procedure, the teacher's role is to monitor the tutoring sessions. The teacher will evaluate the quality of tutoring, correcting tutoring procedures as necessary, and may award bonus points to tutors for demonstrating correct teaching behaviors. In this monitoring role (rather than the traditional lecture or discussion leader role), the teacher is free to respond immediately as students request assistance. This results in increased instructional time and attention provided for students with learning disabilities and other learning challenges in general education classes because the teacher can respond more freely and one half of the students in the class are also providing instruction. One might well imagine an entire school undertaking CWPT as a general education instructional procedure. In such a case, student training would transfer from one classroom to another, and all teachers would find increased time for individual and/or small-group instruction at the Tier 1 level.

Advantages of CWPT

There are many additional advantages to implementation of this procedure in differentiated classes. Because of the careful monitoring on the part of the

Teaching Tip 5.2

Training Students for Classwide Peer Tutoring

1. The teacher starts by explaining how the "game" (i.e., the tutoring) works, including a discussion of winning teams, points, and tutoring. Students are introduced to both worksheets and scoring sheets for various instructional activities. Emphasis should be placed on the concept of good sportsmanship during the tutoring sessions.

2. The teacher then demonstrates by having a student perform the schoolwork as the tutee/student while the teacher acts as the tutor. The awarding of points is demonstrated, as is the appropriate, civil, and very polite error-correction procedure.

3. The teacher then selects two additional students to model tutoring procedures in front of the class while the other students watch and the teacher provides feedback.

4. After two or more such student demonstrations, the teacher has all students practice the tutoring procedure (Arreaga-Mayer, 1998). Actual CWPT may begin the next day.

teacher, CWPT is a system that engages students with the subject matter at higher levels. Students doing CWPT usually spend 75% to 95% of the session engaged in the learning task, and that on-task time is quite high for students with learning disabilities in any educational endeavor (Greenwood et al., 2003; Mortweet et al., 1999; Utley et al., 1997). Further, CWPT has been proven beneficial in a variety of subject areas for both elementary and high school levels. For example, at the elementary level, CWPT is designed to supplement traditional instruction and to replace seatwork, lecture, and oral reading group activities. At the middle and secondary level, CWPT is often focused on practice, skill building, and review of subject matter. Whole-school level CWPT procedures also are available for supporting the implementation of this tutoring system schoolwide (Mortweet et al., 1999; Utley et al., 1997).

Next, CWPT can be used in conjunction with teacher-made instructional materials or with commercial curriculum materials, and thus, one does not have to purchase specific materials to use CWPT. Also, CWPT elicits extensive help from the peer group in the teaching process, and depending on the age of the students involved, this can be a powerful motivation for learning. Students can and often do learn a great deal from each other, and teachers in today's classrooms must learn to take advantage of the power of students learning from other students through tutoring.

Next, the reward system for individual students in CWPT depends not just on their own performance but also on the performance of other members on the team. This offers the advantage of strengthening the social interaction possibilities for students with learning disabilities and other learning challenges. Changing the tutor-tutee pairs weekly and changing the roles within daily sessions keeps the students motivated and provides for a variety of social interactions that may not occur in more traditionally taught classrooms (Burks, 2004; Mortweet et al., 1999; Utley et al., 1997).

Finally, research has demonstrated that this strategy works. The research studies on CWPT are extensive, and have demonstrated the effectiveness of CWPT in the areas of reading, spelling, vocabulary, and math (Burks, 2004; Greenwood et al., 2003; Mortweet et al., 1999, Utley et al., 1997). Several used single-subject and experimental control group designs that included students with learning disabilities, behavior disorders, or mild mental retardation, and all of these studies have shown positive outcomes. Furthermore, CWPT has been reported to be effective for students with mild disabilities as well as other students in inclusive settings. Clearly, this peer-tutoring strategy should be employed in many general education classes.

Peer-Assisted Learning Strategies

Peer-assisted learning strategies (PALS) is another highly structured peer-tutoring system that was developed by Lynn and Douglass Fuchs and their coworkers in the early 1990s. PALS provides general education teachers with an effective, feasible, and acceptable intervention in the differentiated class (Fuchs et al., 2001; Fuchs, Fuchs, & Kazdan, 1999; Fulk & King, 2001; Saenz, Fuchs & Fuchs, 2005; Utley et al., 1997).

In 1995, Fuchs, Fuchs, Hamlett, Phillips, and Bentz observed that general education teachers typically made fewer adaptations in their classes than were needed by students with learning disabilities. This was the case even after teachers had been provided frequent information on the progress or lack of progress of individual students. To address the need for general educators to provide more adaptations (i.e., to differentiate their instruction) in the inclusive classes, these authors recommended that general educators use curriculum-based measurement within the context of classwide peer tutoring to differentiate the instruction for students with learning disabilities and other learning challenges (Fuchs et al., 1995).

The PALS approach is built around the classwide peer-tutoring concept, but it also includes a number of different instructional approaches that are linked to computerized curriculum-based measurement, which was described in Chapter 4. For example, math in PALS provides teachers with group and individual progress reports on a student's learning of specific math skills using classwide curriculum-based measurement (Fuchs et al., 2001; Saenz, Fuchs, & Fuchs 2005). This enables the teacher to provide instruction to the group as well as address the needs of specific students. A PALS tutoring session for a reading lesson is described in detail in Box 5.7.

> PALS is built around the classwide peer-tutoring concept, and includes a number of different instructional approaches that are linked to computerized curriculum-based measurement.

BOX 5.7: A PALS TUTORING LESSON

There are three different instructional tactics included in a PALS reading lesson: *partner reading, paragraph shrinking* (i.e., paragraph summarization), and *prediction relay.*

In a *partner reading* lesson, each student reads aloud for 10 minutes. The higher performing student reads the lesson first. The lower performing student rereads the same material. Whenever a reading error occurs, the tutor says, "Stop. You missed that word. Can you figure it out?" The reader either figures out the word within four seconds or the tutor says the word. Then the reader repeats the word. Next, the tutor says, "Good job. Read the sentence again." Students earn 1 point for each correctly read sentence (if a word-reading correction is required, 1 point is awarded after the sentence is read correctly) and 10 points are awarded for retelling the content of the reading selection. After both students read, the lower performing student retells the text content for two minutes (Fuchs, Fuchs, & Kazdan, 1999).

In *paragraph shrinking* (i.e., paragraph summarization), the tutor guides the struggling student in identification of the main idea by asking the tutee to identify who or what the paragraph was about, as well as the most important thing in the text. The reader is required to put these two pieces of information together in 10 or fewer words. When the tutor determines that a paragraph summary error has occurred, he or she says, "That's not quite right. Please, skim the paragraph and try again." The reader skims the paragraph and tries to answer the missed question. The tutor then decides whether to give points or give the answer. For each summary, students earn 1 point for correctly identifying the who or what, 1 point for correctly stating the most important thing, and 1 point for using 10 or fewer words. Students continue to monitor and correct reading errors, but points are not longer awarded on a sentence-by-sentence basis. After five minutes, the students switch roles (Fuchs et al., 1999).

(Continued)

(Continued)

In *prediction relay,* the reader makes a prediction about what will be learned on the next half page. The reader reads the half page aloud while the tutor identifies and corrects reading errors, (dis)confirms the prediction, and summarizes the main idea of the half page. When the tutor judges that a prediction is not realistic, he or she says "I don't agree. Think of a better prediction." Otherwise, the word reading and paragraph summary correction procedures are used. The student receives 1 point for each viable prediction, 1 point for reading each half page, 1 point for accurately (dis)confirming each prediction, and 1 point for each component (i.e., the who or what and what mainly happened in 10 or fewer words) of each summary. After five minutes, the students switch roles (Fuchs et al., 1999).

Note that PALS incorporates various content enhancements such as requiring students to predict what they might find in a text or to summarize a text. These instructional supports have found widespread support in the research literature (Bulgren, Deshler, & Lenz, 2007; Gajria, Jitendra, Sood, & Sacks, 2007; Mason & Hedin, 2011), and are thus recommended in virtually all curricular areas. As a result of the use of these highly effective teaching techniques, research on the effectiveness of PALS provides convincing support for its superiority compared to conventional general education instruction in reading and math (Fuchs et al., 2001; Fulk & King, 2001; Saenz, Fuchs, & Fuchs 2005; Utley et al., 1997). The results of these studies indicated that all students with and without learning disabilities who were doing peer tutoring made measurably greater progress on test scores in the same amount of time. Further, teachers and students both reported high levels of satisfaction with PALS instruction (Fuchs et al., 2001; Saenz et al., 2005; Utley et al., 1997).

Peer Tutoring in the Differentiated Class

Regardless of the tutoring approach one selects, peer tutoring is one of the most effective tactics available to assist students with learning disabilities or other learning difficulties in the differentiated classroom. Using these methods, teachers can differentiate instruction and address the instructional needs of many struggling students, including students with disabilities, in the general education class. As shown above, research has been supportive of each of the peer-tutoring methodologies, and both tutors and tutees learn more and are engaged more with the lesson content during tutoring situations than in traditional classroom instruction.

These peer-tutoring systems will generally save the teacher time in the class and can therefore greatly enhance the opportunities for implementing various differentiated instructional strategies, as well as Tier 2 interventions for students requiring them. This system also makes the academic goals much more attainable for students with learning difficulties in the general education class, and thus peer tutoring can be considered as one aspect of universal design for the curriculum. For these reasons, most differentiated general education classes should be characterized by various peer-tutoring instructional programs.

RECIPROCAL TEACHING FOR DIFFERENTIATING INSTRUCTION

Reciprocal teaching represents a scaffolded instructional technique in which both the teacher and the other students are providing instructional support. Further, each student will ultimately lead the reciprocal teaching lesson at some point, so each student becomes responsible for teaching the lesson through structured dialogue (Lederer, 2000; Palincsar & Brown, 1986, 1987; Vaughn & Linan-Thompson, 2003). The reciprocal teaching method emphasizes several content enhancements that have been discussed previously to facilitate the students' planning of the task and task completion. In reciprocal teaching, students are supported by the teacher initially and use four specific content enhancement techniques to explore a reading passage:

1. prediction

2. question generation

3. summarizing

4. clarifying

Teaching Reciprocal Teaching

In teaching this procedure to a general education class, the teacher would initially model these procedures while studying a reading passage, while asking questions of the group. After the students learn these techniques, each member of the group becomes the "teacher" and leads one or more class discussions, using these same four content enhancement procedures. Box 5.8 presents a sample reciprocal teaching dialogue.

A teaching dialogue such as this is exciting for anyone who has ever attempted to involve students with learning difficulties in class discussions, because many students with learning challenges are quite reluctant to answer questions in class for fear of potential embarrassment. In a reciprocal teaching lesson, not only are almost all students participating in the dialogue, but the level of these small-group instructional dialogues indicates a great deal of cognitive understanding on the part of the students. In the sample dialogue above, each of the students was aware of the four basic procedures that are included in reciprocal teaching, and even when the students could not complete one of these procedures (e.g., thinking about what came next in the story), they were still aware of the need to complete that particular cognitive task.

In reciprocal teaching, the teacher and the students take turns as instructional leader. Whoever is the "teacher" assumes the role of leading a dialogue about the reading passage. In the example above, the task was a reading passage that the students were required to read silently. Using the reciprocal teaching approach, the common goals of each member of the group were predicting, question generating, summarizing, and clarifying, and each of those goals was taught separately.

> In reciprocal teaching, the teacher and the students take turns as instructional leader.

BOX 5.8: A RECIPROCAL TEACHING DIALOGUE

Student 1: My question is, What does the aquanaut see when he goes under water?

Student 2: A watch.

Student 3: Flippers.

Student 4: A belt.

Student 1: Those are all good answers.

Teacher: Nice job! I have a question too. Why does the aquanaut wear a belt? What is so special about it?

Student 3: It's a heavy belt and keeps him from floating up to the top again.

Teacher: Good for you.

Student 1: For my summary now: This paragraph was about what aquanauts need to take when they go under the water.

Student 5: And also why they need those things.

Student 3: I think we need to clarify the word "gear."

Student 6: That's the special things they need.

Teacher: Another word for "gear" in the story might be "equipment," the equipment that makes it easier for the aquanauts to do their job.

Student 1: I don't think I have a prediction to make.

Teacher: Well, in the story, they tell us that there are many strange and wonderful creatures that aquanauts see as they do their work. My prediction is that they'll describe some of these creatures. What are some of the strange creatures you already know about that live in the ocean?

Student 6: Octopuses.

Student 3: Whales.

Student 5: Sharks.

Teacher: Listen and find out. Who will be our next teacher?

From *Differentiating Instruction for Students With Learning Disabilities: Best Teaching Practices for General and Special Educators*, Second Edition, by William N. Bender. Thousand Oaks, CA: Corwin, 2008. Used with permission.

Initially, the teacher discussed the benefits of *prediction* as a reading strategy. Prediction of what comes next in the text involves relevant background knowledge of the text and provides students with a reason to read further, that is, to confirm or refute their predictions. Therefore, this strategy involves both comprehension of material being read and comprehension monitoring of material that has already been read. The teacher may even prepare a poster or wall chart of the various aspects of prediction and keep it in front of the class to assist the student who is leading the activity on any particular day.

The second phase of reciprocal teaching is *question generation.* Question generation gives the student the opportunity to identify the type of information that may make up test questions. Also, this activity may provide an occasion to discuss the methods of study for various types of questions.

Summarizing is the third aspect of reciprocal teaching. This step provides an opportunity to integrate information from different sections of the text. The most important ideas of the reading sections should be jointly identified and discussed.

Finally, the fourth activity—*clarifying*—encourages students to identify the major points of the reading selection and to identify concepts that may be difficult. Identification of difficult concepts is one aspect of reading comprehension that is particularly troublesome for students with learning disabilities because these students will often read a selection and not realize that they did not understand part of the passage. Seeking clarification also allows the student to ask questions without embarrassment because the role of the student is to "question and clarify" the problem areas for other students.

Each of the four components of reciprocal teaching is taught for a single instructional period, with the teacher conducting these lessons. Initially, each strategy is explained and examples are given along with guided practice. By the fifth or sixth day, the teacher and students are using the strategies together to discuss reading material. At that point, the teacher continues to model the strategies, praises the students for using the strategies, and prompts the students to use additional strategies.

Note the "scaffolded" nature of this student support—the idea that the teacher is constantly modeling, demonstrating, and only selectively turning these responsibilities over to the students as the students' skills increase. By the end of a two-week period, the role of "teacher" can be rotated and the students, each individually, become the instructional facilitators.

Efficacy of Reciprocal Teaching

Reciprocal teaching has been widely supported by research in a variety of academic areas and a variety of grade levels (Lederer, 2000; Palincsar & Brown, 1986, 1987: Vaughn & Linan-Thompson, 2003). The study by Lederer (2000), for example, illustrated the efficacy of reciprocal teaching for students with learning disabilities in a social studies class. Lederer used six inclusive classrooms (two each at Grades 4, 5, and 6), in a comparison of the effectiveness of reciprocal teaching. The students in experimental classes at each grade level were taught their social studies for a 30-day period using reciprocal teaching, while the students in the other classes were taught in the traditional manner. Fifteen students with learning disabilities were in the experimental classes and formed the experimental group, while 10 students with learning disabilities were in the control classes and formed the control group.

The three dependent measures in Lederer's study (2000) were measures of the students' ability to answer comprehension questions, generate questions, and summarize based on a reading selection in social studies. The repeated assessments throughout the 30-day period indicated a consistent advantage in each dependent measure for the students who received reciprocal teaching instruction. The students with learning disabilities in the reciprocal instruction group consistently outperformed the students with learning disabilities in the control group on question generation, comprehension, and summarizing the reading passages.

Other Advantages of Reciprocal Teaching

In addition to strong research support for this instructional strategy, reciprocal teaching offers a number of other advantages. First, reciprocal teaching can be viewed as a scaffold for learning a variety of content areas and can easily be incorporated into almost any general education classroom. Next, this procedure will greatly benefit students with learning disabilities as well as many other learners in the class.

Further, the reciprocal teaching technique has several additional advantages when used to differentiate instruction in the general education class. While it is relatively simple to differentiate by focusing on learning products (i.e., the teacher may merely require different products from various children and associate those product assignments with the students' learning strengths), the reciprocal teaching technique focuses on the "process" of learning. This technique engages each student on several levels, first as a student and subsequently as "discussion leader." Thus, the process of learning is explored from several differing perspectives. For this reason, implementing this technique in the general education classroom tends to strengthen the student's understanding of the learning process, and that understanding can then be translated into other subjects and classes.

This procedure also tends to increase the social acceptance of students with learning difficulties. In this technique, students with learning disabilities and other learning challenges will be viewed as competent and capable class members, even if they do receive a bit more "coaching" from the teacher when they lead the reciprocal teaching lesson. Thus, this technique is likely to support these students' self-concept development as well as academic success.

For these reasons, teachers should incorporate reciprocal teaching into their general education lessons whenever possible. Simply put, this strategy encourages students to take more responsibility for their own learning, even as they learn the processes of comprehending the content under study.

WHAT'S NEXT

This chapter has presented a variety of learning supports for struggling students and students with learning disabilities in the differentiated classroom. Scaffolded instruction, content enhancements, peer tutoring, and reciprocal teaching should all be frequently used in most general education classes, and while no teacher can implement all of the effective instructional practices available, one or more of these strategies should be in evidence in most classrooms. Not only are these highly effective, but they also lend themselves to increased teacher time for individual and small-group instruction, not to mention the option of implementing a Tier 2 intervention in the general education classroom.

The next chapter will continue to present learning support strategies for the differentiated class by presenting a specific class of content enhancements, cognitive strategies for general education.

Cognitive Strategy Instruction for Differentiated Classes 6

Students with learning disabilities and many other learners in the classroom demonstrate a variety of academic deficits as well as deficits in planning and various other organizational problems, and of course, the concept of differentiated instruction places strong emphasis on structuring the learning tasks to address these diverse learning needs (Sousa & Tomlinson, 2011; Tomlinson, 1999; Tomlinson, Brimijoin, & Narvaez, 2008). Whereas appropriate classroom structure and universally designed assignments will support students with learning disabilities in their personal organization of schoolwork, these students will also need highly organized academic instruction and numerous academic supports for understanding the tasks assigned to them. The technology tools discussed in Chapter 3 will likewise help, as will the learning support instructional ideas in Chapter 5.

However, in addition to the instructional strategies described previously, students with learning disabilities and other academic challenges can benefit from various additional instructional supports. This chapter focuses on a specific type of learning support instructional strategy for differentiating instruction in the general education classroom: cognitive strategy instruction. Of course, this term has many different synonyms (e.g., content enhancement routines, learning strategy instruction, metacognitive instruction, or merely strategy instruction), and some theorists perceive terms as representing different instructional ideas. However, in this chapter these terms will be considered roughly synonymous.

Initially, this chapter presents a discussion of the metacognitive concept from which these instructional approaches stem. Next, a profoundly influential early adaptation of this concept—learning strategy instruction—is presented and discussed at length. A case study of strategy instruction as a Tier 2 RTI intervention is presented next. Finally, self-monitoring and self-regulation are described as those instructional approaches likewise have roots in this metacognitive and cognitive strategy research.

From the teachers' perspective, the issues are relatively simple: What has been proven to work in the differentiated classroom, and how do I do it?

It is essential to point out that many of the strategies and tactics presented in the last chapter could, with equal ease, have been presented here. Again, different theorists have different perspectives on how these strategies and instructional ideas relate to each other, but from the teachers' perspective, the issues are relatively simple: What has been proven to work in the differentiated classroom, and how do I do it? This chapter addresses those questions.

METACOGNITIVE INSTRUCTION

Metacognitive instruction has developed over the past 35 years and is one of the most influential concepts in the field of education today as well as the field of learning disabilities (Rosenzweig, Krawec, & Montague, 2011; Palincsar & Brown, 1986; Vaughn & Linan-Thompson, 2003). This emphasis on metacognition is quite understandable, given the characteristics demonstrated by students with learning disabilities and other learning challenges in the differentiated classroom (Rosenzweig et al., 2011). Every veteran teacher has experienced the "dog ate my homework" story from some student with a learning disability. Indeed, most of us have contemplated asking, "Why did you put your homework on the floor, where the dog could reach it?"

In reality, students with learning disabilities often do the homework and then leave it on the desk or a bed where "Rover" can get to it. Alternatively, they may put the paper on their desk at home, on the sofa, or even on the floor—presumably as "dog munchies"—and forget to bring it to class the next day. The point is they often do the work but don't put it in their book bags, which ultimately makes little difference in the long run because they frequently forget to bring their book bags to school anyway! In short, even when students with learning disabilities and other learning challenges do perform the required work, there is no assurance that their relative deficit in organizational skills will allow them to present that work to the teacher.

Organizational difficulties, however, go far beyond failing to turn in work. In fact, many veteran teachers clearly understand why students with learning challenges have so much difficulty with schoolwork. Consider a fifth-grade class in which the teacher makes the following assignment.

OK, class. Since our social studies assignment involves writing our congressperson, I want you to put away your social studies books. Take out your language arts text, and turn to page 189. On that page you will find the format for a business letter, and I want you to use your laptop computers and write a business letter to your congressperson. Use the format for the letter from page 189. Billy will write the address for you on the dry-erase board. When you have finished, e-mail those to me, and we'll share those letters with each other before we mail them.

This assignment involves a minimum of five different instructions—which must be followed in sequence in order to ensure success—as well as several additional critical pieces of information (including one piece of information that is not even available yet—the address). Given the organizational problems noted above, why would teachers expect students with learning disabilities to successfully transition into this new task? In fact, much of the frustration that first-year teachers feel in dealing with students with learning disabilities and other learning challenges stems from failure to successfully transition from one activity to another. Students, in turn, are often left in the dark because of the complexity of instructions offered during transition periods between classes.

What Is Metacognition?

Metacognitive instruction involves providing students with the tools to assist them in improving their organization skills, their thinking and information-processing skills, and ultimately completing their assignments successfully (Rosenzweig et al., 2011; Palincsar & Brown, 1986). The term *metacognition* may loosely be defined as "thinking about one's thinking" and research over the years has shown that metacognitive skills are an important predictor of academic success (Mason & Hedin, 2011; Rosenzweig et al, 2011). Metacognition has been described as "inner language" that students use to guide their behaviors and their schoolwork, and it may include many skills. Again, different authors often list different components of metacognition, but at a minimum, the concept of metacognition includes the following:

- Talking oneself through planning the steps necessary to complete a task
- Ordering those steps into the correct sequence
- Monitoring one's progress on those steps

While the term metacognitive instruction is used less frequently today, terms with similar meaning are frequently found in the instructional literature, including learning strategies instruction, cognitive strategy instruction, or strategy instruction, as noted above. The critical element in these forms of cognitive strategy instruction is that these instructional approaches involve providing a structuring mechanism or planning and instructional support for a child to assist that child in completing the assigned task. Cognitive strategies help students think about their assignment, plan the sequence of steps required, and monitor how they are doing on each step.

Cognitive Strategies and Differentiated Instruction

From the perspective of differentiated instruction, cognitive strategy instruction impacts all three critical components of differentiation, as identified by Tomlinson (1999); content, process, and product. Cognitive strategy instruction often involves reordering the learning content or organizing content in a different fashion as the graphic organizers discussed in the last chapter indicate. Cognitive strategy instruction, likewise, impacts the learning process, since cognitive strategy training typically involves providing

> From the perspective of differentiated instruction, cognitive strategy instruction impacts all three critical components: content, process, and product.

the student with specific process-oriented steps to follow while completing an educational task.

Finally cognitive strategy instruction often impacts the final product of the learning. For example, when using a cognitive strategy, teachers have the option of evaluating not only a completed paper or project from the student but, in addition, teachers can often evaluate the steps the student completed while working on that paper or product. The case study presented later in this chapter provides an example in which teachers could evaluate a student's reading comprehension, as well as his completion of steps in the cognitive strategy that resulted in improved comprehension. The products that frequently result from cognitive strategy training can be evaluated independently, and they often trace the students' thinking during the educational task. Of course, that type of product often provides extensive insight into how the students did the work, and teachers can often troubleshoot the students' thought processes.

Research over the past several decades is strongly supportive of cognitive strategy instruction, and today, teachers typically incorporate a wide variety of these cognitive strategy ideas into their teaching (Bulgren, Deshler, & Lenz, 2007; Lenz, 2006; Lenz et al., 2007; Mason & Hedin, 2011; Mason, Snyder, Sukhram, & Kedem, 2006; Therrien, Hughes, Kapelski, & Mokhtari, 2009). Furthermore, with consistent and regular practice in these cognitive strategy techniques, students will begin to develop their own cognitive strategies; thus, these cognitive skills will generalize across classes and impact achievement positively over the long term (Iseman & Naglieri, 2011). Over time, students with learning disabilities and other learning challenges will be much better able to plan, organize, and complete complex assignments if they are trained using cognitive strategy instruction (Mason & Hedin, 2011; Therrien et al., 2009).

> At a time when knowledge is expanding drastically, the major focus of education should be cognitive mastery of the processes that enable a child to interpret factual knowledge, and both cognitive strategy training and technology-based learning facilitate that paradigm shift.

In some ways, the emphasis on cognitive strategy instruction parallels the current arguments for teaching 21st century learning skills; both suggest that the teaching/learning process is currently being transformed (Bender & Waller, 2011a). Many argue that, at a time when knowledge is expanding so drastically, the major focus of education should be not mastery of discrete factual knowledge but, rather, the mastery of the cognitive processes that enable a child to interpret factual knowledge. Both strategy training and the types of creative, technology-based learning activities discussed in Chapter 3 will facilitate that shift in what "learning" means (Bender & Waller, 2011a).

In this expanded view of the teaching/learning process, the highest goal of education would be to enable every student to develop into a successful metacognitive thinker—one who carefully considers the various aspects of the available knowledge and its relationship to the assigned task and who then completes the required steps in sequence, monitoring his or her own performance while using modern instructional technologies whenever possible. If this is a realistic goal for educating students with learning disabilities—I would argue that it is the only worthy goal—then cognitive strategies should be emphasized in virtually every differentiated classroom in general education.

COGNITIVE STRATEGY INTERVENTIONS IN DIFFERENTIATED CLASSES

Metacognitive strategy instruction quickly evolved into the development of specific cognitive strategies and/or learning strategies for specific academic tasks (Bender, 2008; Gajria, Jitendra, Sood, & Sacks, 2007). As noted previously, students with learning disabilities and other struggling students often demonstrate a variety of organizational problems and can benefit from cognitive strategy approaches that delineate how they should proceed in accomplishing a specific task (Lenz, 2006; Lenz et al., 2007; Therrien et al., 2009; Whitaker, Harvey, Hassel, Linden, & Tutterrow, 2006). A number of researchers now advocate highly involved training in content enhancements or cognitive strategies that are specific to particular learning tasks (Hagaman, Luschen, & Reid, 2010; Lenz, 2006; Lenz et al., 2007; Schumaker & Deshler, 2003).

For example, consider how the organizational problems of a student with a learning disability, as described previously, may play out when the student is expected to complete a complex assignment such as developing a theme or research paper. To complete this assignment, the student must, at a minimum, select a topic, identify questions/issues within that topic, research each of these topics by reading and taking lengthy notes, select the appropriate order in which to present these different issues, write a first draft, edit, and then complete a second draft and a final paper. These steps can be quite daunting for the average learner, and for a student with a learning disability or other learning challenge, these steps actually prevent the student from accomplishing the task. In short, some type of *strategy* that spells out these various steps and the order for them is critical. Thus, cognitive strategy training for students with learning difficulties emerged, whereby specific strategies (i.e., a set of specific planning and monitoring steps) may be taught to the student to help with that specific educational activity (Lenz, 2006; Whitaker et al., 2006).

What Is a Cognitive Strategy?

A cognitive strategy or learning strategy is a mnemonic device or acronym that assists a student in understanding and completing an academic task, usually by specifying the series of steps to be completed in sequential order (Bulgren et al., 2007; Hagaman et al., 2010; Lenz et al., 2007). Many strategies are summarized in the form of an acronym that the student is expected to memorize and subsequently apply.

> A cognitive strategy or learning strategy is a mnemonic device or acronym that assists a student in understanding and completing an academic task, usually by specifying the series of steps to be completed in sequential order.

Although various theorists have developed a variety of strategies (Hagaman et al., 2010; Iseman & Naglieri, 2011), much of the early research on strategy training was associated with Dr. Donald Deshler and his coworkers at the University of Kansas Institute for Learning Disabilities (Bulgren et al., 2007; Lenz, 2006; Lenz et al., 2007; Schumaker & Deshler, 2003). An array of those early learning strategies is presented in Box 6.1.

BOX 6.1: FREQUENTLY USED LEARNING STRATEGIES

Common Learning Strategies

RAP	A reading comprehension strategy for paragraph comprehension	COPS	An editing strategy for checking a paragraph written by the student
R	Read the paragraph	C	Capitalization
A	Ask questions about the content	O	Overall appearance
P	Paraphrase the content	P	Punctuation
		S	Spelling
SCORER	A strategy for taking multiple-choice tests	RIDER	A visual imagery strategy
S	Schedule your time	R	Read the sentence
C	Clue words	I	Imagine a picture of it in your mind
O	Omit difficult questions		
R	Read carefully	D	Describe how the new image differs from the old
E	Estimate your answer	E	Evaluate to see that the image contains everything
R	Review your work		
		R	Repeat as you read the next sentence

NOTE: Learning strategies are available from a variety of sources (see Day & Elksnin, 1994; Ellis, 1994). Also, the University of Kansas Center for Research on Learning (Lawrence, KS) offers training in strategy instruction.

This early research represents only a small percentage of the growing body of research articles supporting cognitive strategy training, but that early work was very influential. That early work indicated that use of cognitive strategies created rather dramatic increases in reading, math, and language arts performance and/or improved performance on many other educational tasks for students with learning disabilities and other learning difficulties (Day & Elksnin, 1994; Gajria et al, 2007; Iseman & Naglieri, 2011; Lenz, 2006; Schumaker & Deshler, 2003).

More specifically, a cognitive strategy may be thought of as a content enhancement or a method of cognitively planning the performance of a learning task, completing the steps involved in the task, and monitoring completion of the task (Chalk, Hagen-Burke, & Burke, 2005; Iseman & Naglieri, 2011). As one example, Box 6.2 presents a simple learning strategy designed by Korinek and Bulls (1996) that may be used to assist a student with a learning disability in a theme-paper writing assignment. By completing the steps designated in this strategy, the student can organize his or her efforts, sequentially complete the correct tasks, and eventually complete the assignment.

BOX 6.2: SCORE A: A LEARNING STRATEGY FOR WRITING A THEME PAPER

SCORE A: A Research Paper Writing Strategy

Strategy steps include the following:

S   Select a subject

C   Create categories

O   Obtain resources

R   Read and take notes

E   Evenly organize the information

A   Apply the process writing steps

    Planning

    Drafting

    Revising

As this example indicates, the steps in this strategy form a heuristic the student memorizes to complete the task (Korinek & Bulls, 1996). This particular strategy would be used by elementary, middle school, and secondary school students in the general education classroom when a report, a research paper, or a theme paper was assigned in a subject area class. Note that cognitive strategy training of this nature can be differentiated from "study skills" instruction. Whereas study skills include such things as writing down assignments and allocating time for homework, a cognitive strategy encompasses a metacognitive plan for completing a specific type of school-related task as well as structuring the inner dialogue of the student to help monitor his own performance on the task.

Researchers have now developed a wide array of strategies that address various educational tasks (Day & Elksnin, 1994; Bulgren et al., 2007; Iseman & Naglieri, 2011; Lenz, 2006; Lenz et al., 2007), and new strategies are being developed all the time and cover an even wider array of activities. For example, Whitaker and her colleagues (2006) developed a new strategy—the FISH strategy—to assist students in decoding words. This strategy provides a set of guidelines to focus the student on parts of the unknown word. Further, coupling the FISH cognitive strategy with the idea of "hooking a fish" can serve as a useful mnemonic to assist students in memorizing this strategy. Also, given enough practice, this strategy can become the basis for word decoding for students over the years (Whitaker et al., 2006). Box 6.3 presents several recently developed cognitive strategies.

Learning strategies have also been developed to provide assistance for students with learning disabilities in nonacademic tasks. Nelson, Smith, and Dodd (1994), as one example, provided a learning strategy—the SELECT

BOX 6.3: RECENTLY DEVELOPED COGNITIVE STRATEGIES

F I S H—a cognitive strategy for decoding words

F—Find the rime (the first vowel and the rest of the word)

I—Identify the rime (by identifying a word you know that ends like that)

S—Say the rime (the word you know without the first sound)

H—Hook the new onset (the new beginning sound) to the rime

S E L E C T—a cognitive strategy for completing a job application

S—Survey the job application

E—Emphasize words about previous jobs

L—Location cues—locate blank lines that cue you for information

E—Enter the information requested

C—Check that all information is accurate

T—Turn in your application

strategy—which was designed to assist students in completing job applications. Their research proved the value of this strategy. This strategy in presented in Box 6.3 above.

As described in Chapter 2, the mandate of universal design suggests that teachers should use a variety of strategies and tactics to make content accessible for students with learning disabilities and other learning challenges in the general education classroom. Cognitive strategies such as those described here can assist in that regard. Strategies have been developed for many tasks that students must complete, including:

test-taking skills	self-questioning
word identification	searching for answers in text
using pictures in texts	visual imagery to improve comprehension
chapter reading assignments	completing job applications.

Some strategies are independent; others include sub-strategies for various steps. For example, note the sub-strategies in SCORE A for the writing process. The level of detail in many strategies and sub-strategies indicated that, from the perspective of differentiated instruction, most cognitive strategy training is directed toward the processes of learning, though many involve reformulating the learning content as well.

Using Cognitive Strategies in the Differentiated Classroom

Judicious application of these cognitive strategies can facilitate differentiated instruction, given the learning-style differences seen in most general education classrooms. For example, in Box 6.1 above, two cognitive strategies were presented that address reading comprehension, RAP and RIDER. Note that the RAP strategy would probably be more appropriate for students with a linguistic learning preference, since that strategy involves linguistic skill, specifically self-questioning on the content and noting linguistically the main idea and details in the text. In contrast, the RIDER strategy may be more appropriate for students with a learning preference for spatial learning, as that strategy depends on using one's imagination to create a mental picture of the reading content, and then revising that picture with each additional sentence.

Although learning strategies can be used in various ways, Dr. Don Deshler and the other researchers associated with the University of Kansas suggest an eight-step model for instruction in any particular learning strategy. These steps are intended to provide guidance for the teacher in implementing strategic instruction, and many teachers employ variations of these instructional steps (Lenz, 2006; Schumaker & Deshler, 2003). While these steps vary slightly from one strategy to another, this general outline is recommended for most cognitive strategy training. Also, for teachers who may be interested, specific strategy instruction training is provided by the University of Kansas Center for Research on Learning in Lawrence, Kansas.

One major strength of this instructional model is that this is one of the few instructional models that specifically addresses the issue of transfer of learning into the general education class. For students with learning disabilities, this strategic instruction can be the single critical component that results in success in the general education class. The steps in strategy instruction are described below.

Step 1: Pretest and Commitment

First, a student with learning disabilities is tested to determine if he or she needs a strategy for a particular task. The results of the assessment are explained to the student, and the student is informed about the level of performance the new strategy would make possible. A decision is then made involving matching a particular strategy to the task and setting (Day & Elksnin, 1994) and determining whether the student will learn the new strategy. Students should be encouraged to "opt in" to learning the strategy; the cognitive strategies instructional approach stresses the need for student involvement in this decision and student commitment to the decision to learn a new strategy. This step usually takes one instructional period.

Step 2: Describe the Strategy

During the second step, the strategy is introduced and the various components of the strategy are described to the student. This step focuses on the key elements of the strategy and how these components are used. Also, the student is told where and under what conditions a strategy may be applied. This also usually takes one class period, although appropriate applications of the strategy will be discussed throughout the course of training.

Step 3: Model the Strategy

On the next day, the teacher models each step of the strategy while discussing the use of the strategy out loud. Thus, the teacher is modeling how a student should give himself or herself verbal instruction (quiet verbal instruction or "inner language") on using the strategy. Each aspect of the strategy is modeled, and students are encouraged to ask questions. This instructional period may include several different tasks, and the teacher may prompt students to model particular aspects of the strategy at various points.

Step 4: Verbal Rehearsal of the Strategy

The expectation for students in this instructional model is that students must learn the strategy by rote; they must state the strategy steps very quickly before they attempt to apply the strategy. The students are also required to identify the action to be taken in each step and tell why each step is important for the strategy overall. This step is intended to facilitate independence in strategy application and can usually be completed by students with learning difficulties in one instructional period.

Step 5: Practice With Controlled Materials

Prior to using the strategy on difficult grade-level materials, the student should master the application of the strategy on simpler materials. The assumption behind this approach is that the difficulty of the material should not impair the student's ability to learn the cognitive strategy. Consequently, the strategy should be applied on "controlled materials." Controlled materials are materials at the student's academic performance level rather than at his or her grade level. For example, if the SCORE A strategy presented in Box 6.2 is being taught, the student would first apply that strategy in a two- or three-paragraph theme paper on material that the student had previously mastered. The student would be coached by the teacher using explicit corrective feedback. If a sixth-grade student with a learning disability was completing science work at a Grade 4 level, he or she should be given a theme assignment at the fourth-grade level to learn the strategy.

A daily record of the student's performance on both the theme and the student's complete and accurate application of the SCORE A strategy would be kept during this step. Typically these data are kept in the form of an X/Y axis chart, making this intervention an excellent progress-monitoring intervention for Tiers 2 and 3 in an RTI procedure. Practice on controlled materials will continue over a period of time (perhaps as many as two or three weeks) until the strategy is totally known and completely understood by the student on lower grade-level materials. In short, the student must master strategy application at something close to 100% before moving on. After the student has demonstrated mastery of the strategy in Grade 4 level materials, he or she should move on to expectations for Grade 5 level, perhaps a four-paragraph themed paper. Also, the student should be encouraged to chart his or her progress on mastery of the learning strategy itself.

Step 6: Practice With Grade-Appropriate Materials

In this instructional model, the level of complexity on which the student practices is gradually increased until the materials approximate grade-appropriate level materials for that particular student. This step also involves the fading out of various prompts and cues the student used in earlier steps. For the student described above, after mastery of the SCORE A strategy on Grade 5 themes, the student would move into expectations for a more complex paper at Grade 6 level. Mastery of the strategy on grade-level materials usually takes between five and 10 instructional periods. Again, this phase is charted to present a daily picture of the student's progress. These charted data should be regularly reviewed with the student to point out progress over time.

Step 7: Commitment to Generalize the Strategy

Once the student has mastered the strategy on grade-level materials, the student must be encouraged to see the value of generalizing the new strategy to other, similar educational tasks in the general education classroom. A commitment should then be elicited from the student to apply the strategy on all theme-writing assignments in all subject areas. This discussion with the student may take as little as a few minutes during one of the instructional periods, but this commitment to generalize is considered a critical step in the learning process.

Step 8: Generalization and Maintenance

After the student makes a commitment to generalize the strategy, several generalization and maintenance phases begin. These generalization and maintenance steps are, in many ways, the most important aspects of this model. There is little advantage in spending the number of instructional periods discussed above to teach a student the SCORE A strategy unless that student is then taught how to apply that strategy throughout his or her schooling. However, if this strategy is mastered, the student then has a skill that can enhance learning in numerous classes in the future—many of which are dependent on one's ability to successfully write extended themes or reports.

The generalization step involves three phases. The first phase is *orientation to generalization*. This is designed to make the student aware of situations in which the new skill may be tried. The student is encouraged to make adaptations of the original strategy for various types of tests. The second phase is *activation*, where the student is given specific assignments to apply the strategy in grade-appropriate materials from other general education classes. Throughout this process, the special education teacher is encouraged to work with the general education teacher in encouraging use of the strategy. The teacher then checks the output of the strategy.

Finally, a *maintenance* phase is implemented. The students who have been trained in a particular strategy should be periodically reminded to use that strategy, and the teacher should check the work output when the strategy is applied.

CASE STUDY

A Tier 2 Cognitive Strategy Intervention

Although much of the research on strategy instruction predates the RTI emphasis of the last decade, the cognitive strategies interventions that have been developed certainly can provide excellent interventions at any level within the RTI pyramid. In particular, the daily progress monitoring that is built into the cognitive strategy training model, as described above, fits nicely within a Tier 2 intervention. In fact, this author has worked with various elementary and middle schools in which the content emphasized within the Tier 2 intervention for struggling students was cognitive strategies training aimed at reading improvement. With that in mind, the following case study describes the use of a cognitive strategy in a Tier 2 intervention.

As described in Box 6.1, the RAP strategy is a strategy for paraphrasing reading material in order to increase reading comprehension (Day & Elksnin, 1994; Hagaman et al., 2010). This was one of the first strategies developed by Deshler and his colleagues, and it is still very applicable from the lower grades up through secondary school. Because this strategy is focused on reading comprehension improvement, it is very appropriate as a Tier 2 or Tier 3 RTI intervention.

Cognitive Strategy Training

Let's assume that a special education teacher, Ms. Rooten, has three students with reading comprehension difficulties and one student with a previously diagnosed learning disability in an inclusive seventh-grade history class during the first period each day. For this example, assume that this class includes 19 other students as well.

The reading level of the students with learning disabilities ranges from Grade 4 to Grade 6, and independent of these three students, the reading level for the entire inclusive class ranges from Grade 1 Level 4 up through Grade 1 Level 11—in short, the typical reading variation in a general education, eighth-grade classroom today.

Ms. Rooten has requested some assistance from Mr. Mosely, the school's reading coach. On the first day, Ms. Rooten and Mr. Mosely review the statewide-assessment reading scores for each of these four targeted students from the previous year as well as their reading performance in Ms. Rooten's class during the first month of school. In many middle and high school grade levels, this type of procedure serves as the screening for Tier 2 interventions (Bender, 2012b). These two educators make a data-based decision and determine that a Tier 2 intervention is necessary for the four students described above.

Mr. Mosely then suggests implementation of a cognitive strategy that will enhance reading comprehension for these students. They decide to use the RAP strategy for the three students with comprehension difficulties and the one student with a learning disability. Mr. Mosely agrees to work in Ms. Rooten's class with the small group of students to get this intervention going. On the first day of the intervention, he works with the entire class and hands out prepared readings on the topic under study in the social studies class, each of which consists of five content paragraphs. He also gives the students a participatory organizer such as the one found in Box 6.4 and tells them to complete the organizer as they read.

BOX 6.4: RAP PARTICIPATORY ORGANIZER

A RAP Worksheet

For each paragraph in the five-paragraph reading passage, the student should list the main idea and two supporting details in the space provided below.

1. Main Idea _____

   Detail 1: _____

   Detail 2: _____

2. Main Idea _____

   Detail 1: _____

   Detail 2: _____

3. Main Idea _____

   Detail 1: _____

   Detail 2: _____

4. Main Idea _____

   Detail 1: _____

   Detail 2: _____

5. Main Idea _____

   Detail 1: _____

   Detail 2: _____

After working through those five content paragraphs and the organizer for 15 to 20 minutes, Mr. Mosely then describes to the class the importance of noting main ideas and supporting details as content material is read. After that, Ms. Rooten teaches the remainder of the class as she normally would, and she agrees to grade the participatory organizers for the class overnight. However, Mr. Mosely grades and scores the organizers for the four target students. In his scoring, he notes each student's score on recognizing the main idea and two important supporting details from each paragraph; each is worth 1 point if correctly identified by the student. Those points are then totaled to get a score ranging from zero to 15. That score becomes each target student's pretest score on implementation of the RAP strategy.

On the second day, Mr. Mosely administers a 10-question comprehension test on the passage to each target student, working with them as a small group in Ms. Rooten's class. The percentage of correct responses becomes the comprehension score for that student on that story. Also on the second day, the test results on the RAP strategy worksheet and the comprehension test are reviewed with each target student. Mr. Mosely talks with these students about their need to improve their reading, and each target student is asked if he or she would like to learn a new strategy to help better remember what has been read. They are told that the strategy is their secret, and they are the only ones that will use it in the social studies class.

The students are then invited to write down a long-term goal stating their commitment to work hard and learn the strategy. Also, an X/Y axis data chart is initiated to show their performance on the first RAP worksheet and the first comprehension test. These data charts will be completed daily for each student, recording daily performance on the RAP scores and the reading comprehension scores. A sample progress monitoring data chart for one of these students, Billy, is presented in Figure 6.1.

The lesson on the next day, involves a description of the RAP strategy. Using a cue card that displays the steps of the strategy, Mr. Mosely will first discuss the meaning of paraphrasing and the use of this skill in various subjects. He and Ms. Rooten may choose to include all the students in the class for this training over the next several days, or they may do this training exclusively for the four target students. Mr. Mosely will point out the advantages of the ability to paraphrase in terms of increased comprehension. Students are then encouraged to set goals for learning the strategy with a suggested guideline provided by the teacher. Mr. Mosely will then discuss the strategy steps in order, carefully giving the students examples.

First, reading is discussed as attending to the meaning of the words. Secondly, several ways to find the main idea (such as looking for repetitive words in the paragraph or studying the first sentence) and details from the paragraph are identified. Next, the need to put the ideas into the student's own words is discussed. Finally, the criteria for a good paraphrase are presented to the student so that they know how their work will be graded.

The third step of strategy training provides the opportunity for the teacher to model the strategy. Mr. Mosely will read an appropriate passage of five paragraphs and implement the RAP strategy. Before starting, he will verbally

Figure 6.1   Tier 2 RTI Progress Monitoring Chart for Billy

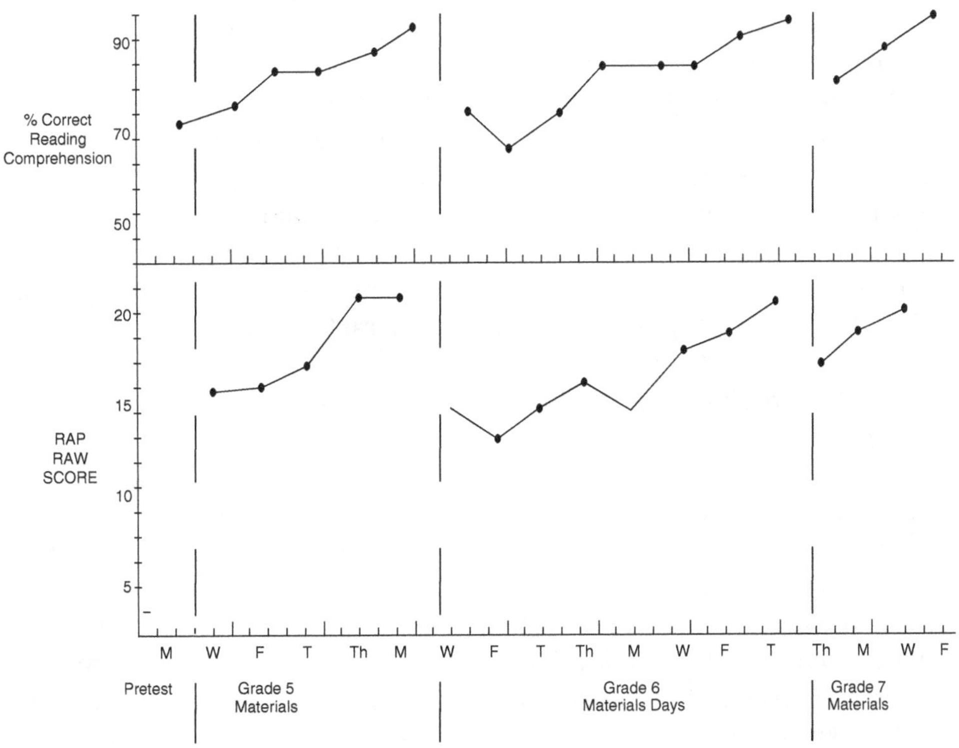

remind himself of the strategy, thus modeling the self-instruction aspect that is critical to cognitive strategy instruction. He will then read the passage aloud and discuss the strategy with himself. "Now that I have read the first paragraph, I have to state in my own words what it was about. After that, I'll list the main idea and some details." After several ideas are specified, Mr. Mosely will put these on his participatory organizer. This is done for the first two paragraphs, and students then become involved in helping with the last several paragraphs.

The next step in cognitive strategy training is verbal practice of the components of the strategy. Each student should be able to name the series of steps from memory and provide information on how to complete each step. With a cue card in front of the small group that summarizes the steps of the RAP strategy, the students should be encouraged to state the next step of the strategy or to answer any question about that strategy that Mr. Mosely might ask. For example, they should be able to give at least two suggestions for finding the main idea of a paragraph (i.e., sometimes it is the first sentence, but other times it is the most frequently stated general idea, etc.).

Practice on Controlled Materials

The next day begins the fifth step, implementation of the strategy through controlled practice for paraphrasing. Each of the target students is given a five-paragraph reading selection at the student's independent reading level. By selecting these reading selections on the topic of study from the social studies class, the Tier 2 intervention will not only build Billy's reading comprehension, it will also help him learn the subject content. Of course, the independent reading level for a student is defined as the grade level at which a student has 95% mastery of the words, and that reading level will typically be several grade levels below the grade-level placement for struggling students.

In this example, the data in Figure 6.1 indicate that Billy's independent reading level was Grade 5, so he would be provided a five-paragraph reading selection on the Great Depression that Mr. Mosely obtained from a fifth-grade level social studies text. To begin the day for this phase, Mr. Mosely briefly reviews the steps in the strategy with the students. Then, the students are told to use the RAP strategy as they read each paragraph, recording one main idea and two major details for each.

The RAP reading worksheet presented in Box 6.4 is given to Billy along with the reading selection. These will be scored using the same criteria as the pretest. If only 20 minutes of the social studies time is devoted to the strategy, the students will probably complete a reading selection and the RAP worksheet on one day. They will then need to take a reading comprehension test on that content on the next day. The data chart presents data collected in that fashion. Again, the comprehension test typically is a 10-question test on the reading passage, and that score, coupled with the score on the RAP worksheet, provides the progress monitoring data for Billy's Tier 2 reading comprehension intervention. Thus, the student completes a RAP reading worksheet and a comprehension test for each five-paragraph passage read, and each of these scores will be placed on the student's individual progress monitoring chart.

Also, each target student's work on both the paraphrase worksheet and the comprehension test for each reading selection should be used as an opportunity to provide corrective and positive feedback. Frequent feedback is a critical component of Tier 2 instruction, and the cognitive training approach facilitates such feedback. To provide appropriate feedback, Mr. Mosely should identify several things that each student did well and share these with the student. Also, he will review the requirements that were not met when a student did not receive credit for an answer on the RAP reading worksheet or the comprehension test. After both a RAP reading worksheet and a comprehension test are completed on a five-paragraph reading segment, the student will read another reading selection at the same grade level. This series of daily lessons is continued until the student reaches mastery level at 90% accuracy in both paraphrasing and comprehension of the material at that grade level.

On average, students may be expected to reach mastery of this step in three to 10 practice attempts at each grade level, though some struggling students or students with learning disabilities may take longer. Thus, if a student's reading level is Grade 5 and the student is in a seventh-grade general education social studies class, he or she may take from 20 to 30 days to achieve mastery at grade-level work in Grades 5 and 6.

Practice on Grade-Level Reading Texts

The next step emphasizes grade-appropriate practice in reading comprehension, and the four target students in the Tier 2 intervention will, in all probability, reach this step on different days. Each student will then be given grade-appropriate materials, such as a five-paragraph reading selection from their social studies text, and the RAP worksheet to use. It is important in this step that the reading passages be taken from a text that is normally used at his or her grade level, as this shows the students, rather dramatically, that their efforts have improved their reading in an important and relevant way. Thus, Billy would begin working on Grade 7 materials from his social studies text during this phase of the intervention.

Generalization of These Reading Skills

The following step involves the post-test and student commitment to generalize the strategy. Billy will be required to complete a paraphrase task and a comprehension test for a passage that consists of five paragraphs of reading from his social studies book. Results of these will be noted on the progress chart, and Mr. Mosely will discuss the entire learning procedure with Billy, pointing out the progress depicted in the chart. He will remind Billy of his goal from the beginning of the intervention and then obtain a commitment from Billy to generalize the strategy to other textbooks in social studies and other general education classrooms. This step takes only one instructional period, but the commitment step must be done with each student individually and is critical for students with reading comprehension problems.

The next day, Mr. Mosely begins the final step with Billy—generalization. Billy is asked to use his textbook, and Mr. Mosely gathers reading material from other settings, such as the home, newspapers, and magazines that interest Billy. Mr. Mosely will discuss with Billy the use of RAP with each reading selection. At this stage, Ms. Rooten—the general education teacher—should become more involved by meeting with Billy and Mr. Mosely outside of class to discuss strategy application in the materials in social studies classes. Billy will make cue cards for the strategy and tape these inside the front of each textbook, and other cues for using the strategy will be discussed. Ms. Rooten will make an agreement with Billy to remind him to use the RAP strategy whenever appropriate on a social studies reading assignment.

The next day begins the activation phase of the generalization step. Mr. Mosely may provide a small pocket-size notebook for Billy and ask that Billy make a note each time he uses the RAP strategy. Billy should be told to note the date and the type of reading material on which the strategy was used: textbook, newspaper, online reading, novel, or magazine. Mr. Mosely might assign specific reading activities for the student to complete sometime within the next 24 hours. These should each be carefully graded by Mr. Mosely and Billy, with corrective feedback given where necessary. Billy should be required to complete at least six different activities of this nature. Mr. Mosely will also discuss the completion of the diary each day with Billy for the first week, but that support will be reduced to weekly meetings on the diary for the final two weeks.

Maintenance is the last phase of the generalization step (Day & Elksnin, 1994). This consists of a series of evaluations similar to the pre-test and is generally completed every other week after the student completes the strategy training described above. At this point, Billy has, in all probability, internalized the RAP strategy, and that is likely to facilitate his reading comprehension across the grade levels and for all types of reading materials. Of course, both

Ms. Rooten and Mr. Mosely should continue to remind Billy to perform the RAP strategy on appropriate reading material during Billy's classes.

Implementation of Cognitive Strategies

As can be seen, the example above uses a number of methods that are the hallmark of both metacognition and differentiated instruction, including modeling, scaffolds for memorizing the task (e.g., RAP), use of inner language, corrective and timely feedback, and repeated guided practice. Use of effective teaching behaviors such as these in a focused, coordinated manner greatly enhances the efficacy of the cognitive strategies instructional approach. Although the example above presented the ideal collaboration between a general education teacher and a reading coach, general education teachers who do not have such a collaborative relationship should also consider implementing this cognitive strategies instructional approach. Of course, this may be a bit more difficult for a single teacher to implement, yet the results of modifying the learning process through cognitive strategies instruction will greatly increase the academic performance for many students in the general education class, and this procedure will certainly help struggling readers over the long term.

From the perspective of RTI, cognitive strategies training may be used at any level of the RTI hierarchy. The data on Billy's performance presented in Box 6.5 indicated both his accurate completion of the RAP worksheet organizer and his comprehension assessments for each reading passage. Remember that these measures come one day apart for each five-paragraph reading selection, as indicated on the chart. On fifth-grade materials, it took Billy 10 days to complete work on five different reading selections. In that time, he reached his goal of 90% accuracy on both the RAP organizer and his comprehension questions. On sixth-grade level materials, it took 16 days to complete work on eight reading selections and reach the goals. However, it only took six days to reach his goals on seventh-grade materials. This chart does not show generalization or maintenance data since such data are collected weekly or every other week.

As these data indicated, it is frequently the case that students speed up on reaching their goals later during these interventions as they master the cognitive strategies. Also, these Tier 2 intervention data indicate that Billy does not have a learning disability because he responded quite well to this cognitive strategies intervention. In his case, he merely needed some supplemental reading comprehension instruction in order to get back on track in his reading performance for subject-area textbooks.

Also note that, in this example, Mr. Mosely and Ms. Rooten found a way to implement parts of this training for all students in the general education social studies class while still targeting four students for a specific, highly effective Tier 2 intervention in reading comprehension. Again, cognitive strategies interventions such as these make excellent Tier 2 and Tier 3 interventions, as well as being quite applicable in Tier 1 for the entire general education class.

Research on Cognitive Strategies

Research over the past two decades has indicated the effectiveness of cognitive strategies instruction (Bulgren et al., 2007; Day & Elksnin, 1994; Gajria et al., 2007; Iseman & Naglieri, 2011; Lenz et al., 2007; Therrien et al., 2009). While a full review of this research is not appropriate in this context, the research above has shown that in-depth instruction in cognitive strategies, such as the implementation training described above, improves academic performance for students with learning disabilities and many other struggling students in the class. This would suggest that implementation of a cognitive strategies training approach would be very appropriate for most general education classrooms.

However, we must stress that implementation of cognitive strategies training involves more than merely copying a cognitive strategy on a poster and pointing in that general direction occasionally. As shown in the implementation guidelines and the case study above, cognitive strategies training does take some time, but the rewards in terms of students' academic performance will typically justify that time. Given the strength of this research, virtually every teacher should be implementing this method of instruction in some form in the differentiated general education class.

SELF-MONITORING AND SELF-REGULATION

Many educators now advocate teaching students to take responsibility for their own attention behaviors and their own learning. This process is typically referred to as self-monitoring and/or self-regulation of instruction (Chalk et al., 2005; McConnell, 1999; Rafferty, 2010; Wery & Nietfeld, 2010). As discussed in the chapter on technology, throughout our nation's history, teachers have taken the perspective that education is a process done to and for students. Students have traditionally been viewed as passive recipients of the educational process, and active participation of students in planning their own learning and monitoring that learning was not widely emphasized. This view was, historically, a serious problem for students with learning disabilities and other learning challenges because these students are much more likely to become distracted and uninvolved in the learning process. That lack of engagement leads, inevitably, to academic deficits.

> Lack of engagement leads, inevitably, to academic deficits.

However, this view of the learner as passive recipient of instruction began to change in the 1970s, with the increasing emphasis on metacognition. Moreover, the concept of universal design would suggest that teachers should teach in a fashion that encourages students to take personal responsibility for their own learning. Daniel Hallahan and his coworkers at the University of Virginia were among the first researchers to postulate that students should begin to assume personal responsibility for their attending behavior and learning (Hallahan, Lloyd, & Stoller, 1982; Hallahan & Sapona, 1983).

Further, the much more recent research on the human brain and learning has demonstrated the importance of "executive functioning" during learning tasks, a term that represents the thought processes involved in planning a task—or considering how to undertake a task—and monitoring the task compared to merely doing the task. Prior to actually initiating a task, most successful students take a moment to consider what a task requires and how a task may be accomplished; this is executive functioning.

Educators now realize that the success of education is in large measure dependent on the responsibility students take for their own learning and behavior (McConnell, 1999; Rafferty, 2010; Sousa & Tomlinson, 2011), and the brain-compatible instructional literature has supported this view quite dramatically. Students with learning disabilities and other learning challenges must be intimately involved in the tasks of learning if learning is to take place. In short, it is very difficult if not impossible to teach anyone anything unless they are willing and motivated to learn. Thus, students must monitor their own learning (Jitendra, Hoppes, & Yen, 2000; Mason & Hedin, 2011), and ultimately take responsibility for it. The self-monitoring strategy presented below is a metacognitive procedure that addresses this requirement.

Initial research of self-monitoring in the 1970s and 1980s focused on students' attending behaviors and on-task time. Hallahan and his coworkers developed a self-monitoring strategy that involved teaching a student how to pay attention (Hallahan, Lloyd, & Stoller, 1982; Hallahan & Sapona, 1983). Attention in the context of the classroom typically means the ability to repeatedly check one's own orientation and focus on a particular task (McConnell, 1999; Rafferty, 2010). Whereas early research concentrated on the use of self-monitoring to enhance attention of students with learning disabilities (Hallahan & Sapona, 1983), more recent work has focused on using self-monitoring procedures to enhance classroom readiness behaviors (McConnell, 1999; Snyder & Bambara, 1997) or help students monitor their own academic proficiency on specific tasks (Rafferty, 2010; Wery & Nietfeld, 2010).

Self-Monitoring for Attending Behavior

Although teachers through the ages have often told children to "pay attention," very few teachers have ever taught a child exactly *how* to pay attention. The fact is, teachers tend to assume that students know what we mean by that frequently used phrase, "pay attention." However, experience with students with learning disabilities and other learning challenges tells us that these students do not stay on task as well as other students; in short, students with learning difficulties often do not really know how to pay attention. Thus, the initial application of self-monitoring procedures involves teaching students with learning disabilities how to pay attention in class.

The self-monitoring training procedure may be done in either a special education classroom or in the inclusive general education classroom by using the following steps.

Step 1: Identification of the Student

As with all aspects of differentiated instruction, the first task of the teacher is to select the right strategy for the student. Again, this will depend on the students' preferred learning styles, the teacher's relationship with the students, and the types of learning problems demonstrated by each student. There are several guidelines for identifying the type of students for whom self-monitoring may be an effective intervention. First, the self-monitoring strategy to improve on-task behaviors is intended for students with learning challenges who demonstrate rather benign attention problems, such as poor task orientation or an inability to complete worksheets on time rather than overtly aggressive behaviors. This strategy is not as effective for children who do not perform their schoolwork because of violent behaviors or noncompliance in the classroom, though variations of self-monitoring procedures have shown some success, even with these severe behavior problems.

Next, self-monitoring should not be used when a student is being introduced to a new topic or learning task. This is not a strategy to be used during the initial instruction phase of learning. Rather, self-monitoring is most effective when a student is in the independent, drill-and-practice phase of learning. Individual computer work, seatwork, and paper-and-pencil tasks in any basic skill area are appropriate. Also, self-monitoring is more effective for "speeding up" a student than for increasing the student's accuracy in problem completion (Hallahan & Sapona, 1983).

Step 2: Developing the Components of the Self-Monitoring Tactic

During a self-monitoring project, the student is trained to periodically ask himself or herself a very simple question—"Was I paying attention?"—to increase his or her attention skills. The only materials used in this self-monitoring procedure are (1) a "record sheet" on which the student will record his or her attention behavior, and (2) a cue to record the behavior—usually a tape recorder with an audiotape of a bell that rings periodically. Various guidelines have been presented on how to create the record sheet (Hallahan et al., 1982; McConnell, 1999; Rafferty, 2010; Wery & Nietfeld, 2010). A record sheet for this procedure is presented in Figure 6.2.

Teachers may copy and use this record sheet or simply make one. In making a record sheet, the question above should be printed on the sheet at the top, along with places to answer either "yes" or "no" to the question. This question provides the student with a simple memory technique that tells what should be done (i.e., paying attention to the worksheet and the problems it contains). Whenever the student is cued to consider his or her "attention behavior," the student should silently ask, "Was I paying attention?" He or she should then answer the question on the record sheet and return immediately to work.

The second component of the tactic is the cue to record. This may be an audiotape, bell, or tone that will cue the student to ask the question and mark the record sheet. Either a simple cassette tape or an MP3 player may be used as the cue to record, and the tape should present a series of bell tones. It is essential that the time interval between these bell tones vary, but they should range

Figure 6.2   Record Sheet for Monitoring Attention In Class

Was I Paying Attention?

YES	NO

From *Differentiating Instruction for Students With Learning Disabilities: Best Teaching Practices for General and Special Educators*, Second Edition, by William N. Bender. Thousand Oaks, CA: Corwin, 2008. Used with permission.

anywhere from 10 to 90 seconds. Overall, they should average a time interval of about 45 seconds (Hallahan et al., 1982). The student will use the tape or recording as the cue to ask the question above, mark an answer, and return to work. For general education classes, teachers may wish to have the student use headphones to listen to this bell tone to prevent disruption to other students during seatwork.

Step 3: Initial Instruction in Self-Monitoring

Hallahan et al. (1982) also recommended a series of instructional steps by which the teacher actually teaches attention skills. On the first day, the teacher begins instruction by suggesting that the student could finish the work faster and more accurately by learning how to pay attention better. This possibility should be discussed with the target student in an attempt to have the student accept responsibility for the self-monitoring procedures. The dialogue presented in Teaching Tip 6.1 was recommended by Hallahan et al. for this initial self-monitoring instruction.

On the first day, the initial instruction in self-monitoring takes about 15 or 20 minutes. The main points in the training dialogue should be repeated

Teaching Tip 6.1

Instructional Dialogue for Teaching Self-Monitoring

"Johnny, you know how paying attention to your work has been a problem for you. You've heard teachers tell you, 'Pay attention,' 'Get to work,' 'What are you supposed to be doing?' and things like that. Well, today we're going to start something that will help you help yourself pay attention better. First we need to make sure that you know what paying attention means. This is what I mean by paying attention." (Teacher models immediate and sustained attention to task.) "And this is what I mean by not paying attention." (Teacher models inattentive behaviors such as glancing around and playing with objects.) "Now you tell me if I was paying attention." (Teacher models attentive and inattentive behaviors and requires the student to categorize them.) "Okay, now let me show you what we're going to do. Every once in a while, you'll hear a little sound like this." (Teacher plays a tone on tape.) "And when you hear that sound, quietly ask yourself, 'Was I paying attention?' If you answer 'yes,' put a check in this box. If you answer 'no,' put a check in this box. Then go right back to work. When you hear the sound again, ask the question, answer it, mark your answer, and go back to work. Now, let me show you how it works." (Teacher models entire procedure.) "Now, Johnny, I bet you can do this. Tell me what you're going to do every time you hear a tone. Let's try it. I'll start the tape and you work on these papers." (Teacher observes the student's implementation of the entire procedure, praises its correct use, and gradually withdraws his or her presence.)

From *Differentiating Instruction for Students With Learning Disabilities: Best Teaching Practices for General and Special Educators*, Second Edition, by William N. Bender. Thousand Oaks, CA: Corwin, 2008. Used with permission.

in a briefer form, for the first several days with the target student. The student should use the self-monitoring procedure every day during the initial stages of instruction. This instruction will require 10 to 15 days. At that point, the teacher will have a number of work activities on which the student had the opportunity to finish the work in class; these successes should be pointed out to the target student.

Step 4: Weaning Procedures

The goal of self-monitoring of attention is the establishment of good attention skills based on the "habits" of attention, rather than being outwardly dependent on behavior charts and tape-recorded bells. Consequently, teachers should wean the students from the recording sheet and the cue to record (i.e., the bell tone), leaving the "habit" of continually monitoring one's own attending behavior. First, the teacher should wean the student from the bell tones. After a successful 15- to 20-day intervention period using the full self-monitoring procedure, the teacher begins the weaning phase by simply indicating that the student's success in attending to task has increased and that it is no longer necessary to listen to the taped bell sounds. During this initial weaning phase, the student is encouraged, whenever he or she thinks about it, to continue monitoring on-task behavior by asking, "Was I paying attention?" The student should then mark the record sheet, and if the student was paying attention, he or she should self-praise (e.g., give yourself a pat on the back!) and then return to the classwork.

During the second weaning phase, the student is weaned from the recording sheet. The student is given instructions to ask the question whenever the thought occurs, to praise himself or herself for being on task, and then to return to the class work. Generally, five or six days are recommended for each phase of the weaning process.

Efficacy Research on Self-Monitoring

The research on self-monitoring has demonstrated that this procedure works for students across the grade levels in both special education and general education classes, making this an excellent strategy for virtually any differentiated classroom (Barry & Messer, 2003; Hagaman et al., 2010; McConnell, 1999; Rafferty, 2010; Snyder & Bambara, 1997). Next, this procedure may be taught to students in groups in general education classes. Finally, the research above has shown that almost every student with a learning disability or other learning challenge can improve his or her attention using this procedure (Digangi, Magg, & Rutherford, 1991). Research has shown that the on-task behavior of some students more than doubled (from 35% to more than 90% on task), when they were taught specifically what paying attention means. That effectively doubles the educational time in any given year for children with learning difficulties!

Research has now addressed a number of additional questions about the use of self-monitoring. First, for students with attention problems severe enough to warrant medication, this self-monitoring procedure can dramatically enhance attention skills above the effects of medication alone (Barry & Messer, 2003; Harris, Friedlander, Saddler, Frizzelle, & Graham 2005; Mathes & Bender, 1997). Thus, even for students on medication for attention problems, self-monitoring procedures should be used.

Of course, this holds serious implications for instruction in almost every general education classroom today. Specifically, how can any teacher justify not implementing a self-monitoring procedure for students on medication for attention problems when there is solid evidence that this procedure will help? To emphasize the importance of this intervention for some students, Box 6.5 presents a personal experience of this author relative to the critical nature of this self-monitoring technique.

BOX 6.5: PERSONAL EXAMPLE OF SELF-MONITORING

To emphasize the importance of this tactic for students with learning disabilities, allow me to share a personal example that demonstrated how critical this technique can be. As a relatively new higher education faculty member, I taught this self-monitoring technique in a methods class for special education teachers at Concord College, in Athens, West Virginia. In that class, I had an older woman who was the mother of a 14-year-old daughter who had recently been diagnosed with learning disabilities. After the author assigned some readings on this self-monitoring idea, the mother chose to try it with her daughter while the girl completed her homework. The mother later shared with me that this seventh-grade girl would sometimes do her homework for up to three hours per night and still not accomplish a great deal. Of course, with self-monitoring implemented, that student began to complete her homework in about 90 minutes each weekday evening. Both the mother and daughter were ecstatic, but that's not the end of the story. Within just a few weeks, the daughter had requested that her teacher also allow her to do self-monitoring on her school tasks in class (that's when I heard about this little experiment). The teacher knew me and called to ask what self-monitoring was—imagine a student with a learning disability asking to try a particular learning method and the teacher not knowing anything about it! Needless to say, I provided some readings and actually met with that teacher to assist her in getting up to speed on this self-monitoring procedure. Still, the importance of this technique in that young girl's life is obvious. She wanted to learn how to use a method that would help her stay on task and save time on her classwork and homework.

This is the only time in my career that I've had this particular experience, and I will never forget how critically important this technique was for one young girl with a learning disability. To state again, I believe that every teacher in general education and special education classes should be using some version of this technique for students with learning disabilities. Given the attention problems these students demonstrate, I can think of no technique that is more critical.

From *Differentiating Instruction for Students With Learning Disabilities: Best Teaching Practices for General and Special Educators*, Second Edition, by William N. Bender. Thousand Oaks, CA: Corwin, 2008. Used with permission.

SELF-MONITORING FOR INCREASING CLASS READINESS

With the research continually demonstrating the success of self-monitoring procedures for increasing attention among students with learning difficulties, researchers began to apply this self-monitoring concept to behaviors other than attention, including increasing the class preparedness of students with learning challenges or decreasing inappropriate behavior (McConnell, 1999; Snyder & Bambara, 1997). An example of this type of self-monitoring scale is presented in Figure 6.3.

Figure 6.3   Self-Management Recording Sheet for Increasing Class Preparedness

Ten Ways to Behave

Name _____   Class _____
Date _____   Teacher _____

Circle one of the three choices: *3 = always, 2 = most of the time, 1 = did not do.*

1. I worked without disturbing others	3	2	1
2. I participated in class	3	2	1
3. I fouced on the lesson	3	2	1
4. I asked for help when I needed it	3	2	1
5. I helped others when I could	3	2	1
6. I followed teacher direction	3	2	1
7. I completed class assignments	3	2	1
8. I turned in completed assignments	3	2	1
9. I completed all homework	3	2	1
10. I behaved appropriately all period	3	2	1

Student Score _____

28–24 points:	SUPER!	19–14 points:	Fair
23–20 points:	Good	13–0 points:	Make a plan to improve

From *Differentiating Instruction for Students With Learning Disabilities: Best Teaching Practices for General and Special Educators*, Second Edition, by William N. Bender. Thousand Oaks, CA: Corwin, 2008. Used with permission.

Training for this intervention would parallel the training described above for self-monitoring of attention, and the intervention may be easily modified to work in almost any class. Again, the research has shown that self-monitoring along these lines will instill in students their responsibility for learning and for being prepared (Digangi et al., 1991; Harris et al., 2005; Rafferty, 2010; Wery & Nietfeld, 2010).

Self-Management and Self-Regulation of Academic Tasks

More recently, the self-monitoring research has been expanded to include a variety of self-management and self-regulation strategies for students with learning disabilities and other learning challenges (Chalk et al., 2005; Digangi et al., 1991; Rafferty, 2010; Wery & Nietfeld, 2010). For example, Rafferty (2010) recently described an array of self-management instructional approaches stemming from this initial research on self-monitoring, including

- *Self-Monitoring*—interventions to teach students to monitor their behavior, including (1) self-observation, such as that process described above, and (2) self-recording, including both completing the self-monitoring record sheet and then charting one's attending behavior over time on an X/Y axis chart
- *Goal Setting*—using the self-monitoring data and having the student set behavioral goals for improvement
- *Self-Regulating*—using interventions that have a student compare his or her behavior with a set standard of behavior
- *Self-Instruction*—interventions that require students to use self-statements to direct their own behavior (e.g., the RAP strategy described above)
- *Strategy Instruction*—interventions that involve step-by-step completion of the learning task until mastery is reached

Research confirms that all of these forms of self-regulated strategy instruction are effective if the intervention is implemented in a systematic manner (Gajria et al., 2007; Iseman & Naglieri, 2011; Lenz, 2006; Rosenzweig et al., 2011; Palincsar & Brown, 1986; Vaughn & Linan-Thompson, 2003). Further, as these strategies indicate, the self-monitoring research has been very fruitful for educators, in that it has led into a variety of instructional strategies. All of the techniques described herein are implemented using guidelines similar to the instructional guidelines presented herein, and these strategies should be utilized in the differentiated classroom to assist students with learning difficulties.

CONCLUSIONS AND AN INVITATION

In conclusion, this chapter and, in a larger sense, this book have presented an array of instructional strategies and techniques that will foster increased achievement among students with learning disabilities and other learning problems in differentiated classrooms. Of course, many other techniques could have been presented, and in some sense, no book on differentiated instructional strategies is ever "complete." Still, the tactics and instructional strategies presented herein represent many, if not most, of the best practices for the differentiated classroom today. Moreover, those strategies selected for inclusion here represent either the latest interventions and instructional techniques or the latest version of instructional intervention ideas that have been available to teachers in recent decades.

As educators continue through the first decades of the 21st century, many changes may be anticipated; indeed, many have already begun. Bender and Waller (2011a) describe the joint impact of these changes (i.e., RTI, differentiated instruction, and technology) as a "Teaching Revolution" that is now taking place in classrooms around the world. As teachers seek to differentiate their instruction, they should likewise be prepared to ramp up their instructional efforts by participation in a variety of these innovative instructional techniques. All of the teaching strategies presented here will enhance the positive impact of every teacher's classroom, and in that sense, these strategies represent the best we can offer in the differentiated class for students with learning disabilities and other learning challenges.

I sincerely hope this book has been and will be of help to all teachers seeking to differentiate their classrooms, and I invite educators worldwide to communicate directly with me on these strategies and tactics and/or variations of them that they might develop. I can be reached directly via e-mail at wbender@ teachersworkshop.com. I do respond to e-mails, but please allow several days for those responses as I do many workshops in schools each year and am frequently traveling to those workshops.

Also, teachers are invited to follow me on twitter: twitter.com/williambender1. I post three to five times weekly about important articles for teachers that I've read and/or other issues in education. I think these posts are helpful to teachers, and I hope you find them useful, just as I hope this book is helpful in differentiating your instruction. I look forward to hearing from you.

Appendix

CURRICULA COMMONLY USED FOR DIFFERENTIATED INSTRUCTION OR RTI INTERVENTIONS

While there are literally thousands of curricula available in education, the curricula discussed below are frequently implemented in differentiated classes and/or within RTI procedures in schools today. This is not an endorsement of these curricula, most of these are discussed in this book, and teachers should be aware of these curricula as they will probably come into contact with them.

Read Naturally

Read Naturally is a supplemental reading curriculum that emphasizes repeated reading to enhance reading fluency using the WPM measure discussed in Chapter 4. The curriculum also targets reading comprehension (www.readnaturally.com). This curriculum features brief stories, typically 100 to 200 words, that are written at a variety of grade levels. The program has received research support, and a new Spanish version is now available, making this an excellent curricular choice for English learners who may require RTI interventions. It includes a variety of research-based strategies for improving fluency, such as teacher molding, goal setting, vocabulary practice and development, repeated readings, and daily or weekly progress monitoring.

Implementation of Read Naturally involves repeatedly reading the same passage. Initially, a teacher listens to a student read a story at his or her instructional level. The teacher then marks oral reading errors, notes the time the student began and ended the passage, and then calculates the number of words read correctly per minute for that initial read-through, which is referred to as the "cold timing." Based on this correct-per-minute reading score, the teacher and the student should jointly set a goal for how quickly the student should read the passage by the end of the instructional period. Next, the student rereads the same passage several times, which may be facilitated in a number of ways. In some cases, the teacher may chorally read the passage along with the student, thus modeling fluent reading. Alternatively, the student may read the passage one or more times chorally with other students or accompanied by an audio version of the story passage from the software. Once the student feels he or she has reached proficiency, the student and teacher again go through the story with the student reading and the teacher noting both the time and words read correctly. This is referred to as the "hot timing." In almost every case, the student's hot timing will represent an improvement above the cold timing, and students may then be reinforced for their improvement. However, over time, research has indicated that most students' cold timing (their reading fluency on new material) increases also (see Bender & Waller, 2012, for a review). This curriculum and progress monitoring system is quite useful in RTI Tier 2 and Tier 3 interventions.

Accelerated Reader

The Accelerated Reader supplemental curriculum by Renaissance Learning has been available for a number of years and is perhaps the most widely used reading instructional software available (www.renlearn,com/am/). In this program, students are assigned specific Accelerated Reader hard-copy books at their instructional level, which they then read at their own pace. When they complete a reading section, they take a quiz on that reading content, which supplies the teacher with information on their reading comprehension on that passage. The curriculum provides reading material for students across the grade range, and a fairly large body of research has shown that this program is effective in helping students progress in every area of reading.

In conjunction with implementation of the Accelerated Reader program as an option for RTI interventions, many schools are adopting STAR Reading, a computer-based progress monitoring system that was also developed by Renaissance Learning. STAR Reading provides norm-referenced reading scores on a variety of reading skills for students in Grades 1–12, as well as criterion-referenced measures of students' instructional reading levels. Like all software-based assessments, STAR Reading uses technology to customize assessments to particular students based on previous responses. By administering test items closely linked to achievement levels, reliability is enhanced and testing time minimized; a student's reading level can actually be assessed in as little as 10 minutes. The software generates a variety of progress monitoring reports for one child or a group of students. For individual progress monitoring, the charts compare student growth to a target line depicting the growth necessary to reach the individual student's goal; this can be very useful for progress monitoring in the RTI context. This is a well-researched program with a proven track record, and we recommend this program for Tier 1 instruction in general education classes as well as Tier 2 and Tier 3 interventions.

Accelerated Mathematics for Interventions

Accelerated Mathematics for Interventions is a supplemental curriculum that was published in 2010 specifically for RTI progress monitoring by the same company as Accelerated Reading. Accelerated Math for Intervention and the related curriculum, Accelerated Math, are research-based curricula and assessment tools for use in RTI interventions (www.renlearn.com/am/). The Accelerated Math for Intervention curriculum presents mathematics practice activities for students struggling in mathematics from Grades 3 through 12 and is specifically intended as either an RTI Tier 2 or 3 intervention program. The program is self-paced and completely individualized. Students see multiple forms of practice problems on the tasks they have difficulty with. The program fosters mastery on mathematics content at each level, so students receive the level of intensity they need on each mathematics objective. An extensive system of ongoing professional development focused on RTI concerns supports this program, including using this program for universal screening, progress monitoring, and providing evidence-based documentation for intervention decisions. This curriculum can generate a wide variety of reports; some focus on a single student's performance, while others focus on schoolwide or districtwide data. Student data reports are highly detailed and identify specific skills on which the student has worked. Research has supported the use of the Accelerated Math curriculum.

Study Island

Study Island, from Archipelago Learning, is a supplemental web-based intervention and instructional program that is tied specifically to each state's standards of learning, making this particularly useful for states that have not adopted the Common Core State Standards. Study Island is also tied to each state's testing program (visit www.studyisland.com for more information). By basing this curriculum exclusively online, the Study Island developers have made these instructional and assessment materials available to licensed users, including teachers and students, both at school and at home, and this can be a significant advantage. Some students will undertake these instructional activities in the home environment, and software programs that are loaded exclusively on computers at school do not have that option.

Instructional activities are available in a wide array of subject areas other than reading. Teachers can either allow students to select topics on which to work, or they can assign specific topics that are based on the exact learning needs and styles of the individual student. The student will then be presented with various computer-based work or educational gaming activities.

Based on adaptive assessment technology within the program, the curriculum adjusts itself according to the learning curve of particular students, either moving students through the reading content faster or moving students into a slower track with more practice on various content items. Once students have mastered a particular lesson and assessment, they receive a blue ribbon and are able to move to the next lesson. However, should a student receive a low score, the program may prompt the student to continue working on the same skills until he or she develops proficiency. Thus, students receive instructional feedback each time they answer a question. This can be implemented as either a stand-alone instructional program or as a supplemental program in conjunction with other instruction. Thus, this program can also be used as the basis for RTI procedures either as Tier 1 instruction or as a Tier 2 or Tier 3 intervention for reading skills across grade levels. The stand-alone nature makes this curriculum intervention and assessment program ideal for RTI implementation in elementary, middle, or even secondary schools. Like more modern computerized programs, reports can be generated either for individual students or the entire class.

Study Island has only limited anecdotal research support, and that research was prepared by an independent firm, under contract with the company. The research can be found on the Study Island website (www.studyisland.com). The Study Island website does present a variety of reports suggesting how Study Island can be implemented in the context of RTI, which will help schools considering RTI implementation in the future. A number of schools around the nation are using Study Island, with some success, in the RTI context.

Language!

The Language! curriculum was developed as a supplemental curriculum to assist struggling students in reading, including language-delayed students and English learners across the grade levels. This supplemental curriculum has received research support for use with struggling readers (www.sopriswest .com/language). It is particularly effective for EL students since it teaches about the English language as well as teaching specific reading and language skills. The program features activities including phonemics and phonics through listening, reading, and comprehending more complex reading material on grade level, and it is useful from elementary grades through Grade 12.

Because difficulties in English only compound learning difficulties in the content areas in the upper grades this curriculum is a great option for Tier 2 or Tier 3 interventions for older students struggling in reading. It is formatted into three levels comprising a total of 54 instructional units. Each unit includes 16 instructional lesson plans, but not all students receive all lessons. Rather, built-in assessments determine the level at which individual students should begin. There are also various performance-monitoring assessments built in, including an online assessment option.

This integrated, comprehensive curriculum includes reading, spelling, and writing, and it teaches these as a complex whole using explicit, highly focused instruction (see www.fcrr.org/FCRRreports/PDF/Language.pdf). It is intended for implementation in two daily sessions of 90 minutes each, though some schools have implemented it successfully in less intensive formats. It is a research-supported curriculum, and while research is limited, the company website does present a variety of anecdotal studies and one controlled study that demonstrate the program's efficacy.

TransMath

TransMath (www.sopriswest.com/transmath/transmath_home.aspx) is a higher-level supplementary mathematics curriculum developed by John Woodward and Mary Stroh that focuses on moving students from elementary mathematics skill levels up to algebra readiness. This curriculum is intended for students functioning at or below the 40th percentile in Grades 5 through 9, but the content covers a wider range of skills, reaching from number sense to algebraic expression. This curriculum covers fewer overall topics than most core mathematics curricula but covers those topics in much more conceptual depth. This program progresses in three levels that focus on specific mathematics areas: number sense, rational numbers, and algebraic expressions.

Three placement assessments (one for each of the levels mentioned) come with the curriculum, and each instructional unit within each level also includes two performance assessments. Together, these assessments allow for frequent progress monitoring, making this a useful curriculum in the RTI context. There is limited research support for this curriculum. This curriculum has been implemented by many elementary, middle, and high schools in their RTI efforts, and given the transitional nature of this curriculum, a focus that is virtually unique in the mathematics area, this curriculum is likely to be implemented in many more schools.

COMPUTERIZED CURRICULA FOR DIFFERENTIATED INSTRUCTION

When implementing RTI in differentiated classes, the teacher's time becomes extremely valuable. Fortunately, modern technology allows for total differentiation of instruction, by virtue of high-quality educational curricula with instruction delivered entirely on the computer. Because the research on many of these curricula consistently demonstrates significant achievement gains, one might well ask several important questions:

> Are there students with learning difficulties who can benefit from these computer-driven curricula who do not seem to benefit from more traditional classrooms?

> Do the attention problems experienced by many students with learning disabilities and/or ADHD necessitate a totally individualized, computer-driven curricula?

> If students benefit from computer-driven instruction, but not in traditional classes, isn't it a moral obligation to provide those students with computer-driven curricula?

As computer-driven curricula become more numerous, these are questions educators should ponder. Of course, one can easily debate whether or not a student working independently on software-based (or web-based) instruction is receiving differentiated instruction or not. However, the curricula below are described briefly in order to help teachers understand these tools as useful for some of their students.

The Success Maker Curriculum

Success Maker is an instructional software core curriculum developed by Pearson Learning that provides individualized instruction for elementary and middle schools students (http://www.pearsonschool.com/index.cfm?locator=PSZkBl). Success Maker is a supplemental program and addresses the core subjects of reading and math. It is currently being used in many RTI intervention programs as it focuses on a wide variety of academic areas including reading and mathematics. Students take an initial assessment when they begin, and those data are used to place each student in specific levels in reading or mathematics. As students complete the lessons, the levels and questions get increasingly complex to move students toward mastery. In addition, Success Maker generates a variety of reports for teachers that make it possible to review student growth individually, in sub-groups, or for the entire class. This is excellent data for RTI implementation, and the teachers can closely monitor students' growth. This program can be used with the entire class, or students needing a Tier 2 or Tier 3 intervention are able to work with Success Maker on an individual basis, at their own pace, with a customized program. Research available at the What Works Clearinghouse is extensive and supports the use of this curriculum (http://ies.ed.gov/ncee/wwc/reports/adolescent_literacy/successmaker/references.asp).

Fast ForWord

Fast ForWord is a supplemental, software-based reading program that is founded in the latest research on brain functioning (http://www.scilearn.com/). It was developed by Scientific Learning and focuses on phonemic-based instruction for students with reading difficulties. It presents a series of comprehensive computer-driven lesson activities that cover reading skills ranging from preschool through high school. Sample tasks involve the blending of sounds to recognize correct pronunciation, word segmentation, oral reading fluency, and passage comprehension. The three levels of this program make it appropriate for nonreaders up through struggling readers in Grade 12. The software tracks individual progress of the students with difficulties and generates progress reports for the teacher. Subsequent lessons within the curriculum present different skills in a variety of ways, most of which involve game-like formats.

This program has been piloted by the publisher, Scientific Learning, in a number of school districts, and the early research results compiled by the company on use of this program among students with learning disabilities are quite positive. In some cases, reading-challenged students have demonstrated one- to three-year gains in reading and language in just one or two months based on this program. Fast ForWord seems to be a highly effective software program for teaching reading and is appropriate for use in the RTI framework.

The Voyager Passport Reading Journeys

Voyager Passport Reading Journeys (www.voyagerlearning.com/prj) is a multilevel comprehensive language arts program structured into three levels: Voyager Passport Reading Journeys, Journeys II, and Journeys III. This curriculum teaches reading and language arts skills in the context of subject-area studies on various topics in social studies, science, and fine arts. All of the lessons include both reading and writing skills, making this a particularly effective program for learners who are struggling in both reading and writing assignments.

The program provides 30 weeks of intervention lessons for each of the three levels, and each daily lesson requires approximately 50 minutes to complete. The third level of the program (Journeys III) is aimed directly at high school students who are at least two years below grade level. The program is motivational, and each level features a variety of "expeditions"; these are structured lesson activities involving nonfiction reading in two-week lesson units related to different high-interest topics. The curriculum includes weekly assessment, making it a good fit within the RTI model for elementary, middle, and high schools. Limited research evidence is available and demonstrates the efficacy for this curriculum (www.bestevidence.org/reading/mhs/limited.htm).

VMath

Like the Voyagers reading curricula, VMath was developed by the Voyagers company (http://www.voyagerlearning.com/vmath/index.jsp). VMath is developed as a supplemental curriculum and benchmarking tool aimed at students who are struggling from Grade 3 up through Grade 8 in mathematics, and that grade range makes this curriculum very useful, even for high schools students who are demonstrating mathematics deficits.

VMath presents a balance of teacher-led, explicit instruction, printed materials, assessment options, and student work online and is intended to fill gaps in student knowledge across the grade levels. In the daily lessons, teachers model the skills, facilitate both group and individual practice, and provide corrective feedback as students experience difficulty. Each lesson addresses conceptual understanding, skills practice, and problem solving.

The program is founded on mathematics standards from the National Council of Teachers of Mathematics and uses CBM as one of the assessment tools. The program aligns well with RTI requirements. Also, intensive training and support are provided once a school undertakes implementation of this program.

The PLATO Curriculum

PLATO is an online learning core curriculum that includes every subject in the school in the upper grades and focuses on mathematics and reading in the elementary grades (http://www.studyweb.com/). It is being widely used in elementary, middle, and high schools today. PLATO Learning offers an extensive product line of technology-based teaching tools from online assessment tools to extended day learning solutions for elementary and secondary students. In the middle and high school level, PLATO offers a version of e-learning with the entire core curricula online.

PLATO curricula are structured around semester-long courses, and initial assessments place students in the course content that they need, and students then work through content at their own pace. Courses are aligned with standards of various professional organizations, including the National Council of Teachers of Mathematics and the National Council of Teachers of English, but no mention is made of alignment with the Common Core State Standards. This program does offer teacher-generated reports that detail student progress.

Courses offered by PLATO include online and offline activities with end-of-course assessments to show completion and mastery. Although the courses are self-paced, users are given multiple resources to ensure success including a teacher's guide, a scope and sequence, instructional pacing, and copies of all tests with grading keys.

References

Abell, M. M., Bauder, D. K., & Simmons, T. J. (2005). Access to the general curriculum: A curriculum and instruction perspective for educators. *Intervention in School and Clinic, 41*(2), 82–86.

Acrey, C., Johnstone, C., & Milligan, C. (2005). Using universal design to unlock the potential for academic achievement of at-risk learners. *Teaching Exceptional Children, 38*(2), 22–31.

Arreaga-Meyer, C. (1998). Increasing active student responding and improving Academic performance through classwide peer tutoring. *Intervention in School and Clinic, 24*(2), 89–117.

Ash, K. (2011). Games and simulations help children access science. *Education Week, 30*(27), 12.

Ausubel, D. P., & Robinson, F. G. (1969). *School learning: An introduction to educational psychology.* New York, NY: Holt, Rinehart & Winston.

Barell, J. (2010). Problem-based learning: The foundation for 21st century skills. In J. Bellanca & R. Brandt (Eds.), *21st century skills: Rethinking how students learn.* Bloomington, IN: Solution Tree Press.

Barry, L. M., & Messer, J. J. (2003). A practical application of self-management for students diagnosed with attention deficit/hyperactivity disorder. *Journal of Positive Behavior Intervention, 5*(4), 238–249.

Barsenghian, T. (2011). *Proof in study: Math app improves test scores (and engagement).* Retrieved from http://mindshift.kqed.org/2011;12/proof-in-study-math-app-improves-test-scores-and-engagement/

Belland, B. R., French, B. F., & Ertmer, P. A. (2009). Validity and problem-based learning research: A review of instruments used to assess intended learning outcomes. *Interdisciplinary Journal of Problem-Based Learning, 3*(1), 59–89.

Bender, W. N. (2008). *Differentiating instruction for students with learning disabilities* (2nd ed.). Thousand Oaks, CA: Corwin.

Bender, W. N. (2009a). *Differentiating math instruction* (2nd ed.). Thousand Oaks, CA: Corwin.

Bender, W. N. (2009b). *Beyond the RTI pyramid: Strategies for the early years of RTI implementation.* Bloomington, IN: Solution Tree Press.

Bender, W. N. (2012a). *Project-based learning.* Thousand Oaks, CA: Corwin.

Bender, W. N. (2012b). *RTI in middle and high schools.* Bloomington, IN: Solution Tree Press.

Bender, W. N., & Crane, D. (2011). *RTI in math.* Bloomington, IN: Solution Tree Press.

Bender, W. N., & Shores, C. (2007). *Response to intervention: A practical guide for every teacher.* Thousand Oaks, CA: Corwin.

Bender, W. N., & Waller, L. (2011a). *The teaching revolution: RTI, technology, and differentiation transform teaching for the 21st century.* Thousand Oaks, CA: Corwin.

Bender, W. N., & Waller, L. (2011b). *RTI and differentiated reading in the K–8 classroom.* Bloomington, IN: Solution Tree Press.

Berkeley, S., Bender, W. N., Peaster, L. G., & Saunders, L. (2009). Implementation of responsiveness to intervention: A snapshot of progress. *Journal of Learning Disabilities, 42*(1), 85–95.

Berkeley, S., & Lindstrom, J. H. (2011). Technology for the struggling reader: Free and easily accessible resources. *Teaching Exceptional Children, 43*(4), 48–57.

Boss, S. (2011). *Immersive PBL: Indiana project reaches far beyond the classroom.* Retrieved from http://www.edutopia.org/blog/pbl-immersive-brings-clean-water-haiti-suzie-boss

Boss, S., & Krauss, J. (2007). *Reinventing project-based learning: Your field guide to real-world projects in the digital age.* Washington, DC: International Society for Technology in Education.

Bulgren, J., Deshler, D., & Lenz, B. K. (2007). Engaging adolescents with LD in higher order thinking about history concepts using integrated content enhancement routines. *Journal of Learning Disabilities, 40*(2), 121–133.

Burks, M. (2004). Effects of classwide peer tutoring on the number of words spelled correctly by students with LD. *Intervention in School and Clinic, 39*(5), 301–304.

Caine, R. N., & Caine, G. (2006). The way we learn. *Educational Leadership, 64*(1), 50–54.

Chalk, J. C., Hagan-Burke, S., & Burke, M. D. (2005). The effects of self-regulated strategy development on the writing process for high school students with learning disabilities. *Learning Disability Quarterly, 28*(1), 76–87.

Chapman, C. (2000). Brain compatible instruction. A paper presented on a nationwide telesatellite workshop. *Tactics for Brain Compatible Instruction.* Bishop, GA: The Teacher's Workshop.

Chapman, C., & King, R. (2003). *Differentiated instructional strategies for writing in the content areas.* Thousand Oaks, CA: Corwin.

Chapman, C., & King, R. (2005). *Differentiated assessment strategies: One tool doesn't fit all.* Thousand Oaks, CA: Corwin.

Coch, D. (2010). Constructing a reading brain. In D. A. Sousa (Ed.), *Mind, brain, and education.* Bloomington, IN: Solution Tree Press (pp. 139–161).

Cole, S. (2009). 25 ways to teach with Twitter. *Tech & Learning.* Retrieved from http://www.techlearning.com/article/20896

Cole, J. E., & Wasburn-Moses, L. H. (2010). Going beyond "the Math Wars": A special educator's guide to understanding and assisting with inquiry-based teaching in mathematics. *Teaching Exceptional Children, 42*(4), 14–21.

Connor, D. J., & Lagares, C. (2007). Facing high stakes in high school: 25 successful strategies from an inclusive social studies classroom. *Teaching Exceptional Children, 40*(2), 18–27.

Cook, G. (2011). A compelling way to teach math—"flipping" the classroom. Retrieved from http://articles.boston.com/2011/09/18/bostonglobe/30172469_1_math-khan-academy-high-tech-education

Day, V. P., & Elksnin, L. K. (1994). Promoting strategic learning. *Intervention in School and Clinic, 29*(5), 262–270.

Devlin, K. (2010). The mathematical brain. In D. A. Sousa (Ed.), *Mind, Brain, and Education* (pp. 162–177). Bloomington, IN: Solution Tree Press.

Deno, S. L. (2003). Development in curriculum-based measurement. *Journal of Special Education, 37*(3),184–192.

Dexter, D. D., Park, Y. J., & Hughes, C. A. (2011). A meta-analytic review of graphic organizers and science instruction for adolescents with learning disabilities:

Implications for the intermediate and secondary science classroom. *Learning Disabilities Research and Practice, 26*(4), 204–213.

Digangi, S., Magg, J., & Rutherford, R. B. (1991).Self-graphing on on-task behavior: Enhancing the reactive effects of self-monitoring on-task behavior and academic performance. *Learning Disability Quarterly, 14*, 221–229.

Digital Trends (2011). *Students with smart phones study more often.* Retrieved from http://www.digitaltrends.com/mobile/study-students-with-smartphones-study-more-often/

Doidge, N. (2007). *The brain that changes itself.* New York, NY: Penguin Books.

Ferriter, B. (2011). *Using Twitter in high school classrooms.* Retrieved from http://teacherleaders.typepad.com/the-tempered-radical/2011/10/using-twitter-with-teens-html?utm_source=feedburner&utm_medium=feed&utm_campaign-feed%3A+the_tempered_radical+%28The+Tempered+Radical%29

Ferriter, W. M., & Garry, A. (2010). *Teaching the iGeneration: 5 easy ways to introduce essential skills with web 2.0 tools.* Bloomington, IN: Solution Tree Press.

Feyerick, D. (Correspondent). (2010). Teen texting in schools [Television series episode]. In D. Garrett (Producer), *American Morning.* Atlanta, GA: CNN.

Fisher, d., Frey, N., & Lapp, D. (2012). *Teaching students to read like detectives.* Bloomington, IN: Solution Tree Press.

Fogarty, R., & Pate, B. M. (2010). The Singapore vision: Teach less, learn more. In J. Bellanca & R. Brandt (Eds.). *21st century skills: Rethinking how students learn.* Bloomington, IN: Solution Tree Press.

Foil, C. R., & Alber, S. R. (2002). Fun and effective ways to build your students' vocabulary. *Intervention in School and Clinic, 37*(3), 152–171.

Fuchs, D., & Fuchs, L. S. (2005). Responsiveness to intervention: A blueprint for practitioners, policymakers, and parents. *Teaching Exceptional Children, 18*(1), 57–61.

Fuchs, D., Fuchs, L., Yen, L., McMaster, K., Svenson, E., Yank, N., et al., (2001). Developing first grade reading fluency through peer mediation. *Teaching Exceptional Children, 34*(2), 90–93.

Fuchs, L. S., Fuchs, D., Hamlett, C. C., Phillips, N. B., & Bentz, J. (1995). General educators' specialized adaptation for students with learning disabilities. *Exceptional Children, 61*, 440–459.

Fuchs, L. S., & Fuchs, D., & Kazdan, S. (1999). Effects of peer-assisted learning strategies on high school students with serious reading problems. *Remedial and Special Education, 20*(5), 309–318.

Fulk, B. M., & King, K. (2001). Classwide peer tutoring at work. *Teaching Exceptional Children, 14*(2), 49–53.

Gajria, M., Jitendra, A. K., Sood, S., & Sacks, G. (2007). Improving comprehension of expository text in students with LD: A research synthesis. *Journal of Learning Disabilities, 40*(3), 210–225.

Gardner, H. (2006). *Multiple intelligences: New horizons.* New York, NY: Basic Books.

Gardner, H. (1983). *Frames of mind.* New York, NY: Basic Books.

Gibbs, D. P. (2009). *RTI in middle and high school: Strategies and structures for literacy success.* Horsham, PA: LRP Publications.

Goleman, D. (2006, September). The socially intelligent leader. *Educational Leadership, 64*, 76–81.

Good, R. H., & Kaminski, R. (2002). *Dynamic indicators of basic early literacy skills.* Longmont, CO: Sopris West.

Greenwood, C. R., Tapia, Y., Abbott, M., & Walton, C. (2003). A building-based case study of evidence-based literacy practices: Implementation, reading behavior, and growth in reading fluency, K–4. *The Journal of Special Education, 50*, 521–535.

Gregory, G. H. (2008). *Differentiated instructional strategies in practice.* Thousand Oaks, CA: Corwin.

Gregory, G. H., & Kuzmich, L. (2005). *Differentiated literacy strategies for student growth and achievement in Grades 7–12.* Thousand Oaks, CA: Corwin.

Guskey, T. R. (2011). Five obstacles to grading reform. *Educational Leadership, 69*(3). 17–21.

Hagaman, J. L., Luschen, K., & Reid, R. (2010). The "RAP" on reading comprehension. *Teaching Exceptional Children, 43*(1), 22–31.

Hallahan, D. P., Lloyd, J. W., & Stoller, L. (1982). *Improving attention with self-monitoring: A manual for teachers.* Charlottesville: University of Virginia.

Hallahan, D. P., & Sapona, R. (1983). Self-monitoring of attention with learning disabled children: Past research and current issues. *Journal of Learning Disabilities, 16,* 616–620.

Harris, K. R., Friedlander, B. D., Saddler, B., Frizzelle, R., & Graham, S. (2005). Self-monitoring of attention versus self-monitoring of academic performance: Effects among students with ADHD in the general education classroom. *The Journal of Special Education, 39*(3), 145–156.

Hess, B. (2012). The fate of the Common Core: The view from 2022. *Education Week.* Retrieved from http://blogs.edweek.org/edweek/rick_hess_straight_up/2012/03/the_fate_of_the_common_core_the_view_from_2022.html?utm_source-twitterfeed$utm_medium-twitter&utm_campaign=Walt+Gardner+Reality+Check

Institute for the Advancement of Research in Education (2003). *Graphic organizers: A review of scientifically based research.* Charleston, WV: AEL.

Iseman, J. S., & Naglieri, J. A. (2011). A cognitive strategy instruction to improve math calculation for children with ADHD and LD: A randomized controlled study. *Learning Disabilities Research and Practice, 44*(2), 184–195.

Jitendra, A. K., Hoppes, M. K., & Yen, P. X. (2000). Enhancing main idea comprehension for students with learning problems: The role of summarization strategy and self-monitoring instruction. *Journal of Special Education, 34,* 127–139.

Jones, C. J. (2001). CBAs that work: Assessing students' math content-reading levels. *Teaching Exception Children, 34*(1), 24–29.

Kay, K. (2010). 21st century skills: Why they matter, what they are, and how we get there. In, J. Blanca & R. Brandt (Eds.), *21st century skills: Rethinking how students learn.* Bloomington, IN: Solution Tree Press.

King, K., & Gurian, M. (2006).Teaching to the minds of boys. *Educational Leadership, 64*(1), 56–61.

Koellner, K., Colsman, M., & Risley, R. (2011). Multidimensional assessment: Guiding response to intervention in mathematics. *Teaching Exceptional Children, 44*(2), 48–57.

Kohn, A. (2011). The case against grades. *Educational Leadership, 69*(3), 28–33.

Korinek, L., & Bulls, J. A. (1996). SCOREA: A student research paper writing strategy. *Teaching Exceptional Children, 28*(4), 60–63.

Larmer, J., & Mergendoller, J. R. (2010). 7 essentials for project-based learning. *Educational Leadership, 68*(1), 34–37.

Larmer, J., Ross, D., & Mergendoller, J. R. (2009). *The PBL Starter Kit.* Novato, CA: Buck Institute for Education.

Larkin, M. J. (2001). Providing positive support for student independence through scaffolded instruction. *Teaching Exceptional Children, 34*(1), 30–35.

Lederer, J. M. (2000). Reciprocal teaching of social studies in inclusive elementary classrooms. *Journal of Learning Disabilities, 33*(1),91–106.

Lee, S., Wehmeyer, M. L., Soukup, J. H., & Palmer, S. B. (2010). Impact of curriculum modifications on access to the general education curriculum for students with disabilities. *Exceptional Children, 76*(2), 213–233.

Lenz, B. K. (2006). Creating school wide-conditions for high-quality learning strategy classroom instruction. *Intervention in School and Clinic, 41*(5), 261–266.

Lenz, B. K., Adams, G. L., Bulgren, J. A., Pouliot, N., & Laraux, M. (2007). Effects of curriculum maps and guiding questions on text performance of adolescents with learning disabilities. *Learning Disability Quarterly, 30*(4), 235–244.

List, J. S., & Bryant, B. (2010). Integrating interactive online content at an early college high school: An exploration of Moodle, Ning, and Twitter. *Meridian Middle School Computer Technologies Journal, 12*(1). Retrieved from http://www.ncsu.edu/meridian/winter2009/

Loveless, T. (2012). *Does the Common Core matter?* Retrieved from http://www.brookings.edu/reports/2012/2016_brown_education_loveless.aspx

Lovitt, T., & Horton, S. V. (1994). Strategies for adapting science textbooks for youth with learning disabilities. *Remedial and Special Education, 15*(2), 105–116.

Lovitt, T., Rudsit, J., Jenkins, J., Pious, C., & Benedetti, D. (1985). Two methods of adopting science materials for learning disabled and regular seventh graders. *Learning Disability Quarterly, 8*, 275–285.

Manzo, K. K. (2010, March 17). Educators embrace iPods for learning. *Education Week 29*(26), 16–17.

Marzano, R. J. (2010). Representing knowledge nonlinguistically. *Educational Leadership, 67*(8), 84–87.

Marzano, R. J., & Heflebower, T. (2011). Grades that show what students know. *Educational Leadership, 69*(3), 34–39.

Mason, L. H., & Hedin, L. R. (2011). Reading science test: Challenges for students with learning disabilities and considerations for teachers. *Learning Disabilities Research and Practice, 26*(4), 214–222.

Mason, L. H., Snyder, K H., Sukhram, D. P., & Kedem, Y. (2006). TWA + PLANS strategies for expository reading and writing. Effects for nine fourth-grade students. *Exceptional Children 75*(1), 69–89.

Mathes, M., & Bender, W. N. (1997). The effects of self-monitoring on children with attention-deficit/hyperactivity disorders who are receiving pharmacological interventions. *Remedial and Special Education, 18*(2), 121–128.

Maton, N. (2011). Can an online game crack the code to language learning? Retrieved from http://mindshift.kqed.org/2011/11/can-an-online-game-crack-the-code-to-language-learning/

McArthur, C. A., & Haynes, J. B. (1995). Student assistant for learning from text (SALT): A hypermedia reading aid. *Journal of Learning Disabilities, 28*, 150–159.

McConnell, M. E. (1999). Self-monitoring, cueing, recording, and managing: Teaching students to manage their own behavior. *Teaching Exceptional Children, 32*(2), 14–23.

McEwan-Adkins, E. K. (2010). *40 reading intervention strategies for K–6 students.* Bloomington, IN: Solution Tree Press.

McMaster, K. L., Du, X., & Petursdottir, A. L. (2009). Technical features of curriculum-based measures for beginning writers. *Journal of Learning Disabilities, 42*(1), 41–60.

Mergendoller, J. R. Maxwell, N., & Bellisimo, Y. (2007). The effectiveness of problem-based instruction: A comparative study of instructional methods and student characteristics. *Interdisciplinary Journal of Problem-Based Learning 1*(2), 49–69.

Merzenich, M. M. (2001). Cortical plasticity contributing to childhood development. In J. L. McClelland & R. S. Siegler (Eds.), *Mechanisms of cognitive development: Behavioral and neural perspectives.* Mahwah, NJ: Lawrence Erlbaum Associates.

Merzenich, M. M., Tallal, P., Peterson, B., Miller, S., & Jenkins, W. M. (1999). Some neurological principles relevant to the origins of—and the cortical plasticity-based remediation of—developmental language impairments. In J. Grafman & Y. Christen (Eds.), *Neuronal plasticity: Building a bridge from the laboratory to the clinic.* Berlin, Germany: Springer-Verlag.

Miller, A. (2011a). Game-based learning units for the everyday teacher. Retrieved from http://www.edutopia.org/blog/video-game-model-unit-andrew-miller

Miller, A. (2011b). Get your game on: How to build curricula units using the video game model. Retrieved fromhttp://www.edutopia.org/blog/gamification-game-based-learning-unit-andrew-miller

Moran, S., Kornhaber, M., & Gardner, H. (2006). Orchestrating multiple intelligences. *Educational Leadership, 64*(1), 23–27.

Mortweet, S. W., Utley, C. A., Walker, D., Dawson, H. L., Delquardri, J. C., Reedy, S. S., ... Ledford, D. (1999). Classwide peer tutoring: Teaching students with mild mental retardation in inclusive classrooms. *Exceptional Children, 65*(4), 524–536.

Nelson, R., Smith, D., & Dodd, J. (1994). The effects of learning strategy instruction on the completion of job applications by students with learning disabilities. *Journal of Learning Disabilities, 27*(2), 104–110.

Niguidula, D. (2011). Digital portfolios and curriculum maps: Linking teacher and student work. In H. H. Jacobs (Ed.), *Curriculum 21: Essential education for a changing world.* Alexandria, VA: Association for Supervision and Curriculum Development.

O'Connor, K., & Wormeli, R. (2011). Reporting student learning. *Educational Leadership, 69*(3), 39–45.

O'Meara, J. (2010). *Beyond differentiated instruction.* Thousand Oaks, CA: Corwin.

Owen, W., (2011, October 3). Google Apps is the hottest thing in schools, but some parents worry about privacy. *The Oregonian.*

Palincsar, A. S., & Brown, A. R. (1986). Interactive teaching to promote independent learning from text. *The Reading Teacher, 39*, 771–777.

Palincsar, A. S., & Brown, A. R. (1987). Enhancing instructional time through attention to metacognition. *Journal of Learning Disabilities, 20*(1), 66–75.

Partnership for 21st Century Skills (2009). *21st century learning environments.* Retrieved from www.21stcenturyskills.org/documents/1e_white_paper-1.pdf

Pemberton, L. (2011, December 18). With iPads, Olympia students have world at their fingertips. *The Olympian.* Retrieved fromhttp://www.theolympian .com/2011/12/18/1918639/with-ipads-olympia-students:have.html#storylink-cpy

Pierce, R. L., McMaster, K. L., & Deno, S. L. (2010). The effects of using different procedures to score Maze measures. *Learning Disability Research and Practice, 25*(3), 151–160.

Pisha, B., & Stahl, S. (2005). The promise of new learning environments for students with disabilities. *Intervention in School and Clinic, 41*(2), 67–75.

Rafferty, L. A. (2010). Step by step: Teaching students to self-monitor. *Teaching Exceptional Children, 43*(2), 50–59.

Rapp, D. (2009, January). Lift the cell phone ban. *Scholastic Administrator.* Retrieved from http://www2.scholastic.com/browse/article.jsp?id=3751073

Reeves, D. (2010). A framework for assessing 21st century skills. In J. Bellanca & R. Brandt (Eds.), *21st century skills: Rethinking how students learn.* Bloomington, IN: Solution Tree Press.

Reeves, D. B. (2011).Taking the grading conversation public. *Educational Leadership, 69*(3), 76–79.

Richardson, W. (2010). Blogs, wikis, podcasts, and other powerful tools for educators. Thousand Oaks, CA: Corwin.

Richardson, W., & Mancabelli, R. (2011). *Personal learning networks: Using the power of connections to transform education.* Bloomington, IN: Solution Tree Press.

Rock, M. L. (2004). Graphic organizers: Tools to build behavioral literacy and foster emotional competency. *Intervention in School and Clinic, 40*(1), 10–37.

Rose, D. H., & Meyer, A. (2006). *A practical reader in universal design for learning.* Cambridge, MA: Harvard Educational Press.

Rosenzweig. C., Krawec, J., & Montague, M. (2011). Metacognitive strategy use of eighth-grade students with and without learning disabilities during mathematical problem solving: A think-aloud analysis. *Journal of Learning Disabilities, 44*(6), 508–520.

Rushkoff, D., & Dretzin, R. (writers). (2010). Digital nation [Television series episode]. In R. Dretzin (Producer), *Frontline.* Boston, MA: WGBH.

Saenz, L. M., Fuchs, L. S., & Fuchs, D. (2005). Peer-assisted learning strategies for English language learners with learning disabilities. *Exceptional Children, 71*(3), 231–247.

Salend, S. L. (2005). Report card models that support communication and differentiated of instruction. *Teaching Exceptional Children, 37*(4), 28–35.

Salend, S. J. (2009). Technology-based classroom assessments: Alternatives to testing. *Exceptional Children, 41*(6), 48–59.

Saltman, D. (2011). Flipping for beginners: Inside the new classroom craze. *Harvard Educational Letter, 27*(8), 1–2.

Sawchuk, S. (2012). Universities, districts to partner on Common-Core secondary math. *Education Week,* retrieved from http://blogs.edweek.org/edweek/teacherbeat/2012/05/_there_has_been_quite.html

Schlemmer, P., & Schlemmer, D. (2008). *Teaching beyond the test: Differentiated project-based learning in a standards-based age.* Minneapolis, MN: Free Spirit Publishing.

Schumaker, J. G., & Deshler, D. D. (2003). Can students with LD become competent writers? *Learning Disability Quarterly, 28*(2), 129–141.

Shah, N. (2012). Special educators borrow from brain studies. *Education Week, 31*(17). 10.

Shaughnessy, M. (2011). *Assessment and the Common Core State Standards: Let's stay on top of it!* Retrieved from http://www.nctm.org/about/content.aspx?id=30169

Sheehy, K. (2011). High school teachers make gaming academic. Retrieved from http://education.usnews.rankingandreviews.com/education/high-schools/articles/2011/11/01/high-school-teachers-make-gaming-academic?PageNr=1

Silver, H., & Perini, M. (2010a). Responding to the research: Harvey Silver and Matthew Perini address learning styles. *Education Update, 52*(5), Alexandria, VA: Association for Supervision and Curriculum Development.

Silver H., & Perini, M. (2010b). The eight Cs of engagement: How learning styles and instructional design increase student commitment to learning. In R. Marzano (Ed.), *On excellence in teaching.* Bloomington, IN: Solution Tree Press.

Silver H., Strong, R., & Perini, M. (2000). *So each may learn: Integrating learning styles and multiple intelligences.* Alexandria, VA: Association for Supervision and Curriculum Development.

Simos, P. G., Fletcher, J. M., Sarkari, S., Billingsley-Marshall, R., Denton, C. A., & Papanicolaou, A. C. (2007). Intensive instruction affects brain magnetic activity associated with oral word reading in children with persistent reading disabilities. *Journal of Learning Disabilities, 40*(1), 37–48.

Smutny, J. F., & Von Fremd, S. E. (2010).Differentiating for the young child: Teaching strategies across the content areas, PreK–3.Thousand Oaks, CA: Corwin.

Snyder, M. C., & Bambara, L. M. (1997). Teaching secondary students with learning disabilities to self-manage classroom survival skills. *Journal of Learning Disabilities, 30*(5), 534–543.

Sousa,, D. A. (2001). How the special needs brain learns. Thousand Oaks, CA: Corwin.

Sousa, D. A. (2005). How the brain learns to read. Thousand Oaks, CA: Corwin.

Sousa,, D. A. (2006). How the special needs brain learns (3rd ed.). Thousand Oaks, CA: Corwin.

Sousa, D. A. (2009). How the brain influences behavior. Thousand Oaks, CA: Corwin.

Sousa, D. A. (2010). *Mind, brain, & education.* Bloomington, IN: Solution Tree Press.

Sousa, D. A., & Tomlinson, C A. (2011). Differentiation and the brain: How neuroscience supports the learner-friendly classroom. Bloomington, IN: Solution Tree Press.

Sparks, S. D. (2011). Schools "flip" for lesson model promoted by Khan Academy. *Education Today, 31*(5), 1–14.

Spectrum K12/CASE. (2008, March).RTI adoption survey. Washington, DC: Author.

Stansbury, M. (2011). Ten ways schools are using social media effectively. Retrieved from http://www.eschoolnews.com/2011/10/21/ten-ways-schools-are-using-social-media-effectively/?

Sternberg, R. (1985). Beyond IQ: A triarchic theory of human intelligence. New York, NY: Cambridge University Press.

Sternberg, R. J. (2006). Recognizing neglected strengths. *Educational Leadership, 64*(1), 30–35.

Stiggins, R. (2005, December). From formative assessment to assessment for learning: A path to success in standards-based schools. *Phi Delta Kappan, 87*(4), 324–328.

Stone, C. A. (1998). The metaphor of scaffolding: Its utility for the field of learning disabilities. *Journal of Learning Disabilities, 31,* 344–364.

Strange, E. (2010). Digital history review: The portable past. *American Heritage, 60*(1), 66–68.

Sturm, J. M., & Rankin-Erickson, J. L. (2002). Effects of hand-drawn and computer-generated concept mapping on the expository writing of middle school students with learning disabilities. *Learning Disabilities Research & Practice, 17*(2), 124–139.

Swanson, P. N., & De La Paz, S. (1998). Teaching effective comprehension strategies to students with learning and reading disabilities. *Intervention in School and Clinic, 33*(4), 209–218.

Tate, M. L. (2005). *Reading and language arts worksheets don't grow dendrites.* Thousand Oaks, CA: Corwin.

Therrien, W. J., Hughes, C., Kapelski, C., & Mokhtari, K. (2009). Effectiveness of a test-taking strategy on achievement in essay tests for students with learning disabilities. *Journal of Learning Disabilities, 42*(1), 14–23.

Tomlinson, C. A. (1999). The differentiated classroom: Responding to the needs of all learners. Alexandria, VA: Association for Supervision and Curriculum Development.

Tomlinson, C. A. (2001). How to differentiate instruction in mixed-ability classrooms (2nd ed.). Alexandria, VA: Association for Supervision and Curriculum Development.

Tomlinson, C. A. (2003). *Differentiation in practice: A resource guide for differentiating curriculum: Grades K–5.* Alexandria, VA: Association for Supervision and Curriculum Development.

Tomlinson, C. A., (2010). *Differentiating instruction in response to academically diverse student populations.* In R. Marzano (Ed.),*On excellence in teaching.* Bloomington, IN: Solution Tree Press.

Tomlinson, C. A., Brimijoin, K., & Narvaez, L. (2008). *The differentiated school: Making revolutionary changes in teaching and learning.* Alexandria, VA: Association for Supervision and Curriculum Development.

Tomlinson, C. A., & McTighe, J. (2006). *Integrating differentiated instruction and understanding by design: Connecting content and kids.* Alexandria, VA: Association for Supervision and Curriculum Development.

Tomlinson, C. A., Kaplan, S. N., Renzulli, J. S., Purcell, J., Leppien, J., & Burnes, D. (2002).*The parallel curriculum: A design to develop high potential and challenge high-ability learners.* Thousand Oaks, CA: Corwin.

Toppo, G. (2012, May 2). *Common Core standards drive wedge in education circles. USA Today.* Retrieved from http://www.usatoday.com/news/education/story/2012-04-28/common-core-education/54583192/1

Toppo, G. (2011, October 6). "Flipped" classrooms take advantage of technology. *USA Today.*

Tucker, M. (2012). How the Brown Center report got it wrong: No relationship between academic standards and student performance? *Education Week.* Retrieved from http://blogs.edweek.org/edweek/top_performaners/2012/02/how_the_brown_report_got_it_wrong_no_relationship_between_academic_standards_and_student_perf.html

Ujifusa, A. (2012). ALEC's Common Core vote now under public microscope. *Education Week.* Retrieved from http://blogs.edweek.org/edweek/state_edwatch/2012/05/alec_common_core_vote_now_under_public_microscope.html

Utley, C. A., Mortweet, S. W., & Greenwood, C. R. (1997). Peer-mediated instruction and interventions. *Focus on Exceptional Children, 29*(5), 1–23.

Vaughn, S., & Linan-Thompson, S. (2003). What is special about special education for students with learning disabilities? *The Journal of Special Education, 37*(3), 140–147.

Waller, L. (2011). Is your kid's classroom connection high speed? Six easy ways to engage students with technology in reading! *Teacher's Workshop Newsletter, 4*(1), 1–3.

Ward-Lonergan, J. M., Liles, B. Z., & Anderson, A. M. (1999). Verbal retelling abilities in adolescents with and without language-learning disabilities for social studies lectures. *Journal of Learning Disabilities, 32*(3), 213–223.

Watters, A. (2011a). Why wikis still matter. Retrieved from http://www.edutopia.org/blog/wiki-classroom-audrey-watters

Watters, A. (2011b). Khan Academy expands to art history: Sal Khan no longer his only faculty member. Retrieved from http://www.hackeducation.com/2011/10/19/Khan-academy-expands-to-art-history-sal-khan-no-longer-its-only-faculty-member

Watters, A. (2011c). Distractions begone! Facebook as a study tool. Retrieved from http://mindshift.kqed.org/2011/09/distractions-set-aside-facebook-as-a-study-tool/

Wery, J. J., & Nietfeld, J. L. (2010). Supporting self-regulated learning with exceptional children. *Teaching Exceptional Children, 40*(4), 70–78.

Whitaker, S. D., Harvey, M., Hassel, L. J., Linder, T., & Tutterrow, D. (2006). The FISH strategy: Moving from sight words to decoding. *Teaching Exceptional Children, 38*(5), 14–18.

Wiliam, D. (2011). *Embedded formative assessment.* Bloomington, IN: Solution Tree Press.

Williams, J. P., Nubla-Kung, A. M., Pollini, S., Stafford, K. B., Garcia, A., & Snyder, A. E. (2007). Teaching cause-effect text structure through social studies content to at-risk second graders. *Journal of learning Disabilities, 40*(2), 111–120.

Wilmarth, S. (2010). Five socio-technology trends that change everything in teaching and learning. In H. H. Jacobs (Ed.), *Curriculum 21: Essential education for a changing world.* Alexandria, VA: Association for Supervision and Curriculum Development.

Wurman, Z., & Wilson, S. (2012, summer). The Common Core Math Standards: Are they a step forward or backward? *Educationnext, 12*(3). Retrieved from http://educationnext.org/the-common-core-math-standards/

Index

CORWIN

A SAGE Company

The Corwin logo—a raven striding across an open book—represents the union of courage and learning. Corwin is committed to improving education for all learners by publishing books and other professional development resources for those serving the field of PreK–12 education. By providing practical, hands-on materials, Corwin continues to carry out the promise of its motto: **"Helping Educators Do Their Work Better."**

CPSIA information can be obtained
at www.ICGtesting.com
Printed in the USA
BVHW012117230722
642199BV00013B/151